KRYSTAL'S REVENGE

THE UNTOLD STORY - REVISED EDITION

MAXINE O'DAY

authorHOUSE®

AuthorHouse™
1663 Liberty Drive
Bloomington, IN 47403
www.authorhouse.com
Phone: 833-262-8899

Published by AuthorHouse 09/29/2020

ISBN: 978-1-7283-7201-3 (sc)
ISBN: 978-1-7283-7199-3 (hc)
ISBN: 978-1-7283-7200-6 (e)

Library of Congress Control Number: 2020916368

Print information available on the last page.

Introduction

This is a revised edition of the original book published in 2004. The reason for the revision is that a lot more information came to light after the original publication.

If you were given an awesome message to present to government officials, how would you go about it to have the greatest effect? Could you change the world by this message? Would it take a lifetime to accomplish it?

These are questions that underlie this true story. It is said "truth is stranger than fiction." This is not Hollywood make-believe. This is not a "reality series TV show" where individuals have to survive on some deserted island. The events depicted really happened to the people involved. The names of these people as well as some of the places have been changed to protect innocent lives. The innocent victims in this story survived because they were determined to find the truth and reveal it.

This was not an easy story to write. There are a lot of disturbing events that the people involved had to work through. As a private investigator a lot of research had to be done, and where necessary, references are cited in the appendix to support government claims that were made by the individuals involved.

"People who do not learn from their mistakes are doomed to repeat them." Let's hope that those related to the events depicted in this story learn from their mistakes. This is not a story that needs to be repeated.

Acknowledgements

Most of the material for this revised edition was taken from the original edition of this book. At the time of the first printing, not all the facts had been revealed. It was only after the first publication, that more relevant material came to light. Due to the fact that the message in the original publication had a profound effect on some individuals, it was deemed best to include as much information as possible. As in all messages given, some will accept the message, others will not.

In this revised edition, then there is evidence brought forth that indicate there was much interference from some FBI and CIA efforts to manufacture alternate facts and distort the truth. This revised edition, therefore, is to present the truth and not alternative facts.

We may not discover all the falsehoods, but eventually this book goes up to the Heavenly Father, who knows the whole truth and nothing but the truth!

CHAPTER
1

Agent Mark Mullins cried out, "Why did you kill me? – There's more I could have told you about that child! Now you have to find out for yourself that she will destroy you!"

When he had finished, the black snake that had been encircling him as he spoke, opened its gaping jaws and swallowed him whole. The snake turned to Agent Damian and in a possessed-sounded voice claimed, "You're mine now! You will find this child with my help!" His fangs shone brightly as he laughed.

Damian sat bolt upright in his bed, sweat running down his pale face and into his hands. He blinked his blue eyes several times as he stared around the room, attempting to get his bearings. "That must have been just a dream," he muttered to himself, hurriedly throwing off his bedsheets and blanket. He got up, pulled back the drapes of his hotel room, and looked out into the darkness. As he ran his fingers through his chestnut-brown hair, he could see the brightly lit Holiday Inn sign partly illuminating the dark parking lot across the street. Two white signs with black lettering blatantly brought reality like a smack in his face. One sign said, "Whites only," and the other sign said, "Coloreds." In the far distance he could see the rest of the city of Shreveport. Yes, he was definitely aware he was in present time in the 1960s and he was definitely in the Deep South.

As he became more awake and cognizant of his surroundings, he glanced back around his room, eyeing the empty bed where Agent Mullins would have slept had he survived. Damian walked back to his bed, glancing at the dimly lit 3:35 from his nightstand. He turned on the light by the desk and sat down. *How am I going to explain this to the bureau?* he wondered as he poured a half glass of scotch in his previously used glass. He reached down into his briefcase and pulled out several bureau report forms. He stared at the heading for a long time, "Federal Bureau of Investigation - Philadelphia Office"

He downed the scotch and began writing his report. At 7:00 a.m. he would call the office to report what had happened, or at least what he said had happened. By then his report would be finished. There would be no discrepancy in what he would say and what he would write:

> On Wednesday, June 7, 1967, Agent Mark Mullins and I arrived at the Shreveport Regional Airport in Shreveport, Louisiana. We rented a car under our assumed names and found a Holiday Inn close by. We rented a room and spent the rest of the evening talking about various cases and general material about this investigation. Later on we changed into our undercover clothes, bib overalls and T-shirts, and went into Shreveport, stopping at several bars. We began making small talk with the white locals as part of our true purpose, which was to uncover where the next church service for the alleged "snake enchanting" session would be held. At Tony's Tavern, we at last found that the Little Church of Faith was a local group that frequently held their "snake enchanting" sessions on Friday evenings. We were able to establish that east of Shreveport, outside the little town of Cotton Corners, near the Bodcau Bayou, two days later there would be such a church service taking place.

On Thursday, June 8 and Friday, June 9, 1967, we spent much of the day in Shreveport, mostly milling around, trying to blend in, so as not to arouse suspicion. On Thursday afternoon we drove out to Cotton Corners to get more acquainted with the surroundings as we would be driving there again Friday night after sunset.

On Friday, June 9, 1967, at 8:30 p.m. we arrived in Cotton Corners. We were told to take an abandoned farm lane back to a small barn. Inside we found a room full of white people, fully engaged in clapping and doing a "jig." One man – who we assumed to be the minister, as he was referred to as Reverend Jeb – was in the center of the room twirling around in a rhythmic motion as he carried a snake in his hands. He worked his way around the room, frequently shoving the snake closer and closer to the bystanders.

At that point Damian stopped writing. He put his pen down and poured another half glass of scotch. His eyes widened as he recalled how the cottonmouth water moccasin had reacted when Reverend Jeb brought the serpent extremely close to Damian. The black adder had made a screaming-like sound as he bared his fangs at Damian. Damian shook his head, bit his lip, and decided not to include that part in his report. He started writing again, but he immediately had stopped as he searched for the wording he needed. He sat there for a few moments nervously clicking his ballpoint pen.

Mark knew all about this religious mumbo jumbo. Maybe he's got something written down about what these snake sessions were supposed to be about. After searching through Mark's suitcase, he found some scribbled notes with several biblical references. Damian looked down and saw the Catholic Bible Mark had brought with him. He hesitated to open it. Inhaling deeply, he quickly padded through it, finding the reference he needed. Throwing it hastily down and closing the suitcase, he then moved back to the desk and continued writing.

At some point Reverend Jeb began preaching about having faith and stating that it was faith that enabled Moses to lift up the snake in the wilderness. Likewise, if Moses could touch a snake and not be harmed, anyone else could handle a poisonous snake and not be harmed. At that point several bystanders in almost trancelike fashion began handling the snakes as they mimicked Reverend Jeb's motions and "jigging" around the room. In two cases the snakes retaliated and bit their handlers. When this happened Reverend Jeb called on the rest of the "congregation" to pray for healing and more faith for these members. After some time. it became apparent no one was going to seek medical aid for these two bitten people. Rather they continued with their chants. As the wailing crowd continued, Agent Mark Mullins and I eased ourselves out of the barn to discuss what our next move.

I, of course, wanted to do something to stop this, but surprisingly Agent Mullins was against this.

Damian once again stopped writing. *It would be better if I assumed Mark's thoughts and let the bureau think Mark was the one who was too scared to do anything. After all, Mark is dead now and can't refute this.*

Agent Mark Mullins and I began to argue, stating that we could not go back to town and get help. He reiterated that it would blow our cover and that we were here to report, not become involved. We would have to wait until the two victims actually died, so we could report them as murders.

Then Damian ceased writing as he recalled what had happened next. He and Agent Mullins argued over whether or not they should render aid to the victims.

"I'm not helping these poor schmucks! If they're gullible enough to believe this, then they can suffer the consequences. Let them die!" Agent Damian said.

"You can't just walk away like that!" Agent Mark demanded as he grabbed hold of Damian's short shirt sleeve. "Don't you even care that they could die? What if that were us?"

Damian tore away from of Mark's grip.

"What do I care about crazy beliefs anyways? They got themselves into this!" He walked ahead of Mark turning his back on him. As he did so Damian reached down into his pocket.

Mark once again stretched out his arms and grabbed Damian by the shoulders, but as he did so Damian pulled his Ruger out of his pocket, and rapidly spinning around and fired into Mark's chest. No one heard the quiet snap of the silenced pistol over all the chanting going on inside the bar. Damian immediately took the car keys from Mark's pocket as Mark's body went limp, and he pushed Mark's body into the murky waters at the edge of the bayou. Several alligators came to claim the prize. Damian wanted to make sure the body sank, but he could not reach out in time before the alligators came to feed. He stepped back as they began devouring the fresh meat. Before most of the flesh was gone, one alligator climbed on top of the corpse and stared at Damian as he ripped the flesh from Mark's hand. Damian could hear the tendons snapping as the alligator continued to feast, blood dripping from his razor-sharp teeth. Damian froze, standing silently like a statue in fear that he would be the alligator's next meal. It seemed like an eternity before the alligator stopped staring at Damian and moved back into the water, dragging down the remainder of Mark's body.

As Damian now sat at the desk, he quickly shook his head, trying to rid himself of the memory of what had really happened. *How can I write this?* As he asked himself that question, a sudden downpour startled him. He got up and looked out the hotel window to find rain coming down in sheets. *What luck!* he thought. *Now any tracks will definitely be covered. They'll have a hard time finding evidence.* Feeling more relaxed he sat back down with a confident smile and continued writing.

It was at that point that we settled our argument and decided to go back to the hotel and wait for the report of deaths of these two bitten victims. As we walked back towards the car, it was dark and Mark missed his footing and slipped into the nearby waters of the bayou. I did not realize that this had happened until I turned around and could not find him. I could still hear chanting in the background, and if he had cried out, it was obscured by the noise. I back-tracked to where I thought he might have been, and saw several alligators pulling the last of the remains into the water. There was no time to grab his legs. He was already gone by the time I reached him.

Damian at last put his pen down. Breathing a sigh of relief, he leaned back in the chair placing his hands behind his head, staring at the ceiling. He could hear the pounding of the rain outside and feeling calmer, drowsiness at last began to take hold. Then he crawled back in bed, set the alarm for 6:45 and went to sleep.

At 6:45 a.m. as Damian awoke, he noted that the rain had stopped and the early morning sunlight was breaking through the half-pulled back, pale green drapes of his hotel room. He washed his face and then called the Philadelphia office and was immediately connected to Agent John Simmons. Damian relayed the story as he had written it, embellishing on parts and choking up on others, giving the impression of how distraught he was about his partner's death.

"Oh, my God!" groaned Agent Simmons. "Oh, my God! How could this have happened?" Then sucking in a deep breath, he said, "I'll be taking a flight this afternoon with several other agents. Meet me at the airport later."

Damian hung up the receiver and then remembered he had to clean his gun. When the barrel had been swabbed out completely and the remainder of this clip emptied back into the box of bullets, he dressed and walked into the hotel lobby where some fresh brewed coffee aroma scented the air. It was a relaxing inhalation that set his mind further at ease as he poured himself a cup. Glancing around the brightly decorated lobby, he noticed a nicely groomed blonde sitting on a sofa dressed in United Airlines blazer and skirt. The outfit fit her well as Damian eyed how well her rounded breasts filled out her top and how well the split skirt revealed her delightfully tantalizing thighs. He stood for a few minutes lustfully taking in the view when he realized that she was staring at him.

Moving towards her he politely and charmingly asked if he could join her. The conversation began with the superficial nonentities and then moved on to matters close at hand.

"So you're here on business?"

"Why, er, yes." Damian stated trying to quickly come up with a good story.

"Alone?"

"Well, my sales partner had to leave early, and I'm just finishing up some loose ends." He smiled trying to pour on the same enchantment that he used when he was with his fraternity brothers at Phi Beta Kappa. "We could spend some time upstairs getting to know each other better."

"We, no," she declined rapidly, "I'm on my way to the airport now to fly back home – last flight for a few days, and then back in the air again." She started to gather her purse and belongings together.

"And home is where?"

"Cleveland – well, on the outskirts of Cleveland."

"So you're a Buckeye," he smiled. "I'm from Philadelphia, but perhaps I can get up to Cleveland sometime, Karla." He noted her name tag on her uniform.

"Well, you can get a hold of me at the airport terminal. That's how all my friends find me when I fly so much."

She parted and sauntered out the front door as Damian watched her go. His thoughts were abruptly interrupted as he overheard two gentlemen who had entered the lobby discussing the latest fighting between Arab and Israel which predominated the headlines of the newspaper one was carrying in with him.

He returned to his room to make sure things were neatly in order for the later confrontation with Agent Simmons and his group. After conveniently burying his gun and bullet in the belly of his fully packed suitcase, he slid into the bed, crossing his hands behind his head and stared at the ceiling. He thought over the words that Mark relayed to him in the dream he had. He recalled the conversation Mark and he had Thursday evening when they were discussing about the case they were involved in.

"Yeah, I've seen some strange things occur," stated Mark emphatically. "Religious events can bring out some really wild happenings – unexplained things, although I do recall a different case that I stumbled across."

"In Philadelphia?" inquired Damian.

"No, Cleveland. I was on assignment at the Cleveland office of the Bureau for several years. I had to pick up on a case of a former agent, Agent Skip Clarabelle who the Bureau moved up in the ranks. We were watching this Polish family who were continually sending packages over to Poland. Of course, Hoover wanted to know every step they took because of suspected Communists being in this country. Agent Skip felt that they were a real threat to national security especially since the CIA wanted some property owned for ulterior motives. Anyway, as I was on assignment having the family under surveillance, the youngest child kind of caught my eye. The sweet kind, you know, kind of reminds you of an angel or something. Anyway, we had their church bugged and I viewed the catechism class and was amazed at a well-educated response she gave to the teacher. The child told how St. Michael, the archangel, defeated the devil. It was very well relayed as to the specifics according to what the Bible says. The teacher wasn't a nun or anything, just a lay teacher. I am sure she, as well as I, was taken back by this. And the teacher's response to the child took me by surprise, too, because she told her that someday she, the child, was going to do something special for Jesus. It was almost prophetic the way the teacher said it to this child."

Damian immediately shifted uncomfortably in his seat and perplexed he responded with, "but I thought you said they were Communists or suspected Communists?"

"Well, we were never sure if they were just a good inside contact in this country – you know, make it appear like they're churchgoers, religious people. So I had on my assignment to view all their contacts with the church, trying to see if there was anybody in the community who would have been another contact."

"So were they?"

"We don't know, but I was asked to be reassigned to Philadelphia to look into this case we're working on now – I guess, because of my knowledge of religious practices."

"So this is just a very young child?" scoffed Damian.

"Well, that was back then, I guess about 10 years ago."

Damian lay on the hotel bed now mulling over this conversation and the possible reference to what he had dreamed about. *How could a child hurt me?* he thought and tried to dismiss the notion. He closed his eyes and let his mind wander in an almost transcendental state, but he could not achieve the relaxation he needed and this thoughts began to arouse questions of 'what if' especially in view that if the child was young then, 10 years down the road she would possibly be grown up. He laid in bed a long time twisting and turning over and over, attempting to cleanse his mind of any related thoughts. When he was unsuccessful, he finally got up and drove to the airport to await Agent Simmons' arrival.

When at last the plane arrived, Damian's attention was now diverted to Agent Mark and his dealings with their case of investigation. Upon leaving the airport, they immediately drove out to Cotton Corners to view the crime scene. There were several agents who had come so there was quite a commotion being made as agents scrambled along the edge of the bayou scrutinizing every inch of the muddy banks and into the water itself.

Damian stood nervously nearby watching as the painstaking event seemed to go on for an agonizingly long period of time. He was aware that Agent Simmons, who stood next to Damian, frequently looked over at him.

Not wishing to arouse any suspicion, Damian was able to give the appearance that tears were filling his eyes.

"I just can't take watching this," he bitterly tried to explain. "The whole thing was so horrible – to watch him be dragged away – there was nothing I could have done." He nervously fingered his lips as he spoke, sporadically wiping the superficial tears from his eyes.

Agent Simmons put his arm across his shoulder, "It's understandable; he was a good agent." Yet Agent Simmons could not help but notice how Damian ever so slightly cringed at his gesture.

"Hey, I got something!" yelled an agent that had ventured further out into the bayou. He produced a skull, devoid of most of the flesh, but definitely with a few patches of scalp with Agent Mark's black wavy hair attached. The agent waded to the edge and as he climbed out, another agent had produced a large plastic bag to place it in. Other agents strode out to where he had been and found more remains, although disemboweled of any body tissues.

Damian turned his back to the scene, nervously fingering his lips. Agent Simmons instructed the agents to find as much as they can and then they would meet back at the hotel and for the rest to go to the coroner's office to go over dental records, and other items of identification that they had brought with them. After Agent Simmons acquired from Damian what hotel room they would be in, he passed on the information to the other agents and drove Damian back to the Holiday Inn.

Once back in his room, Damian brought out his bottle of scotch. As he did so, he handed Agent Simmons the report he had written about what he said had happened. Agent Simmons poured scotch for both as they sat down in opposite chairs across the room. The room was eternally quiet as Agent Simmons silently read Damian's report.

"You know," began Agent Simmons, pulling his glasses down from the bridge of his nose and looking up from Damian's report. "I put the two of you together because you both were so opposite. I chose Agent Mark because he had a degree in business as well as religious studies. You know that he graduated from John Carroll University in Cleveland, Ohio."

"Yes, we had some discussion about his background the other night."

"He actually came from the Cleveland office some time back as we started looking into building the case. We though his input would be an asset to understanding the religious nature in connection with some possible related murders."

Damian sort of smirked at his words, but nodded his head indicating that he was following along the train of thought.

"And I brought you into this case because you had a degree in psychology from Temple University. Your input would provide more of the paranormal aspects. We thought the combination would give us a broader input of all aspects in the case."

"Yes, I gathered that was the general idea."

Agent Simmons then paused a little bit. After another sip of scotch he began to focus on Damian. "We got you out of the military draft by recruiting you from campus."

"Well," Daman uneasily replied, "I felt my services would be better served in doing something for my country at home."

"Just what would you like to do in the agency when we finish here?"

"I have an excellent command of the Russian language, as you know." Then the thought came to Damian to pursue a more purposeful intent. "I am aware of the search for Communists and Communist-sympathizers in this country. And I feel my efforts might better be served if I pursue those lines rather than be on the front edge of some rice paddy in Vietnam." Damian smirked dryly as he spoke.

Agent Simmons pondered over what Damian relayed.

Eagerly gaining more calmness in the conversation and assurance in his newfound quest to locate the family with the young child, Damian continued, "You know Mark and I were talking about other cases the other night and he relayed a case he had worked on in Cleveland. It sounded like something I might be interested in." By now Damian was sitting on the edge of the chair leaning forward towards Agent Simmons.

Noticeably aware of Damian's change in outward presentation and anticipation in Damian's voice, Agent Simmons remarked, "I'll give it some thought."

Just then the phone rang. Damian answered it. He turned the receiver over to Agent Simmons and for a short while Damian paced the room. When Agent Simmons had finished, he stated they needed to get to the office. "They have a lot of things to show us."

Damian swallowed hard, but obediently followed Agent Simmons out the door.

"We were able to piece together just about all the bones of the skeleton. And of course, the dental records do match. So we know this is definitely Agent Mark Mullins," affirmed the one agent. "But there is something interesting. Right here," he pointed with his gloved fingers to the pieced together torso, "just to the left of the sternum, between the fourth and fifth ribs, is a slightly rounded nick in the sternum. Any ideas what caused that?" He asked the tightly crowded group encircling the table.

At that announcement Damian covered his mouth with his hand and turned pale. Agent Simmons thought Damian was just reacting to the entire scene and fearing that Damian was responding to the loss of his partner, instructed Damian to go outside and get some fresh air. Damian eagerly did so and when he stood outside the red bricked building in the late afternoon sun, he once again was able to regain better composure.

When the group of agents had completed their assessment of Agent Mark Mullins' body, Damian and Agent Simmons returned to the hotel room. After much discussion it was agreed that Agent Simmons and Agent Damian would fly back to Philadelphia with the rest of the entourage following later.

Several days later back in Philadelphia, as the tolling church bells of St. Peter's Roman Catholic Church resonated inside, Agent Damian uncomfortably sat with a multitude of other agents. The solemnness of the funeral service bored him, but he knew he had to make good impressions to the rest of the brotherhood if he wanted to achieve his goals. As he gazed at the various people in the church pews ahead of him, he could not help but notice the black-veiled head of Mark's wife. He focused on her for quite some time. When the final dirge began and the slow procession started to exit down the church aisles, Damian took note of Mark's wife as she passed by his church pew.

Once the drive to the cemetery was over, and Damian crawled out of one of the procession cars, he maneuvered himself in the crowd until he was behind Mark's wife. Her grief continued to spill forward like a breaking dam, when at last Damian reached forward and put a simulated comforting hand on her back attempting to soothe her. As the other agents filed past the casket expressing their last goodbye, Damian began to converse with Mark's wife.

"We all feel your sorrow," Damian began passionately. "It's a very hard time for all of us." Then wetting his lips with his tongue and after offering a barrage of shrouded condolences he said, "Perhaps we could get together – er, later on, that is – and have a drink or two – maybe share some good memories of your husband." Damian's eyes scanned up and down her body, envisioning what an evening of drinks and conversation could produce. It was something that always worked at Phi Beta Kappa a year or so ago. After all, his one fraternity brother had gone out for beer one night while Damian seductively engaged in carnal satisfaction with his fraternity brother's girlfriend.

Mark's wife, to Damian's dismay, only wiped the tears once more from her face and laying one last rose on the casket, was joined by her sister as they made their way to the waiting car.

Damian's actions at the cemetery had not gone unnoticed by other agents. Several days later at the Bureau's office meeting, Damian's performance was brought to light as the discussion revolved around what Damian's next assignment would be. Since Agent Simmons was the Agent-in-Charge of the Philadelphia office, the responsibility laid heavily upon him as to the future of Agent Damian in the Bureau.

"I'm not really sure you can handle other cases," began Agent Simmons as he partly sat on the edge of his desk. Facing Damian, he pulled his glasses from his face and pensively began to explain his rationale.

"J. Edgar has some strict standards for his agents, and you border on infringing on those standards."

"What are you saying?" demanded Damian.

"It is the opinion of the fellow agents of the Philadelphia office that maybe you would be better suited to operate as more of an informant. – Now don't get me wrong here," Agent Simmons held his hand up as he stood up and moved to a more commanding position seated at his desk. "We'll still allow you to work with us, but we want you to use your background in a more applicable fashion. You expressed a desire to use your Russian language with regards to Communist infiltrators. That we can accommodate you with. But we want you to set yourself up as a psychological counselor. Be somewhat more of a confessor-type informant and let us in on possible suspects."

"Licensed psychologist?" rebuked Damian.

"Yes, we can get you set up with that, but there is another matter. With all the publicity and questions around Agent Mark Mullins' death, we want to mask your identity – we need you to alter your name."

Damian jerked nervously at the suggestion, but continued to listen.

"How about instead of Damian Lear, you become Damian Lear Madden? – Now we can get you the proper identity and diplomas changed, so we'll take care of the formalities."

Damian sat there half-stunned, not knowing what to do for a moment or two. At last, he spoke, "I guess, but I'm really not happy about this." After more discussion was held on the specifics Damian left the Federal Building in deep contemplation and anger.

CHAPTER 2

"Here's some more clothes that I don't fit into anymore!" stated Krystal who handed her mother several pairs of well-worn pants and a few faded sweaters.

The Kruczyinski household was busy gathering up spare canned goods, outgrown clothing and a patch quilt that Grandma Kruczyinski was putting the final touches on. Henry, Krystal's father, was boxing up the goods to take to mail as Martha, his wife, made sure the clothes laid neatly in the boxes, yet compressed to save space. It did not seem like much to send to Grandma's remaining family who lived in Communist-controlled Poland and from whom she had left many years back when she was 13. Now in her late 70's she still tried to provide something to what remained of her relatives. When Krystal saw how Grandma carefully concealed money in the bottom of the coffee can by replacing all the coffee on top, to Krystal it seemed to say, *we care*. Krystal admired Grandma for her bravery and diligence.

When Henry had the car ready to go to the post office with Grandma, Krystal settled back on the sofa. Picking up the newspaper to finish a project for her senior high school government class, she read several articles hoping to get enough information to write her essay.

It was April 28, 1968, almost three weeks after Dr. Martin Luther King Jr., had been assassinated. The Vietnam War continued. Krystal wanted to quickly bypass those articles. They were depressing to read because more and more soldiers died every day and it seemed like the war just dragged on and on with no end in sight. Krystal still had not gotten over the death of Dale, a high school upperclassman who never made it to his 19th birthday. She would think often times how she sat across from him and Richard Sadick in study hall conversing on various topics. Now Dale was gone, killed in action in Vietnam. Even though President John F. Kennedy's assassination shocked and saddened her in 1963, with Dale's death in 1966 it seemed like it happened right next door. She personally knew Dale and she felt he was snatched away right before her eyes. Then came Dr. Martin Luther King's assassination, a man she felt was trying to do something positive to help others. She has listened to several of his speeches including "I Have a Dream" and she saw nothing wrong with people wanting equality in their lives. She was appalled when she saw the retaliation that took place in the South and she wondered how so much hate could fester inside some white people. She realized why the black people then began to form militant groups, and even though she did not agree with many of the tactics promoted by Malcolm X, when he was assassinated too, she sensed a loss there as well.

Krystal turned the next page of "The Cleveland Plain Dealer." Various protests and riots fill other articles. Columbia University in New York suffered a student sit- in, incited by the Students for a Democratic Society (SDS) who eventually closed the college down. Civil rights riots were proliferating several places prompting police to clamp down strongly with law and order. Two nuns were killed in Nicaragua, supposedly working for the CIA.

At that point Krystal put the paper down. She thought how earlier in her life she had wanted to become a nun, how a lay teacher in her catechism class had planted a "seed" in her mind on doing something special for Jesus someday. For many years Krystal thought to become a nun was her destiny. When she reached her 16th birthday, two years prior, Henry and Martha took her to a nearby convent to talk with the mother superior. Giving prudent advice, the mother superior told

Krystal to live a little and wait until later to make a decision. Now, as Krystal read about these two nuns working for the CIA, she was very glad she had waited and decided against becoming a nun. If the CIA was using nuns, she certainly did not want to be one of them. She had read other articles previously about the CIA and how they were involved in other countries with assassination plots of various leaders, how they "disposed" of people who did not cooperate with their agenda. She just did not want any part of such covert and sometime devious actions on the part of the CIA.

Although Krystal did not count out a career with adventure included, working for the CIA would be just too much adventure. So for two years now she has spent much of her time deciding what she wanted to do career-wise. She had thought of nursing, but looked at other options, still not making any concrete decisions.

Then as Krystal picked the paper back up to work on her essay project and scanned across the page from where she had left off, she noticed a very brief article in the far bottom right corner.

PHILADELPHIA, PA – Former Agent Damian Lear had filed a complaint against the FBI citing discontent over the FBI's handling of the death of Agent Mark Mullins, a partner of Agent Lear's.

Krystal read it again. It was so short without detail. Yet it said quite a bit. She knew nothing about anyone by the name of Damian Lear or Mark Mullins. However, from what little the article did say, it sounded like there was enough conflict going on. The one agent was listed as a former agent who sounded like he might be quite discontented. Krystal wondered, *What would a disgruntled FBI agent do if he left the agency on a note of discord?* Krystal surmised a little of what form of possible revenge or retribution that would take. Yet she knew that J. Edgar Hoover had a very tight hold on his agency and underhandedly Hoover could make it very difficult for that person to find employment elsewhere.

Upon reading this little article Krystal thought about how becoming an FBI agent had been one of her other possible career choices. It was true she had toyed with the idea of working for the FBI. She was impressed with Ephrem Zimbalist Jr.'s role in the TV series, "The FBI." She felt that the character presented by him performed the role of a true FBI agent and lived up to the standards of the agency of Fidelity, Bravery and Integrity which were supposedly upheld in the Federal Bureau of Investigation. Of course, she would later discover that that was exactly what Hoover himself wanted to portray about the agents and his agency, and so had utilized the TV media to make his point. Krystal, in fact, was quite impressed by this production. However, she soon discovered at that time that there were no women FBI agents, only secretaries. Yet she was intrigued by the possibility of becoming an agent.

She would discover four years later had she pursued this career choice, she would have become the first women FBI agent, happening to someone else in 1972. At this time she thought about the possible harassment she might encounter by the male counterparts for her undertaking such an endeavor. Even though Henry almost went out of his way to have her stand up for herself in whatever she tried to do and provided lots of support and encouragement for his younger daughter, this was a time when many occupations were not open to women. Krystal was aware that trying to break into occupations dominated solely by men could bring about reactions from them in the order of cruel jokes played upon women to get them to quit as well as outright harassment such as sabotaging their specific duties at work. At this point in Krystal's life she felt that she was not quite strong enough to put up with all that she might encounter, particularly at such a male dominated agency. Krystal blinked rapidly to erase the thoughts of how far harassment could go. She put the paper down and then decided to visit her girlfriend across the street.

Chrysha was from another Polish family in amongst many in the neighborhood. As they sat and reminisced their younger years, they laughed as the two of them looked back on how they took old clothes and scarves, and dressing up like gypsies. They had set up a card table on the front lawn, complete with crystal ball, Ouija board and a toy cash register - to collect profits from their fortune-telling of any passerby. No one ever stopped, of course, but a lot of people sure slowed down as they drove past.

There were other adventures that had been involved in, and at times although they were humorous, they could take on a deeper and more serious tone.

"What do you think happens when you die?" Chrysha asked on one occasion when the two of them were about 14. "I wonder if you feel anything."

"Me too, but I hope we go up instead of down," replied Krystal jokingly. Then she proposed the idea. "I wonder if your dog and my dog will be in heaven." They both sat there and contemplated the idea. Both were fond of their dogs, even though they were just crossbreeds.

After discussing their interpretation of purgatory as a waiting place on the way to heaven, that the Catholic Church taught them, Chrysha excitedly responded with, "I've got an idea. Let's build a church for dogs, so we can pray for them and they can be in heaven." With that the two of them eagerly began tying some sticks together in a very basic frame to form their "church." It was built in Chrysha's backyard partly into the heavily shaded grove that bordered on a much larger woodland area.

One such time when they were praying in their church, Ernie Wilson and a group of boys came out from the woodland area that lay beyond their church and began talking with Chrysha.

"I remember Krystal" said Ernie to Chrysha. "I remember talking to her outside of St. Michael's Church. I wonder if she remembers me."

Chrysha turned to Krystal asking, "Do you remember Ernie?" Krystal stared intently at the young man. He did seem familiar, although he had black hair and was of medium build - nothing particularly outstanding about him, but right at this time Krystal could not place him. It had been at least three years since she had last seen him. He had been in a neighboring school so would not have had much contact with even the upper classmen in her school. He was obviously older and had already graduated quite some time back. So there had not been much contact between the two of them. A lot had happened in the meantime and she just did not recall his name, but he remembered her.

"He said he really liked you," Chrysha continued. "He said he had watched you play in the town marching band." Krystal did vaguely remember someone who looked like him every so often standing off from the bandstand on the town square watching as the band would perform weekly summer evening concerts. Yet he was not around that much, and it was pretty much light conversation that took place between the two of them when they did meet, at least that is what Krystal remembered at this time. After the boys joked a bit with the girls, they soon left and Chrysha and Krystal became engrossed in their project.

They spent some time working on their new endeavor. When they took a break, they decided to go visit the priest at St. Michael's Church and tell him about it. They were saddened after he spoke with them, because he told them that dogs have no souls. When they questioned him whether dogs would be in heaven, he reiterated his point again that they had no souls. Krystal and Chrysha left disgusted, but undeterred.

Now as the two friends sat in Chrysha's kitchen recalling this and other events that they had been involved in, they began to laugh.

"I'm really going to miss you," stated Chrysha sincerely as tears of sadness began to form in her eyes. "And with you going to Kent State and me going to Ohio State, we'll only get to see each other just at break."

"Me, too," heartily agreed Krystal. "Just keep the booklet I gave you, and maybe that will make you laugh." They both hugged each other and then Chrysha went to find the booklet. It was comic-book style in layout, rather crudely drawn by Krystal, who never claimed to be an artist. She had tried to capture the various escapades and troubles both of these two young girls had gotten involved in. Krystal had put plenty of humor in it, so as the two them paged through the booklet, they both laughed recalling how their fond friendship had solidified.

Yet this friendship had had its time of testing and there were differences that stood out between the two. Chrysha had black hair and had definitely blossomed out in body shape during her adolescence. Krystal, on the other hand, was more slight of bodily features, short-stature, and had medium-length straight brown hair. She was not unattractive, but not stunningly beautiful as others might have wanted her to be. Henry felt she was the apple of his eye, and of the four children with her being the youngest and smallest, he gave her plenty of encouragement and support when others bullied her at school.

Henry often told Krystal, "I was the smallest and youngest not only in the family, but at school as well. I didn't let it get me down. I was able to be an avid swimmer on the swim team and won many awards."

"Did you get to go to college?"

"No," Henry sighed. "There wasn't any money for that. You know Grandma was a widow and raised the family when she was in her late 20s. She also owned a store, and we helped her out with that."

"Wasn't that during the Great Depression?"

"Yes, but we never had to stand in a bread line. Grandma was very resourceful. She had a garden and grew much of what we ate. She also had a butcher shop, so we never went hungry."

"What else did you do in school?"

"I was part of a debate team, which I really enjoyed, and I also was the school newspaper editor – it was a lot of fun. So going to college did not bother me as much."

Henry spent much time with Krystal not only sharing his life story, as well as Grandma's, but encouraging Krystal to be willing to go the extra mile to help others in need. Yet he also taught her to be less gullible of other people's statements and to check things out for herself if they were true or not.

Unknown to Krystal at the time, Henry was advised by the church to expose Krystal to other cultures and history. So there were times he would purposely watch TV programs about the Holocaust and what happened to the Jews in Nazi Germany and elsewhere. Yet, Henry sensed there was something more he needed to give her, and so spent many times in the library searching for anything spiritual that he could get his hands on to help him with this quest. At some point he came across the hymn, "How Great Thou Art" and he immediately took to heart the hymn becoming his favorite. Yet this was a Protestant hymn and not included in the Catholic Church. In time, this hymn became one of Krystal's favorites as well.

Krystal loved and respected her father, but she was also aware of the emptiness that lingered within Chrysha over the death of her own father, Frank, several years back. That death had actually occurred before Krystal had met Chrysha. The family had lived several streets away from Krystal's family. Frank apparently had been hassled by a large shopping center development firm for some time. They had wanted to buy him out so they could take the property. Apparently he was not so eager to be bought out. When he returned home late one night he never made it inside his home. His wife later found him shot to death in the driveway. The entire incident was covered up and Krystal wondered if there was more to it. Yet she never asked Chrysha much more about it as Krystal was well aware that Chrysha had a lot of deep-seated pain. Chrysha's mother, now a widow, had to make do with what they had. They had moved their house to across the street from Krystal. As neither family was rich by any means, both Chrysha and Krystal learned how they had to make do with what they had. So it was easy for Chrysha and Krystal to come up with many make-believe situations and use whatever props were on hand for their activities. Both were frugal about what they spent on what.

Chrysha had boys interested in her, although she did not date much. Krystal had her first date when she was 17, when the brother of another friend of hers, invited her to go visit Kent State University campus. They had a good time, but the relationship never matured. As with card playing that was a favorite Saturday night activity in the Kruzyinski household, Krystal was never good at playing the Ace of Hearts. It seemed like the deck was always stacked against her. Even though several card games were played including Pinochle, Hearts, and Canasta, Krystal seemed to excel better by playing the Queen of Spades or some trump cards. So Krystal's dating history would not be that embellished as that of other teenagers on the brink of adulthood.

Both Chrysha and Krystal attended the local Catholic Church, but Chrysha had gone through parochial school to the fourth grade and then transferred to public school. Krystal on the other hand, had always gone to public school. When both entered public high school, they both attended the same catechism class on Saturday mornings. Many times Chrysha would become disenchanted with what the priest was saying and what questions she had. Krystal, too, began to feel the same way. Even though the Catholic Church had made some major changes in the mass, going from Latin to English, there still seemed to be a lot more that needed changing. Both Krystal and Chrysha questioned various aspects of doctrines trying to find answers that both would satisfy them. When many of the questions were brought up in class, including the doctrine concerning purgatory, the priest leading out would dismiss the questions stating that some things had to be accepted by faith and never questioned. After some time Chrysha stopped attending. Krystal continued for quite some time, but she, too, later dropped out.

Sometimes when Krystal would view the newspaper headlines and watch the evening news, it seemed like an innocence had died. Now at 18 she began to question why there was so much hate, so much killing, so much horrible crimes and so little love. In her own grieving pain for President Kennedy, Dale killed in Vietnam, Dr. Martin Luther King, Jr., all occurring within five years, she questioned the whereabouts of God. When in June of 1968, Robert Kennedy was shot, Krystal's grief only compounded. God, as the church portrayed Him, was always there when "the sun was shining." Yet as Krystal's dissection of church doctrines continued, she wondered, *Where was God when the bad times hit. Why didn't He intervene? When would all the hate and the killing end and why did it seem like evil in the world was escalating, almost out of control?*

Although the Kruczyinski family were Catholics, Krystal would never classify any of them as overly devout. Yes, they did attend church very regularly, but they were not fanatics and did not go overboard on topics. When President Kennedy died, all of the family felt a very strong loss, especially since he had been a Catholic. Krystal remembers being in a study hall when the announcement was made that he was shot. By the time she got home it was already on the news that he was dead. No one in the household spoke much that evening after it occurred. For several days after his death, Grandma Kruczyinski moved nervously about the house. After about a week or two, she finally admitted what bothered her. She claimed that the night before President Kennedy was shot she had a dream. President Kennedy was sitting in a chair. She said she saw a dark figure, she called Satan, strike him down out of the chair. She regarded the dream as somewhat of a premonition. Yet it was too late to do anything about it.

Grandma was not the only family member who had dreams like this. Krystal had several different dreams as well. One such dream that she could not explain had her "flying" through the air very fast hovering over the ground in search of something. There were no trees and the earth seemed almost barren. It was extremely dark, and yet a light appeared as the clouds above were rolled back like scrolls. At the time she could not understand if it meant anything or not, but it was so stunningly odd, that she remembered it for a long time. Then she dreamed the exact same dream the very next night. Every so often she would think about the dream and wonder about its significance. Yet she found nothing in the Catholic Church that could give her any insight.

She was raised to believe everyone had a guardian angel, and in the Catholic Church she was taught to pray and ask for protection from her guardian angel. Although she never saw an angel, she remembered an incident when she was home by herself at age 11 and some bullies from the neighborhood came into her yard and began taunting her. One of the bullies, George, even had a knife that he liked to wield in a show of power, although at that particular moment, he kept it concealed. They wanted her to come to the edge of her property and show where they should not cross over into hers. Since her property, like Chrysha's, bordered on a much larger woods, there were no fences up to mark the borders. She would have naively obliged the request of these bullies and gone with them, yet she felt a hand grasp her right shoulder and actually hold her back preventing her from moving forward. Although there was no one standing by her, she was sure that her guardian angel had kept her safe, as she found out later these boys meant to do her harm had she followed them.

There were other incidents that sharpened her discernment skills making her more aware of her surroundings. After her older brother went to work for a government research company, the family talked for quite a long time about how the FBI had made inquiries from the neighbors making sure of his character. As they discussed this, Krystal was sure they had to be watching the family continuing to mail these packages overseas to Communist Poland. Yet no one ever told them to stop, at least not at this time.

After World War II and sometime before 1950 the Soviet Union had taken over Poland, as well as other European countries. Grandma Kruczyinski, kept in contact with relatives who were behind the "Iron Curtain", a so-called barrier set up by the Soviet Union to block contact with any western countries. Grandma Kruczyinski was separated from relatives in Poland, and as a result, she would send "care" packages to these relatives. Sometimes the packages made it through; other times, no.

Relatives who emigrated from Poland before the Iron Curtain went up, entered the US through Ellis Island at the Statue of Liberty. When Krystal studied the history of Poland and the layout of the land, it was easily invaded by various armies, and races were mixed. So some of these relatives had more Russian blood in them, some more German blood, some mixing occurred from Eastern Europe and Russia that comprised of Czech Republic, Slovakia, Poland and Lithuania especially in central Poland surrounding the Warsaw area. Grandma's family came from this area between 1871 and 1918. The family, however, could not emigrate all at the same time. She was left behind in Poland and came over at age 13 on a freighter. With the Russian Revolution occurring in 1917 between the Whites or elite, Bolsheviks and the Reds, which were the common people of peasants and working class, it became necessary to emigrate Grandma then. Because of this instability in the area and the family origin of more central Russia, this caused unduly concern from many U.S. government officials.

The fear of communism in the U.S. at that time along with McCarthyism, which were based on false accusations without evidence, made everyone distrustful of everyone else. So the Kruczyinski family was a target as well. J. Edgar Hoover head of the FBI, was just as distrustful of anyone coming from areas of Polish and Russian connections.

Krystal loved spending time with Grandma. There were times when Krystal became sad not having known her other grandparents. She could only rely on what Martha told her about her mother and father. Martha's mother had a beautiful singing voice and sung many German songs. Since Krystal took German in high school, she wished she could have conversed with this grandma. Martha's father was a farmer, and from what Martha relayed was a very kind man. One night when the barn caught fire, he rushed in his bare feet to rescue the horses. Although the barn was a loss and he eventually developed asthma from smoke inhalation, he still was able to farm.

As far as her other grandfather, Henry described Grandma's

Kruczyinski's husband as a very distant and unhappy man. He often noted to Krystal that he was not sad that his father was gone, as he was very selfish. Though Henry was not bitter, he described his father one time buying a loaf of Polish bread, bringing it home and eating the entire loaf in front of the children without ever sharing a piece. Yet Henry was always loving and sharing towards others, not wishing to be like his father. Krystal noted all these actions that her dad performed along with his various instructions and strategies. He also taught her to play chess, and of course, the family enjoyed playing card games, which Grandma Kruczyinski was an avid player.

Damian Lear sat for a long time in his room contemplating his next move. He scowled with eyebrows drawn tightly on his forehead. Although the FBI had set him up as a licensed psychologist in Pennsylvania, and he was still an agent of the bureau with a new name, he was not satisfied. He wanted to get closer to Cleveland, find the Polish family Mark Mullins had talked about and find that child, the one who was going to destroy him, supposedly. He also felt he had more abilities that the Philadelphia FBI office was not utilizing well. It had been over a year since he received credentials with his new name, Damian L. Madden, Ph.D., Psychologist. He had been working in Philadelphia renting office space with some other medical doctors. He was hoping to get referrals from them, but the clients were not coming to him in the numbers he wanted. As he looked over his various credentials provided to him, he contemplated attending some sort of seminar, something that might enhance his career. As he looked through a list he received in the mail he noted that there were workshops on recognizing signs of schizophrenia available in the Cleveland area within the upcoming weeks. One such seminar/workshop was going to be held at Case-Western Reserve University. As he looked over the agenda and the map, he looked to see how far away he would be from the Federal Building housing the Cleveland office of the FBI. He then began to make plans to attend, hoping to stop by the Cleveland office and gain more information that he really wanted.

After all, he said to himself, *I can write off my trip as business expense.*

When he boarded the plane he could not help but notice that Karla, the stewardess he met in Shreveport, was on the plane as well and headed for Cleveland. Damian felt that at least the trip might have some interesting outcomes after all and with eagerness anticipated his arrival to Cleveland. They spent much of the trip conversing about their likes and dislikes, and Damian used his wiles and charms easily convinced Karla to go out with him the following evening as they parted at Hopkins International Airport. Damian made his way to Case-Western Reserve University to sign up for the afternoon seminar. Then he boarded a bus and made his way to the Federal Building on East Ninth Street.

He flashed his badge as he introduced himself with his new name to Agent Robert Snuggles whose desk was encountered first. Damian took note of the large portrait of J. Edgar Hoover that hung on the wall behind the agent's desk. The portrait was so positioned it almost appeared that Hoover himself was watching over Agent Snuggles' shoulder. The receding black-haired agent in his early 30's was finishing a conversation with another person. He had shoulder length hair that was becoming speckled with gray, wore a black leather jacket, and looked more like someone off the street rather than anyone with the bureau. When their conversation ended and the stranger moved away, Damian introduced himself.

Agent Snuggles replied, "Oh, yeah, I've heard about you."

Damian stood with a little puzzled look on his face, not knowing how to take that comment, but let it pass for the time being. After some small talk Damian decided to get to the point of his visit.

"I understand my former partner, Agent Mark Mullins, used to work out of this office," he began.

"Yes, Mark was a pretty good man. Too bad what happened to him down there in Louisiana; who'd have thought that alligators would be the ones to do him in."

Damian anxiously fidgeted with the change in his pockets as Robert spoke, wanting to get past the death of Mark and move on to more important matters. After a few moments, Damian then inquired, "I know that he was a pretty devout Catholic, and he was watching a

Polish family that were Catholics. Do you happen to recall what case that was?"

Robert replied bluntly, "He worked on several cases like that."

"Well, these were people believed to be Communist sympathizers - they had a young girl in the family."

"That's pretty vague. Got any more to go on than that?"

"Well," Damian continued, "Maybe if I could look through the files that he worked on, I could locate that one."

"That could take quite a while."

"Well, I think he said he took over a case that Agent Skip Clarabelle worked on with this Polish family."

Agent Snuggles stared at Damian for quite a while before he answered. "Maybe after your seminar is over, we might be able to locate those files," stated Robert, hoping to put off Damian's request for some time. "I assure you that is not going to be easy. We cover the entire northeastern section of Ohio and there's a lot of Polish families we have kept tabs on."

Damian left the office abruptly feeling rather like a jilted lover. As he walked down the sidewalk from the Federal Building, the man he had seen inside was standing smoking a cigarette when Damian approached him.

"Didn't find what you wanted?" the stranger asked. His weathered face made him appear older than his age. Damian just stared at him wondering who he was.

"I'm Elliott, CIA. – We've been watching you for some time. We know you were partners with Agent Mark Mullins and that you now have a new identity." Then he repeated his first question, "Didn't find what you wanted?"

"No, I guess just lots of bureaucracy inside." He sighed and then added not wanting to give away his true intent. "I was trying to find the family he investigated so that I can pick up on any leads possibly going into the Soviet Union. - You know, I am well versed in the Russian language."

Elliott inhaled a long drag on his cigarette eyeing Damian as he did so. "My car's over there. I need to show you some things." They both walked to the parking lot and got inside whereupon Elliott continued

— 28 —

his conversation. "I need to take you over to the hotel where several other agents are. We have some things to discuss with you." As they drove to their destination, Damian once more felt encouraged that he was pursuing his goal, or at least getting closer to his sought-after answers.

Once inside the hotel room he was greeted by three other CIA agents, who introduced themselves by first name only. It appeared that they had been waiting for him.

"We know that you and Agent Mullins were looking into odd religious cults as well as possible murders in these cults outside Shreveport," began one older appearing agent.

"Well," corrected Damian. "That's true about the murders, but I was to observe and report as to what paranormal events I saw. Mark was the religious one."

"Yes, we understand that, and that is why we want your input at this time." As the agent looked over at Elliott, Elliott flipped the lights off and another agent began running a small projector. Using the plain light-colored wall as a screen, they viewed some surveillance film of a Russian hospital room.

"This is one of our operatives who was captured and severely beaten. We thought he was left for dead and would not pull through the night. He was taken to a hospital in Moscow, where we were able to get this clip. If he was going to die, we wanted to make sure that no traces would lead to us." The agent continued. "Now watch this as the Soviet guards return to their posts outside the door. There is no one in the room except our informant lying on the bed near death. No one come through the door. Yet from the shadows this glowing figure appears to come over and stroke our man's head."

Damian squinted at the screen. He could see the glow, but he could not make out any figure of a person in that glow. When he voiced that objection, the other agent stopped the projector and commented, "We know it's hard to see. Not everyone sees a man in that glow." Then the film viewing continued. The glowing figure then disappeared. The film went on for several more minutes and then was shut off.

"Now Agent Mullins claimed when he saw this, that the glowing figure was an angel - Oh, yes," chuckled the agent, "our informant made a miraculous recovery and lived." At that statement Damian coughed forcefully.

"I'm sorry," he stated, I just have a hard time believing this." He paused and then continued.

"Well," continued the first agent. "We want to keep this sort of thing quiet. We don't want the public to know. - It's almost like we have something special going for us in the CIA. We want some sort of cover for this, maybe something that would go along with our UFO cover for our newly designed military aircraft so the Soviets can't get a hold of it."

"I'm not sure I follow exactly where I fit in," queried Damian.

"We need some documentation to support that these figures are some sort of figment of people's imaginations or something like that. Maybe aliens from other planets or something. – Something that would give them the idea that it's scary and not to indulge in."

"I think I can come up with something. I could give clinical studies of patients or something to that effect."

"That would be good, maybe write a few papers – maybe even a few books. - Whatever you need we'll help you get it in print."

"Is that all you need?"

"For now. You know Mr. Nixon is hoping to win this election and now that Robert Kennedy is out of the way, it looks pretty good. He relies on us for a lot of backup for his plans. We supply a lot of covert information that he can use for his political advantage. After all, you know that Democrats will try to get the Negro vote."

"Yeah, I guess getting Martin Luther King out of the way helps too," stated Damian. As he made that statement, the others in the room agreed. Damian began to think about how he could conjure something up really good for the CIA's purpose. At last he spoke again, "You know, of course," Damian began to sneer, "Those Negroes are below us far as intelligence and all. If we have these supposed beings helping us, then the Negroes must be on the side of Satan. It's simple black and white concept." Damian then cleared his throat and speaking with a more authoritative voice he commented, "If this is an angel that glows then why don't we see any angels from the dark side? It would just have to mean that the Negroes are from the dark side with their skin color and all. – Yes, I think I can get a lot of cover for you on this."

Then looking at his watch, he commented that he needed to get to the seminar, at least to put in his attendance. The others nodded in agreement with everything he said and produced a phone number for Damian to contact Elliott when the seminar was finished.

"We have some other matters to go over with you about some other things that we are working on," confirmed Elliott. "We'll be in a different hotel when your seminar is done, so you'll have to contact me then to find out where we'll meet next."

Damian left the hotel with Elliott and they drove to University Circle, where he was dropped off at the hospital for the seminar. Damian bore an air of confidence about him now, feeling that at last someone in the government was recognizing that he had some talents to be tapped into. This thought kept him occupied during the lecture. When another doctor leaned over and asked Damian what the lecturer had just said, he suddenly found himself wondering what really was being discussed.

"I'm sorry," he apologized. "I lost the train of thought."

"Yes, it is pretty boring. – I see by your name tag that you're from Philadelphia. - How are things there?"

"Well, actually I've been looking to perhaps start a practice elsewhere." With that the other doctor introduced himself. He was from another area of north central Ohio and had been looking to take on a new partner. When the lecture broke for a dinner recess, the two of them continued their discussion with the doctor offering Damian an incentive to come join him. Damian told him he would give him an answer when the seminar was over and he could give more consideration to the proposition. Besides, he still wanted to find out what he could about this so-called child, and if she even existed. And he still had a date to keep with Karla the next night, as well as meet again with the CIA before he went back to Philadelphia.

Krystal had only a few more weeks of summer left working at a small snack counter before she would be off to Kent State. She was looking forward to that time with anticipation of starting something new in her life. She had not really enjoyed high school, and her senior year was still overshadowed by a group who were seeking revenge in the form of harassment. She and her other friend, Hattie, whose brother Krystal went out with just that one time, managed to avoid most confrontations with this group of classmates. Yet there were times when they could not avoid them. Both Hattie and Krystal were never sure just how serious the group was regarding carrying out of their threats until they noted that a teacher's brake line was cut by one of them. At that point both girls tried to avert any confrontation with that group. Now that graduation was over and most of her classmates were busy with summer jobs like her, she saw no more of this harassing group.

Yet her school years were very enlightening. Her school was one of a few that incorporated learning other cultures from around the world including folk dances, games, and songs. Krystal enjoyed these games and learned so much about other peoples and yet how very alike they all were in some way or another. Even in grade school, Krystal was interested in learning about others. There was only one classmate with a darker skin tone, and Krystal made friends with her. However, at some point the family moved away and Krystal never saw her again. Krystal wondered if it was because of her skin color.

This particular day after working the morning and lunch shift, she came home and took a stroll through the back woods of Henry's property. The 15 acres of mostly wooded property had a continually flowing spring of ice cold water. It was frequently referred to as a well, although it was not really a well. The spring surfaced at the bottom of a hill, and formed a shallow pool that drained down into a creek. Scattered in several parts of the wooded areas were smaller springs that kept the ground wet most of the year. The wooded area appeared to be undisturbed except for the road that traversed the middle of the property and leading back to what was once was Army Nike Site. The military base had been abandoned several years back in the early 1960s. The property on the west side of the road Henry had dreamed of dividing it up for his four children. Krystal, being the youngest, had her property at the end which bordered on an open field on the north side. Chrysha and Krystal had wandered several times on the north side going west up a hill to where Chrysha's house used to sit before it was moved. A shopping center now engulfed the area. Across the street from the shopping center was the local Catholic Church.

Today, however, Krystal just wandered past the spring well and towards what was to be her property. She sat down on a large boulder that was close to one of the smaller springs. As she listened to the quietness of the woods she could fee her body relax. She knew once she left for Kent, she would not return here very often. As she enjoyed the secluded atmosphere, she was joined by Henry himself. He enjoyed coming back here as well. So the two of them sat for quite a while talking over things.

"Why did the Army ever build this Nike Site here?" questioned Krystal. "It doesn't seem like they used it a whole lot. Did they really need it?"

"Well, I guess because of the tension between the Soviets and the U.S. they felt they needed to build up our defenses," replied Henry.

"But there's still a lot of tension between us and the Soviets with the arms race and space race – don't they need that base now? Yet it has been abandoned. It just doesn't make sense."

Henry had no answer for that question, as he had asked that himself, yet he knew there was more to why the Nike Site was built here and now left with empty buildings and desolate landscape.

"It just seems strange to me to pick the middle of someone's property to build a road back here to get to it, especially when it can be reached from the other side."

"Oh, I guess they felt they need two entrances. Anyway we still own the land under the road. They wanted me to sell the property, but I wouldn't do it."

"I remember you plowing up a cornfield before the road was there."

"Yeah, I was trying my hand on bringing in a little extra money by part-time farming."

"So when did they build this?"

"1954 they began. I have pictures back in the house when they started." Henry said dryly. His face had become quite serious as he talked. Krystal wondered if there was more to the story than her father was telling her, but she did not know what.

"I remember when the Nike Site opened up and we went down and toured the place when the Army had an open house. We went took an elevator down several floors beneath the surface where there were several huge missiles stored. I take it that those were for defense purposes in case the U.S. got attacked by the Soviet Union."

"Yes, they sure had a lot of heavy munitions buried there, but they moved that all out when they abandoned the site. I think they also sealed those floors as well."

"Let's go back to the house. I'd like to look over those pictures," declared Krystal. "I know you always took a lot of pictures of all us kids and all our activities." The two set out for the house.

Inside Henry brought out several albums. He enjoyed looking over the pictures down through the years of all his children growing up and as he paged through several albums he chuckled at the antics of his children that the pictures brought to mind. Henry had begun making albums for each of his children. Krystal started looking through her album which began when she was just a few weeks old and moving upwards.

"These are pictures of the old house," she commented. The old house sat just below where the spring well was. Henry had built their present house on the hill above where the spring well emerged.

"I remember these pictures that you took as you were building the new house," she said.

Henry looked over at them and then commented, "Yeah, I had someone approach me telling me I couldn't build a house here and start arguing with me. But I built it anyway."

Krystal commented, "Did it take a lot of money to build our new house?"

Henry sighed and said that he borrowed money from other family relatives. As Henry commented as he viewed the pictures of the Army building the military site, Krystal leaned over to look at them. Henry had always marked his pictures with dates so there was no question when the pictures had been taken.

Krystal then continued looking through her album. She found a picture with her holding a clown doll.

"Where was this picture taken? It's not our house."

"No," said Alvin as he stiffened somewhat. His lips were drawn tight as he spoke. "I took that picture at Grandma's house back in Cleveland."

"I remember that doll. It was yellow on one side and red on the other and it was made with silk. It had a cone head and was almost as big as I was at that time. Whatever happened to that doll?"

Henry stumbled over his words a little bit, and then said, "I bought you another one – a different one. I guess that first one got lost."

"But I don't have a picture of that other doll, do I? That was a doll that had straps on the feet so I could put them over mine and dance with it. I remember that doll, too, but there's no picture of it."

Henry sat up and contemplated what had happened when he had taken that picture and then replaced the doll. *That's true,* he said to himself. *I never took a picture of the other doll.* He made no comment and as he noticed Krystal paging through the rest of the album he decided not to tell her the true story behind the clown doll, not just yet.

The old stone house

As Krystal viewed other pictures, Henry recalled that he and Martha moved to this old stone house property in 1951, when Krystal was one year old, and had about 15 acres of mostly wooded area. The original property also contained a sandstone quarry, which was shut down long ago, but which provided stone for many sidewalks in Cleveland. There was also a spring of water that surfaced between the stone quarry and this stone house and was called "the well." It really was an underground spring that surfaced. In the basement of the stone house was a trough in the floor through which this spring water flowed. In early years when the Cleveland suburbs were mostly farming communities, farmers would bring their milk cans to the stone house, to let the milk cool before transporting them to market. In time Krystal's family moved from this old house to the new house built nearby.

Krystal posing with clown doll

CHAPTER
3

Agent Snuggles sat in the darkened film room viewing the latest surveillance tape made of the Kruczyinski family. He was a little uneasy as he viewed Henry and Krystal sitting at the dining room table going through the picture albums. He noted that Henry did not reveal any more about the clown doll to Krystal. This reassured him and relaxed him somewhat. He thought about Agent Damian Madden and his request to view Agent Mark Mullins' previous cases. Agent Snuggles did not want to give this case up. He still felt there was something here. During the Kennedy and Johnson administrations the bureau had backed off from this family somewhat. Yet they still continued to monitor the packages that went overseas.

Agent Snuggles took over the case when Agent Mullins was transferred to the Philadelphia office in the mid-1960s. Agent Mullins along with other agents had approved the acceptance of Krystal's older brother for work in government research in the early 1960's. Agent Snuggles felt that there was no problem here. Nor did he feel there would be too much problem with Krystal's sister, Darlene, as she appeared to be taking a conservative approach in her outside interests. However, Krystal's other brother, Matt, had a little more of a rebellious attitude to him. They were close in age as well as activities. Agent Snuggles was concerned that some of this rebellious attitude might rub off on Krystal. Yet there was nothing so far to support his viewpoint. As he pulled out some older surveillance tapes of Krystal seven years back, he viewed Krystal when she was 11 and Ernie Wilson who was 21, occasionally talking outside of St. Michael's Catholic Church.

In one particular tape Ernie expressed a sobering thought to Krystal. "I have to get married. My girlfriend's pregnant."

Krystal appeared to take on a distraught facial expression as Ernie continued.

"But I'll come back. Just wait for me, and don't date anyone else." He claimed as he departed and left Krystal standing on the church steps appearing shocked and stunned from his statement.

That was the last surveillance tape Agent Snuggles had of any interaction between Krystal and Ernie. Yet that was not the last encounter that Krystal had with Ernie. Another agent had gathered some information on Ernie, but there was nothing substantial to go on. Ernie had served in the Army and had been an Honor Guard at the White House serving under President Kennedy. When he was honorably discharged in 1962 he returned home and soon after securing training at the Ohio State Highway Patrol, he married. He was transferred to begin work as a highway patrolman at the northcentral Ohio post. So Agent Snuggles surmised that Krystal never saw Ernie again and that this broken relationship may be a source for rebellion.

Agent Snuggles pulled out another surveillance tape of Krystal in high school in 1966 when the teacher announced to her that a senior who had just graduated the previous year had been killed in Vietnam. This was Dale who had sat across from Krystal in study hall with his friend Richard Sadick. Agent Snuggles could see that Krystal's facial expression once again displayed distraught and shock over Dale's death. Yet there was never any outward display of any type of dissatisfaction with the Vietnam War on Krystal's part. When Matt signed up to join the Air Force upon graduation in 1967, Krystal appeared to express high respect and honor for his decision.

Agent Snuggles looked over Krystal's high school records. She certainly was not inattentive. Her test results from a standard IQ test revealed that she was quite bright at 140. She also had a close friendship with Hattie, who likewise was just as intelligent. Yet with the family continuing to send packages overseas to a Communist country, J. Edgar Hoover himself still insisted that the Kruczyinski family be maintained under surveillance.

As Agent Snuggles thumbed through Henry's file, he was interrupted by his secretary.

"This just came through," she claimed as she handed him a memo and left the room closing the door behind her.

Agent Robert Snuggles:

> In response to the recent protests and un-American activities of various groups on college campuses I am stepping up my COINTELPRO program. As you may be aware this is a covert operation within the FBI using individuals to blend in on the campuses with the sole purpose to infiltrate suspicious groups. This information is being provided to you for your awareness and not to be shared with the general public. Danny Boy will be arriving at your office within the next few days and will be following suspects on several Ohio campuses. He is allowed access to file information that you may have.

> J. Edgar Hoover

He folded the letter back up and placed it on the table. He continued to thumb through Henry's file noting that he had never served in World War II because a heart murmur made him ineligible to serve. This was what a previous agent working on the case had discovered. Yet when Agent Skip Clarabelle began covering the case he viewed this information about Henry as being un-American. Agent Clarabelle, working under orders of J. Edgar Hoover, Senator Joseph McCarthy, and Senator Richard Nixon, all of whom endeavored extensively to uncover any Communist sympathizers, was bolder in his approach towards the Kruczyinski family. When Nixon became Vice President under Eisenhower in 1951, he, along with Hoover, increased efforts to discredit anyone who had any connections in whatever possible way to Communists, even if there was no conclusive evidence of such. When Hoover instructed Agent Clarabelle to use more forceful tactics in attempting to remove the Kruczyinski's off their property, he decided to outright threaten the family. He had a special doll made in the form of a clown and dressed in red and yellow colored silk fabric, the colors of the Soviet flag, denoting that the family was Communist sympathizers.

Agent Snuggles viewed the surveillance tape of early 1954 when Agent Clarabelle approached the Kruczyinski family at the old stone house. Agent Clarabelle entered the kitchen as the family was eating lunch. He handed Krystal the doll which she eagerly accepted, not knowing what it signified. Then an argument ensued between Agent Clarabelle and Henry. With Agent Clarabelle threatening Henry if he did not move off the property, he would make sure that Krystal would be taken and as Agent Clarabelle put it, "used as a sacrifice for the country."

Martha was visibly upset and Henry became enraged as Agent Clarabelle called Henry "nothing but a dumb Polack!" As Henry stood up from the table to show his resistance to this agent threatening him, Martha grabbed Krystal and the doll she was clutching and removed her to another room.

Henry called Agent Clarabelle "a damn son of a bitch!" and then ordered him out of the house as he raised his fist at him. It appeared from the film that had Agent Clarabelle not left, Henry would have bodily thrown him out of the house.

Agent Snuggles then brought out another film of Grandma Kruczyinski's house in Cleveland. They family had gathered for Krystal's fourth birthday soon after the above incident. Krystal had brought her clown doll along as instructed by Henry. Krystal was dressed in a red dress with white trim, a Polish ceremonial costume. At one point, Henry had Krystal "pose" with the doll. She held the doll in front of her with it facing the camera as she was. Then Henry told her to put her arm around the doll's neck to appear like she was choking the doll. He also had her eyes looking up towards heaven.

As he snapped the picture he said to Krystal, "We're going to get those damn bastards!"

Later on when the other birthday presents were opened, Henry presented Krystal with a new doll that Krystal really liked. The straps on the feet enabled her to dance with it and as she was engrossed in playing with this new doll, both Henry and Marth disposed of the clown doll in Grandma's Kruczyinski's trash. There apparently were so many other presents that when the family departed for home, Krystal clung to her new doll and never asked where the clown doll was.

As he put the surveillance films away Agent Snuggles sat at the table contemplating his next step. He decided not to share these files with Agent Damian Madden. He wanted to receive credit for uncovering un-American activities in this family himself. The "well" may come in handy, too, although he was not sure how it would fit in.

Agent Damian Madden made his way to the Federal Building that afternoon. He had quite a confident air about him. His date with Karla had progressed quite well and with the offer made to him from a fellow doctor at the seminar, he felt a change in his professional as well as personal life was in order.

"Here's some of the files Agent Mullins worked on," stated Agent Snuggles and he promptly shoved a stack of manila folders across the desk. Agent Madden began to quickly go through them placing several aside right away. "Just what are you looking for?"

"One of these families had a young girl who Agent Mullins remarked about. I would like to see that file."

Agent Snuggles located the file of Chrysha's family and handed it to him hoping to fool Agent Madden. As Damian thumbed through the file and found a picture of Chrysha, he smiled. She indeed was a cute child as Agent Mullins had remarked. Damian then noted that the father, Frank, had been killed in 1960 and that there was no more in that file.

"Do you have any more on this family? Any more pictures of Chrysha?"

Agent Snuggles produced a very thin file on the remainder of Chrysha's family with a high school yearbook picture of Chrysha. Damian smiled as he looked at the picture and asked if he could have a copy of the file and picture. Confident that he had located the "child" he had been looking for he left the building and contacted Elliott for his next meeting with the CIA.

When Damian had left, Agent Snuggles placed all files of the Kruczyinski family into a special file drawer and locked the cabinet. He left instructions to the secretary that Agent Madden was not to receive any information from those files. Then he left for the day.

As Damian entered the hotel room he had been directed to go to by Elliott, he was greeted by the same people he had met the last time. Knowing that the CIA and FBI were not always on good terms with each other, Damian asked if the CIA had anything of importance on the Chrysha's family, particularly the death of the father.

"That's very interesting that you should ask about him. He had been under our surveillance for some time after his mother-in-law managed to be smuggled out of Poland and came to the Cleveland area. Of course, the CIA, as you know, is not supposed to maintain any surveillance on American citizens in the United States, but at that time she was not a citizen yet, so we continued our surveillance. In the late 1950's, Chrysha's father, Frank, had spoken with someone about buying some property behind his, but apparently then decided to stay where he was at. We had connections with the Scambolini family who operated a development firm for shopping malls. The Scambolini family approached the father and wanted to buy him out. He would not accept the offer saying it was not enough. We had tried to provide an 'incentive' for him by offering more money if he provided information on another family that owned property we were interested in, yet he refused to do this to another Polish family." At this point the agent stopped talked and looking at the others in the room then said, "Frank had a misfortunate happening occur and he was found shot in his driveway."

Another agent quickly inserted. "We want to discuss this other Polish family with you. - Well, actually about the land they own."

A third agent produced a file of memos from overseas agents that had been translated into English. "In the southern borders of the USSR some of our agents discovered some ancient writings that talked about the hand of God directing his people to an ever-flowing well. They had searched several Assyrian writings which indicated that somewhere there was some kind of imprint of the hand of God that would lead the way."

The second agent produced aerial and satellite photographs of the Great Lakes area. He commented, "Since we wanted to find some imprint of the hand of God, the only place we could locate was the five Great Lakes, possibly indicating the five fingers of the hand. Three of these lakes are considered to be some of the largest lakes in the world, and with three being in close proximity, we felt this has to be it."

"Also," continued the third agent, "when you look at the main part of the Michigan it appears in the shape of a gloved hand."

Damian started at the photos and had to agree with their conclusions. Then he commented. "Well, this had to be it, because the acronym of the names of the five lakes spells HOMES – Huron, Ontario, Michigan, Erie and Superior." The other agents agreed with Damian's analysis and continued.

"We have looked for some sort of indication land-wise to where this well may be and after a lot of discussing with the U.S. Geological Survey and other departments we came to the conclusion that the well is somewhere in Ohio."

The second agent brought out a map of the cities of Ohio and began. "If you look at these three cities, one of which was Burning Bridges, you can see they form an arrow from Cleveland to Burning Bridges."

"And," continued the third agent, "if you follow that arrow over, it points directly to the area of the Kruczyinski property."

"Here," pointed the second agent, "is where there is an underground spring."

Damian sat for a long time absorbing this information, and then asked, "So what is the problem here?"

"There's a Polish family on that property. We've tried to move him off in the early 1950's, but he wouldn't do it. So we had the Army come in and build a Nike site to protect that area. We didn't want Chrysha's father to buy property close to this area because we don't want the well to get into the wrong hands, and with his connections to Communist Poland with his mother-in-law, the government was suspicious of any attempt of Communists to infiltrate the U.S."

"Yes, wasn't it the father who was sending packages to Poland?"

asked Damian remembering that Agent Mullins had made this statement about a Polish family.

"Well, no," claimed the third agent. "That was Henry and Martha Kruczyinski and Henry's mother who have sent and still send the packages."

"So then, this Kruczyinski family…" choked Damian, "Do they have a daughter named Chrysha?" inquired Damian.

The Kruczyinski family have four children. - If Richard Nixon wins this election, he wants to use the idea of this being a God-given well to the U.S. to try to convince the Communists that we have the upper hand here."

"So where do I fit in on this?" inquired Damian. "The family that you asked about now lives across the street from the Kruczyinski family. Both families have had close interaction in the past, particularly the daughters. We need you to get what information the FBI had on this family as well. In the past they have not been as forthcoming with us as we would like."

"I'm curious," stated Damian. "Agent Mullins remarked about having surveillance on one of the children of the family sending packages. She would have been a small child then. He claimed he had surveillance set up on one of the catechism classes."

"That would have to be the Kruczyinski family. The other family had sent Chrysha to Catholic school. Since she received religious instruction every day, there was no need for her to attend catechism classes until she transferred to public school."

Damian sat stunned at the revelation that he had picked the wrong family.

"Well, I'll certainly do what I can. By the way, I just may be relocating to this area soon, so it will be easier for me to do this." With that Damian quickly exited the hotel room not wishing to display the jolt of reality and the folly of his assumption.

As Damian stopped in the hotel lobby he quickly looked over the family file once more. There was mention that Chrysha frequently visited the Kruczyinski household and had a close friendship with Krystal of similar age.

Damn! He cursed to himself. *I need the Kruczyinski family file!* He quickly gathered up his files and made his way back to the Federal Building. His attempts to contact Agent Snuggles failed as he had left for the day and was unable to be reached. Although discouraged at the moment Damian was unrelenting in his effort and vowed to return and find out all he could. In his anger and frustration at being somewhat derailed in his quest, he thought about what Krystal might be like. Not wanting to reveal any more about his true intentions on finding her, it was imperative for him to return to Philadelphia and prepare for his move to Ohio.

As he sat on the plane he contemplated more about how he could pay the bureau back. He still felt unappreciative that the Philadelphia office had purposely put an article in the paper regarding his former name as being a former agent. Nor was he happy just being an undercover informant disguised as a psychologist. He had no determination to kill another agent, yet inside he secretly wished to upend the bureau in whatever way he could. *Working with the CIA on a special assignment just might lend a special hand in my efforts. Maybe then the bureau would view me in a more positive light than they had.*

Krystal was busy gathering up what she would need to start fall quarter at Kent State. She would be living with her sister, Darlene, in a rented house close to campus. Darlene was now pursuing a master's degree and secured temporary guardianship so that Krystal could live off campus providing a more economical means for Krystal to attend college.

After she had filled several boxes, she sat down to read the newspaper. The Vietnam War continued and the number of casualties was running well beyond tens of thousands. Although her brother, Matt, was still stationed in the states, he was scheduled to begin duties in Thailand soon. Krystal hoped that he would be safe there. She turned the pages of the newspaper and began reading about the upcoming Presidential election and predictions of the outcome. Jeanne Dixon, a well know psychic, whose previous predictions were felt to be quite reliable, had foretold that one of the presidential candidates if elected would eventually ruin the presidency. Of course, she mentioned no names, but Krystal wondered who that would be. She was interrupted in thought as Darlene entered the room and mentioned that they were ready to load the car up and head for Kent.

After Darlene and Krystal had settled in their house, Krystal felt quite excited about being in a different environment that her all-white home town and her high school. She was hoping opportunities would open up to her. Yet the next day as she walked to her classes, she encountered jeering from other male students. They seemed to be judging any female student who walked passed them by criteria built only on outward appearance. Krystal was aware of her slight body proportions. She had hoped they would just ignore her, but they did not. Instead they only jeered louder about how nobody would want someone like her. She bit her lip and restrained from saying anything to these students, but it left her with an ill feeling. Maybe she was being too idealistic in her thinking of how different campus life would be compared to high school. She would just have to wait and see.

As the fall quarter continued she made casual acquaintances, but certainly nothing that would ripen into any romance. She began to feel somewhat distant and desired to find some other way to fit in with a group of some sort, something she could feel wanted by.

Darlene and Krystal had taken on a new roommate that quarter, who was a friend of a friend. Darlene admitted that she did not know much about Joan, but that her friend knew her and that she needed a place to stay. The living arrangement helped financially and for some time everyone got along okay.

When Darlene hung Matt's Air Force picture in the living room, then the atmosphere began to change. Joan had been attending meetings of the Students for a Democratic Society for several weeks. When she saw the picture appear on the living room wall she immediately flew into a rage and wanted it taken down. She said she opposed war of any kind, was opposed to the Vietnam War and did not want to have to look at it. This protest of hers continued for several weeks and increased intensely particularly when she would return from the meetings she attended. Neither Darlene nor Krystal had any interest in attending any of these meetings, and Joan's attitude only solidified that conviction. They maintained that the picture would stay on the wall just where it was.

At times Joan would invite male members of the SDS to the house where they spent the evening drinking and talking. They were loud, boisterous and had no consideration for anyone else in the household. When approached the next morning about the noise, Joan would take on an attitude that she was being victimized by Darlene showing no consideration for Joan's feelings.

Other than that, fall quarter went relatively uneventful until the Presidential election results came in showing Richard Nixon to be the winner. Henry admitted he voted for him because he felt the "law and order" talk was needed for the U.S. Krystal, on the other hand, had no liking for Richard Nixon. She vaguely remembered his attitude displayed during the Kennedy-Nixon televised debates in 1960 when Nixon lost to Kennedy. Although she was 10 when she viewed the debate, and was not all that cognizant of everything being discussed, Nixon's mannerisms, anger and attitude bothered her. Now that he was elected President in 1968, she thought about Jeanne Dixon's prediction and wondered if this would be true. *Would Richard Nixon ruin the presidency?*

Joan, of course, would not have cared for anyone elected President and as her involvement deepened with the SDS, both Krystal and Darlene were beginning to conclude that the SDS seemed bent on anarchy rather than democracy as their group name indicated. When Joan became too outspoken during another confrontation in the household, Darlene told her to leave. Joan tried to threaten both Darlene and Krystal stating that her father was with the Mafia, and there would be repercussions if they threw her out. Although it was true that Joan was of a Sicilian family, how much the family was involved with the Mafia remained unclear. After Joan had stormed out of the house with insults, criticisms and threats, both Darlene and Krystal spent the night wondering if any Mafia repercussions would occur. They joked a little bit about being shipped down the river in concrete. When morning came and nothing happened, they were just relieved to be rid of her and any connections to the SDS.

Even though they did not see Joan again, the SDS became more prominent on the Kent State campus, organizing several protest and anti-war demonstrations. Krystal was torn between the ideas behind the anti-war movement and with the death toll rising rapidly, she understood why many young men were avoiding the draft and protesting. Yet she had her brother in the Air Force and she upheld his convictions of serving his country and doing his duty. She had not forgotten that she had already lost Dale, a high school acquaintance, in the Vietnam War and that still weighed on her mind. Then in January 1969 Darlene told her that Richard Sadick, the friend of Dale whom Krystal knew as well, likewise was killed in Vietnam. Krystal wondered how many more soldiers would die before the war would be over.

Though Nixon vowed to reduce the troops in Vietnam and bring some of the soldiers home, Krystal only received a flag-draped coffin of someone she wished she could have got to know so much better. She recalled the many times she sat in study hall and how she and Richard Sadick had many conversations and jokes. Both Richard Sadick and Dale would tease each other and if they ever had to go to war, they wanted to know whom would Krystal write to. Now both of them were gone and whatever romantic interests could have been cultivated were buried with the coffins. Krystal hid her grief deep inside her, never really expressing what she felt to anyone else. In her disappointment she reached out to the Catholic Church on campus for some answers. Although the campus Newman Center was much more modern and relaxed in their thinking than the Catholic Church she had grown up in, she still was not comfortable with their answers. When one priest began explaining that Jesus would come back again in judgment, Krystal questioned him intently.

"If when we die we are judged then and go to either heaven or hell at that time, then when Jesus comes back, what is He coming back for?" she reasoned. When the priest could provide no solid answer for her, Krystal walked away from the church.

On one weekend visit back home as the family gathered to play Pinochle, Krystal contemplated the cards she was playing as she thought about the lack of romance in her life. Now with losing two more romantic prospects to a war that only seemed to be deepening she felt she was losing just like when she played the Ace of Hearts. That card could easily be lost to a trump card.

When she returned to Kent, she began frequenting the downtown bars hoping that the beer she drank would somehow ease the pain and fill the emptiness that now seemed to linger inside her.

CHAPTER
4

"What do you have on Joan K.?" inquired Danny Boy as he sat across from Agent Snuggles. The portrait of J. Edgar Hoover hanging behind the agent's desk was now joined by a portrait of President Richard Nixon. Both figures appeared to loom down over his shoulder. "We found she's been pretty involved in the SDS at Kent State. - We know she was living in an off campus house with a couple of sisters."

Agent Snuggles produced a file on Joan's family and slid it across his desk to Danny. "There have been some gambling debts in that family, and a few minor traffic tickets, but nothing else so far."

Danny quickly paged through the manila folder. "Just how involved are the Kruczyinski's with the SDS," asked Agent Snuggles.

"That's what we're trying to find out. So far we have no indication they are involved."

"Well, we've been wanting to get something on this family for some time. Now that President Nixon and Hoover have put a push on anti-American activity, we're more eager to find something. Since you're undercover on campus with COINTELPRO, why don't you get in some classes with Krystal. Darlene seems to be okay so far and apparently working on her master's degree keeps her busy. Krystal, though, we have noted spending some of her time on weekends at several Kent bars and we want to know who she contacts there."

When Agent Snuggles produced Krystal's picture for Danny, Danny could only comment, "Not exactly someone you'd want to take home." He put the picture in his shirt pocket. "There's a couple of us who've been hanging out in the bars. We'll see what we can find." Danny left the Cleveland office and headed back to his campus apartment.

Krystal stared at her high school graduation picture. She was not happy with it. She remembered the downpour that occurred when she went to get her pictures taken. It literally was a "bad hair day." She set the picture aside now as she dressed for class. She grabbed her books for her first day of spring quarter classes. She had signed up for a basic geology class taught by Dr. Glenn Frank, and as she walked to the class her spirits improved. Although the lecture section was large and held in an auditorium, she enjoyed Dr. Frank's humor as he strove to instill geological basics for his students. The laboratory section, in addition to the lecture, was held in a small classroom, and Krystal met several other students there who enjoyed the class as well. One such student was Joe Barnes. He was of short stature like Krystal and had a great sense of humor. He and several other male students worked along with Krystal on several laboratory projects. Joe caught Krystal's eye for several reasons. While many were protesting the Vietnam War by wearing Army jackets and other military garb, Joe maintained a look from the 1950s with slicked-back hair, black leather jacket, blue jeans, white socks and black loafers. When not in class he frequently had a cigarette in his mouth, and when the weather was warm he would roll his pack of cigarettes in his short-sleeve of his white T-shirt. He was quite different, certainly not blending in well with the rest of the students, and that Krystal liked.

There were only about 20 students in that particular lab section and although engrossed with Joe and his friends, Krystal frequently noted someone watching her from the other side of the room.

"She seems to be enjoying this group," Danny Boy whispered to his coworker, Don Klapper. "Let's see if we can talk with her."

They motioned for Krystal to come to their side stating that needed some help with their lab exercise as well. After some light conversation Krystal returned to her seat by Joe.

Joe leaned over to Krystal and remarked, "They're not too swift back there are they?"

"No, they don't seem to know too much. It's probably that they have to take this class as a requirement."

Krystal remained with Joe and his friends until the class was over. For several days after that Krystal did not see Danny or his friend in the lab class and so thought they may have dropped the class. When at last Danny did reappear in class, his friend was no longer with him.

Krystal had fit into the study group which Joe had named "The Lunch Bag Five." They all got along well and enjoyed one another's company. When class was over Joe asked Krystal if she would join them at the Student Center for a break. Joe remarked they played cards and drank Pepsi and just hung out. Krystal obliged as it sounded like perhaps this might be an interesting group to have as friends. When she found out that Pinochle was one of Joe's favorite card games, she readily joined in. In addition to his 1950s dress, Joe carried did carry a six-inch knife "just in case." Although he would often talk about his experiences with the "kids on the street" back home, Krystal noted he was always thoughtful towards her. He was intelligent and remarked that he like to keep his mind sharp by playing "Dell Pencil Puzzles and Word Games." This attraction for challenging one's mental talents rubbed off on Krystal and she, too, enjoyed the magazine as well. Often the two of them were seen solving a puzzle together.

"What do we know about this Joe?" Danny asked Don in Danny's apartment several weeks later.

"He's from the west side of Cleveland and has a fiance there. He used to belong to a group of tough kids. Never got into too much trouble, mostly pranks, but every now and then that group would have fights with the group of kids from other blocks in their neighborhood. They always managed to disappear conveniently when the cops showed up - at least that is what the Cleveland cops told me," stated Don matter-of-factly.

"So we can tell Agent Snuggles that Krystal's hanging around some street punks. "What did you find out about who she met in The Lounge?"

"That's what's kind of strange. She goes in, sits at a table, smiles at a few people and just basically nurses her beer. Sometimes she drinks two, but not often. She seems to just watch people and then when she's done, she walks home. I don't really see her talking to anyone. Sometimes she just sits and stares at the table or the wall."

"Hmm," Danny wondered, "do you think she knows you're watching her?"

"I don't think so. She never seems to even notice me."

"Well, I'm going to talk with her when I see her in class on Monday. Go see what she does this Friday night? Does she only frequent The Lounge?"

"That's the only place I've ever seen her."

Krystal had to admit she really did not enjoy the taste of beer, but it did seem to have a soothing effect on her. Sitting alone at the table and sipping her beer, she enjoyed just observing other people. Once in a while someone would sit down for a short time with her and carry on light conversation, but most of the time she sat alone. Sometimes as she stared at the table or the wall she would think about Chrysha and the fun times they had. Now that Chrysha had announced to Krystal that she was engaged to Sam Hill, a career military man and captain, Krystal knew she probably would not see much of Chrysha after the wedding. She had just been home the week before, and as she and Chrysha compared notes of the boys they met on campus, both had to admit that the boys seemed too immature for them. With the upcoming wedding, Chrysha had told her that they would be moving to New York where Sam was stationed. Krystal sipped her beer contemplating that she would miss her good friend and childhood playmate.

Damian Madden sat in his office staring at Chrysha's picture. The business of his move and marriage to Karla had preoccupied most of his time. Now in late spring of 1969, things had started to settle down and he could spend more time on his projects for the CIA. Karla only knew him as a psychologist and being gone much of the time with the airlines, she was unaware of his true background or activities. Neither Damian nor Karla had wanted children and so Damian took measures to avert any chance of pregnancy that might arise. Yet with Karla being on so many flights and out of town several days at a time, Damian began to look elsewhere for his satisfaction. He contemplated somehow approaching Chrysha on one of his trips to Ohio State where she was at and fantasized on the outcome. This aberration was suddenly shattered when Elliott announced that Chrysha's wedding was just around the corner and afterwards the two newlyweds would make their move to New York. Still, as Damian gathered up the remaining chards of his fractured illusion, he kept the door open to the possibility that he still had a chance with Chrysha. His fantasy was fueled by the thought that he and Elliott had made plans to attend the Woodstock music festival to be held on a farm in New York in August, and perhaps she might be there as well.

His wandering imagination was interrupted when the last patient for that day entered his office. Damian quickly set Chrysha's picture aside as a somewhat disheveled man in his 30's sat down in the chair.

"The court ordered me to come for counseling, so what can you do for me?" He demanded.

After Damian panned quickly through a few notes and forms sent along with Leonard Blare, Damian knew that he really had no experience in dealing with patients charged with sexual offenses. Yet he managed to get this patient to open up some and relay his story. As Damian listened, he continued with the conversation obtaining information about where some of this patient's pictures ended up. When Damian had secured information who he could contact in Columbus, he ended the session and had the patient schedule another appointment the following week. As it was still early in the afternoon and his patient roster was empty, Damian made the drive to Columbus and found the porn shop.

Though Damian engaged in a somewhat fantasy life concerning both Krysal and Chrysha, he did so because of his desire to know them more. The reality was that there were few patients coming to him. When he spoke with his partner about this, he decided to open some other offices in neighboring communities including Scoria and Burning

Bridges. *These areas, being larger in population size, should provide a larger clientele,* he surmised.

He still was needing to get information on the Kruczyski family. Yet each time he went to the Cleveland office to try to get any files on them, Agent Snuggles snubbed him off by telling him that they were working on the case and did not need anyone else, nor were they sharing that information with him. He was miffed by the attitude and approached Elliott about the matter in mid-July. Elliott did manage to get Damian a photocopy of Krystal's graduation picture, but that was all Damian had to go on.

From time to time he would refer back to this picture and wondered what the rest of her looked like. In the multitude of mental images of how he could accomplish getting more information about the Kruczyinski family, he approached Elliott once more.

"What if you threaten the Kruczyinski family with taking their daughter away? You know, Krystal being the youngest child, that might make a greater impact on Henry," Damian suggested.

"Actually something like that was tried a long time ago when she was quite small. One agent had threatened the family about taking her as a sacrifice. Henry, as we understand, was very upset with the agent and swore at him to leave the house."

Damian conjectured, "Well, maybe he would be more obliging if something detrimental happened to his daughter – like unfortunate circumstances, you know?"

"We're trying to keep that sort of thing covered up here. The public doesn't know we're keeping tabs on American citizens, and if something suspicious turns up, that could blow our cover. We took quite a bit of heat over Frank's death," Elliott stated vehemently.

"Well, I didn't mean it had to be us," Damian stated. "I just meant maybe we could do this another way – find someone else with a reason for getting rid of her."

"Yeah, but who is that person going to be?" Elliott eyed Damian and Damian just shrugged his shoulders innocently. "All we know is that she is spending some time with someone in Kent. We've seen the two of them on occasion. It sounds like they're romantically involved." Elliott paused, "We'll have to come up with something else. You know

President Nixon is really putting a push on snuffing out anti-Americans. He also wants that well in U.S. hands for his purposes. We need to work on that angle somehow."

"So you're telling me that you have someone following her?" asked Damian somewhat surprised and rebuked.

"Yes and no. We're using some of Hoover's informants from the COINTELPRO. Several of them are campus police officers and they've been watching her from a distance. Nothing to go on, though." After making arrangements for their trip to Woodstock, Damian departed for home.

Krystal had ended spring quarter in quite an uplifted mood. She decided sciences were her best subjects and strove to obtain a double major in biology and geology. The Lunch Bag Five had signed up for more geology courses together for fall quarter and said a temporary summer farewell to each other. Krystal was planning on staying in Kent over summer working at a local restaurant and cleaning house for an invalid. It would bring in some money. Darlene was pursuing studies out of state for the summer, and she and Krystal planned on a trip out west at the end of August. In the meantime a restaurant customer took a liking to Krystal and so the two of them spent much time together.

When Krystal returned home for Chrysha's wedding, Martha remarked about someone coming to visit Krystal.

"He was such a nice, pleasant, good-looking man, black hair, average height. He said he remembered you when you used to play in the town band. Oh, I wish I could remember his name – was it Ernie something?"

At first Krystal had too much on her mind to recall Ernie Wilson, and it had been so long ago when she last had any contact with him. As she tried to remember, though, she urged her mother to tell her more.

"He just kept asking about you and that he said he would come back for you. Of course, I told him you weren't here, but were at Kent State now. He seemed a little disappointed, but said he would stop back another time."

With only that to go on and with Krystal's attention diverted elsewhere she figured she would wait until he returned again. She spent very little speculation about Ernie being more involved with work. With all the flurry of Chrysha's wedding, there was no time to even think to ask Chrysha if she remembered anyone named Ernie, and Chrysha and her husband departed for a short honeymoon and then to set up their household in Syracuse, New York. After the ceremony Krystal returned to Kent.

She spent the summer working with all of her free time taken up by her new boyfriend. Things looked up for her, yet when he insisted that they marry soon and immediately start a family, Krystal began to back away from the relationship. It seemed too restricting too soon and she enjoyed herself quite a bit with her other friendships. After the trip out west with Darlene, Krystal ended the relationship. Her boyfriend soon found someone else to fill the void he was looking for, and once more Krystal felt the Ace of Hearts being trumped again, though this time she felt it was necessary. Although she felt somewhat guilty for the breakup, her dissatisfaction resolved when she returned to classes and renewed her friendship with the Lunch Bag Five.

Danny was still not sure about this group Krystal continued to spend much of her time with. Managing to secure a position as a campus officer brought him in contact with several others who likewise were with COINTELPRO. The general public knew nothing at that time about this collection of individuals who used whatever devious tactics they could come up with. J. Edgar Hoover himself had authorized them to "do whatever they had to" with regards in seeking out anti-American sentiment especially in organizations. And Hoover had no intentions of letting the general public know about this underhanded group of his. With the SDS being held under scrutiny, any associates, no matter how minor, were monitored.

Danny had met Elliott on a few occasions exchanging whatever information they had with each other. On this particular fall day Elliott and Danny met in Akron, far enough away from the campus so as not to arouse suspicion.

"So you've found nothing to link Krystal with any SDS groups or activities?" inquired Elliott somewhat exasperated.

"Well, I saw her at one rally, but she was way in the back, like me. In fact, she recognized me and waved. But she never got involved with any of the rally. In fact, she approached me and asked why I was there. I told her I was with the campus police and making sure things did not get out of hand. She really did not seem too interested in the rally at all, just came to see what it was like. After she finished talking with me, she left."

'That's it?" Elliott remarked disappointedly. "We need something more substantial. We're getting desperate. We really need something to upset the Kruczyinski family."

"What exactly do you want me to do?" asked Danny.

Elliott's face became contorted in anger. He stood up to leave. "I don't care what you do as long as the job gets done." Shoving his fist at Danny's face, he continued, "And if you don't come up with something soon, I'll make sure you don't have a job on campus - or anywhere else for that matter."

When Elliott and Danny departed company, Danny decided to contact Krystal claiming that he wished to see her again. Krystal was taken by the gesture and as Danny continued to pour on some charm, Krystal became quite captivated by Danny. He quickly pressured Krystal in becoming intimately involved with him, and after the string of disappointing relationships in Krystal's past, she finally gave in thinking that the relationship would only strengthen. So from late 1969 and well into 1970, Krystal sexually involved herself with Danny. They did not go out on dates, but only spent an afternoon or evening in the bedroom at his apartment, and even this was not all that frequent. Although she continued to do well in classes, she did not see Danny very often, having no more classes with him. She noted that when they did get together for a passionate rendezvous, Danny was quite cold in his approach, rarely if ever embracing her for any period of time. She wondered if it was her, or just the way he was or something else. When she remarked that she did not get to see him as often as she would like, he always responded that he had "business to tend to." As she wished for a deeper relationship with him and it did not appear to be forthcoming, she returned to The Lounge and began spending more of her weekends there looking over the clientele.

In the meantime she managed to get a part-time job on campus working in one of the biology labs. Mostly she did clean-up work in the laboratory and her schedule was pretty much open to whenever she could fit some time in. This made it easy for her to put in some hours between classes, and she enjoyed the opportunity of doing something more related to her major.

In April 1970, President Nixon announced escalation of the Vietnam War to extend into Cambodia. With this he demanded 150,000 more troops be drafted. Bitter sentiments were set off in various parts of the country, and the SDS took a front seat in monopolizing anti-war demonstrations on campuses. As Kent State was already inundated by a fair number of SDS members, plans were made for more violent rallies.

On April 22, 1970. Kent State held the first Earth Day rally. Krystal participated in this nonviolent rally by standing in the sparse crowd. She could see there were observers in the distance and she was not sure who they were, but with tensions rising on campus, she decided to stand behind a poster. Later on Krystal returned to her house, yet felt uncomfortable knowing that there were those watching for any type of unrest.

A week later Darlene and Krystal were startled by the sounds of fire engines rushing up the street the Friday evening of May 1ˢᵗ. Although they could not see beyond the hilltop from their house, they sky was well lit. As the two of them crested the hill, they could see the former ROTC (Reserved Officers Training Corp) wooden building engulfed in flames. There appeared to be a lot of commotion going on and the two sisters returned to their house, not wanting to venture any further. Later on that evening they heard the rumbling of military personnel carriers of the Ohio National Guard head in the same direction as the fire.

That weekend sparked more riots and disturbances in downtown Kent. As a result other law enforcement agencies were called to quell the disruptions. These other agencies included city police, campus police, sheriff's departments, and state patrol. Combined with the National Guard the agencies announced martial law in effect. As the decree was made via the media, there were explicit declarations prohibiting the gathering of groups in the city as well as on campus.

By Monday, May 4ᵗʰ tensions were running very high on campus. As Krystal walked to a chemistry class, she first walked past a building close to the top of the hill where she had observed the ROTC fire three nights prior. She noted that a black-haired State Trooper stood guard by the one door. She quickly moved on down the hill and passed the burned-out remains of the ROTC building. It was heavily surrounded by National Guardsman. She continued on and had to pass through a make-shift guardsmen camp. They appeared very tired having been pulled directly off a turmoil in the trucker's strike in recent weeks. As Krystal made her way through the camp, she felt they watched her with begrudging eyes. By the time she reached the chemistry building doors, she felt uncomfortable about what could happen.

During her class she overheard that there was to be a rally and large demonstration at noon on the central portion of the campus. Some students began to argue that martial law was in effect, and arrests could possibly result. Krystal was somewhat inquisitive about the demonstrations, yet the uneasy feeling she had before class persisted.

She arrived back at her house and prepared to go to work at noon. She contemplated once more just observing the rally from a distance, but a pervading feeling encompassed her. She felt something inside her say, "Don't go up there!" It was so strong and emphatic that she chose to forget about going to see the rally and to go to work instead. As Darlene also had to go to the biology building she drove both of them to the parking lot. When the two sisters got out of the car, they heard the shots.

They looked at one another across the car both commenting. "I hope those aren't gun shots."

They entered the building and Krystal walked down the long glassed-in hallway to clock in. As she did so, she could view a good portion of the back of the main part of campus. All the students that she could see had "hit the dirt" and were lying prone on the ground. By the time she got to the lab and turned the radio on the shocking news of "Four students shot dead at Kent State" became a reality. She continued to listen as reports poured in and for several hours she found that she literally was locked in the building until some order could be obtained on what was transpiring outside. When she finally was let out, she learned the campus was closed indefinitely and courses would have to be finished another way.

Krystal did not know any of the four students who had died. There were listed as Jeffery Miller, Allison Krause, William Schroeder, and Sandy Scheuer. She noted that the paper had displayed not only their high school graduation pictures, but the most recent pictures of them as well. In many cases there were remarkable differences. As Krystal looked at Sandy Scheuer's pictures, she noted the similarities between Sandy's and Krystal graduation pictures. She felt it just to be a coincidence about the similarities, but when Krystal read that Sandy had come to the rally just to observe, was not involved, but stood a distance off, and was in fact walking away when she was shot through the throat, a dreadful thought came over Krystal. *That could have been me! I would've done the same thing and stood in the same place, then walk away. Had I gone to attend the rally I might have been the one shot instead of her.* She ruminated over this for the next several weeks until another pressing matter occupied her attention. Her brother, Matt, had written home that he was volunteering to serve in Vietnam.

To finish the quarter's classes, students met off campus various public buildings. Krystal learned that because of the campus being closed, there would no longer be a job for her when the campus would reopen. As she met with several classmates in a church to try to finish their class, they began talking over about what all had taken place in the preceding weeks. Several other discussions occurred, and it was here that she heard what she thought at first was just a rumor.

"Nixon was looking for a female student to shoot," stated one classmate to another. Krystal contemplated the thought behind such an action.

"What would he gain by shooting a female?" she asked.

"Not just any female. There's one he was looking for in particular."

Later when the campus reopened, Krystal was walking around the campus. Ahead of her were two men, Gary Scambolini and Art Castle, both FBI agents. These two agents among others later sat in on Krystal's philosophy class in the hopes of finding other dissidents. Although up to this time Krystal was aware of Nixon's push for uncovering anti-Americans, she had no idea that it was the supposed "well" on the Kruczyinski property that he wished the government to have possession of or of all his methods of how he would obtain this. She thought about all the packages the family had sent to Poland over the many years, and wondered if there was a connection with that action and this rumor she now was listening to.

When Krystal returned home she began reading through the newspaper. There was a lot of speculation expressed as thy why these four had been shot. It was pretty much agreed that Jeffrey Miller had been in the front section antagonizing the guard. There were also various reports that Allison Krause had been an active participant as well. It was not clear about William Schroeder, a ROTC candidate, and as far as Sandy Scheuer, a very limp excuse came forth indicating that she was shot because she was promiscuous and deserved to die. This statement, however, was attacked fervently by her friends, family, and classmates who said she was never like that. Krystal disliked the notion of utilizing such a lame excuse when it was clear that she was walking away from the rally. The discrepancy finally warranted an investigation to inform the public of what really happened.

Another thing that happened when the campus was shut down was that Krystal had a hold put on her bank account. Apparently, the towns people were afraid all the students would take their money out of the banks and so put holds on their accounts so that would not happen. This made it difficult to pay bills, but Krystal was able to draw some money from the savings account. Later on after the campus reopened, Krystal closed out both accounts and transferred them to an Akron bank branch outside of Kent.

Also after the campus reopened, a Kent city policeman stopped at the house and began asking Krystal and Darlene several questions.

"We have some photos here of several SDS members that we were not able to arrest. We want to know since you lived with Joan, an SDS member, if you recognize any of them and just who they are."

Both Krystal and Darlene explained that they knew nothing of Joan's contacts and that they had thrown her out because of her conflicting belligerent attitude. Neither wanted anything to do with Joan and could give no information that would help the police out.

Damian sat at his desk waiting for the next patient to arrive. Now instead of contemplating about Chrysha, he held the picture of Krystal in front of him. His Woodstock trip, although exciting, had not brought him any closer to Chrysha. She had not been there and subsequently he lost interest in pursuing her any more. Just then his secretary broke into the room and asked if he had heard the news.

"Four students have been shot at Kent State!"

They listened to the news reports on the radio, with Damian sitting somewhat forward in his seat. He was hoping Krystal Kruczyinski would be among the four named. As it was unclear at the beginning of all the reports exactly who had died, Damian was eager to hear more. He decided to cancel his afternoon appointments and return home whereupon he sat in front of the television hoping Krystal's picture would appear on the screen. In anticipation he laid Krystal's graduation picture on the coffee table in front of him. *There could be no mistake,* he thought. *If my dream would come true, she should be dead.*

When at last pictures and names were released of the four dead students, Damian's enthusiasm disintegrated and his anticipated dream of winning the FBI's as well as Nixon's favor vanished before his eyes. Yet he needed confirmation that Krystal was definitely still alive. Elliott was unable to be reached and Damian could only wait for Elliott to contact him. He nervously paced the floor for a long period of time when he finally decided to return to the Cleveland FBI office once more.

When summer quarter began and the campus was once again opened up, Krystal wandered down to the restaurant she previously worked at to see if she could pick up some part-time hours. As she spoke with the owner she noted what she thought were several businessmen sitting at the counter. When she had worked here previously, many times businessmen decked out in nice dark suits would come in for lunch, so she thought nothing of this.

As she talked with the owner the conversation turned from job opportunity to news on campus since the reopening. Krystal mentioned that she had heard a rumor about a possible retaliation by the SDS for the student deaths and that a rally was possibly being planned soon. She just happened to be looking in the direction of the businessmen as she spoke when one with a receding hairline, Agent Robert Snuggles, spoke to Agent Art Castle, claiming, "That's her!" and hoped that Krystal had not heard him.

Krystal finished her statement and wondered what the man meant by that. When Agent Robert looked in her direction, she was staring back at him. She quickly exited the restaurant and began walking back to her house. Agent Robert waited until she left the restaurant and then ordered Agent Castle to go speak with her.

Damian Madden had been sitting out in the parking lot waiting for the other agents to come out. He was determined to discover whether Krystal was alive or not, or was Agent Snuggles brushing him off once again. He had followed Agent Snuggles from the Cleveland office to Kent knowing that the Cleveland office would be conducting an investigation into the shootings. While the agents sat inside the restaurant, Damian bided his time by lingering inconspicuously in another parked car. He picked up on their transmitter frequency when they emerged from the restaurant and entered their cars. As they stated that Krystal was walking home, and that they would have to wait until she reached her destination, Damian viewed Krystal through his binoculars hoping to visualize her up close. He was shocked at the discovery that there was really nothing stunning about her. She gave him the impression of being some of a waif, and she did not match any of his conjured images of Krystal.

As Krystal's hand barely reached the doorknob, she was startled by screeching tires of several cars abruptly stopping in her driveway. A man in a dark pin-striped suit jumped out and ran up to the porch.

Holding his FBI badge in front of Krystal's face, he announced, "Krystal Kruczyinski, I'm Agent Art Castle of the FBI. We want to talk to you." The flurry of this activity as well as his serious demeanor scared her, but she motioned for the agent to come inside.

He was tall, had a full head of pepper-colored hair and wore gold-rimmed glasses. He sat down in an overstuffed chair facing Krystal as she sat on the couch. He began by asking her about the rumor concerning another rally, and she declared that she had heard it through Darlene, and that she was only relaying secondhand information.

He then asked Krystal, "Why didn't you attend the rally on May 4th?"

"I heard a voice, you know, 'the voice within,'" she answered trying to indicate that it was something on the order of one's own conscience. "It told me not to go up there, so I didn't."

She was uncertain whether he agreed or understood what she was trying to convey, but she noted that he had either smirked or faintly smiled. He took note of what she said on a pad of paper that he had produced from his suit pocket. The faint smile that she saw made her relax somewhat as the conversation continued. As he wanted more information about the proposed rally, she indicated that she would have to get Darlene to talk about it. She left the room briefly to let Darlene know what was transpiring. She then returned to the living room as both waited for her sister.

In the meantime Agent Castle inquired, "Just out of curiosity, have you ever heard any rumors about Nixon wanting a female shot?"

Krystal felt a lump immediately form in her throat and she started breathing faster. She turned her eyes away from the agent and shook her head as she softly replied, "No." She was hoping to convey the idea that she really did not want to talk about it, but yet had indeed heard something. He then quickly changed the subject, and asked if the picture hanging on the wall behind her was her boyfriend.

Returning to look directly at the agent, she said, "That's my brother Matt." It's his Air Force picture. Once again she noted a faint smirk on the agent's face.

Then Darlene entered the room and he began to question her about the rally. However, she too, could only give secondhand information and so offered Agent Castle little more than Krystal did. When nothing more could be given to him, the agent left.

The next day when Krystal entered her summer philosophy class, the professor announced that there could be some FBI agents sitting in on the class. Krystal became aware when the agents did arrive in their dark suits and polished shoes, that they were the same agents whom she had seen in the restaurant. They stuck out so vividly because no student on campus dressed like that. She began to surmise that they probably did not believe her statements that she knew nothing and would follow her to find out who she was contacting.

At first no one wanted to respond openly in class, but as weeks passed, classmates became bolder in their comments, even to the point of deriding them for sitting there looking for dissidents. When it came time for the final exam, the agents disappeared. Krystal, however, was not comfortable that they possibly had followed her, and one afternoon made her way to the Student Center for lunch. She spied a young black man sitting alone at an outside picnic table and then asked if she could join him.

He was very polite and as they talked she asked if he ever felt he was being followed or checked on by the FBI or other agencies. He readily relayed that the CIA had hounded black people using many unsuspecting individuals as "guinea pigs" in various drug experiments. It sounded to Krystal that the CIA felt themselves to be "superior" to others and could "use others to their advantage." It was true that the CIA had recruited on campuses many top scientists, psychologists and others in research on groups and individuals. They did a lot with "mind control" and studied how one's thinking could be totally changed using such methods as subliminal messaging and others. They were very discrete in their testing and when finished, they would abandon the individual. If there were any residual ill effects from their experiments, the CIA took no responsive action. The blacks, this gentleman noted, had been hounded for having spiritual beliefs.

"What do you mean?" inquired Krystal.

"Well, you know, if we're strongly religious or have had any dealings with casting out demons, then these people seemed to have been singled out. Most of the time they either disappeared or ended up harmed in one way or another."

"Why don't you band together?"

"We have. We learned that if we stick together, we have a better chance of fending them off."

"Did the FBI ever bug your telephone or house?" she finally asked.

"Oh, yeah, - But they never did find anything on me, because there's nothing to find!" He laughed and Krystal laughed as well.

Then she stated, "It's only a matter of time before they find me." She didn't know what made her say that at the time, but as she did so she noted that this man was staring directly into her eyes. She thanked him for being so blunt with her and then left. What she didn't realize at the time was that this black man, who agents had noted talking with Krystal, disappeared after that, and they could find no record of him being a student at the campus, or any way to trace him. He just disappeared. Many years later as Krystal gained more spiritual knowledge, she realized that she had actually been talking to Elijah and his influence made her make the statement about 'it's only a matter of time before they find me.'

A short time later the FBI released their initial report on the investigation. They claimed "there was no violation of Federal law," and therefore it was a closed case. When there was a tremendous outcry from the public for an in depth investigation into the shootings, J. Edgar Hoover had to retract the statements and that the case needed to be opened and further investigated.

Krystal watched the news one evening upon hearing about the case being reopened. She thought about coming forward concerning the rumor about Nixon that she heard. However, she was immediately discouraged when the announcement was made that the hearings would be in closed session and that only those directly involved on campus at that time would be allowed in. She was excluded as her information was only secondhand and she was not involved in the rally on that day of the shootings. Then she watched a segment of TV transmission portraying J. Edgar Hoover commenting about the reputation of Sandy Scheuer in reference to her "promiscuous activities."

He chuckled as he said, "Well, she sure was having a lot of fun!" Krystal stared at the TV long after the segment had disappeared from the screen enraged as she thought about what he was saying.

She reasoned, *if everyone says she was not promiscuous and Nixon wanted a female shot – what if they have my information about my life and are using it to justify the shooting of her? If I was meant to die, according to Nixon, they would lie about someone else's reputation to cover up everything about this rumor.* Then she began to wonder about Danny. *Did he supply some information to them?* She was not sure.

As the summer of 1970 neared an end, she noted one day that Danny's car had pulled in next door. She went out to talk with him, but he totally brushed her aside, claiming he had no time for her. His demeanor and mannerism emotionally hurt her inside.

She was further devastated when a few days later, a picture appeared on the front page of the newspaper. She noticed Danny squarely in the center of the photograph with a young boy on his lap and a woman seated next to him. The caption read that Danny Boy was enjoying a sporting event with his wife and two-year-old son. Krystal gasped when she saw this.

I've been fooled all along. He was married all this time, and I didn't know it! No wonder he was so cold. She surmised that somehow he had communicated their activities to the FBI and this is what Hoover was using to justify the shooting of Sandy Scheuer. She did not know of any other connection Danny might have had, but she kept that information in the back of her mind.

As she entered The Lounge later that evening, she became lost in the number of beers she drank, wishing only to numb the pain and disappointment she felt. When the alcohol began to make her drowsy, she left for her house.

She had just entered the door, when two men came up behind her and asked to speak with her. They easily pushed their way in and while one tried to impress Krystal that he was genuinely interested in her, the other began combing through her refrigerator. Still reeling from the effects of alcohol, she was unable to resist them. The one was insistent on having sex with her, and as she looked at him face-to-face through the dimly lit room, she thought he might have looked familiar. When they were finished, they promptly left and Krystal fell asleep on the floor.

"I've got word from J. Edgar Hoover himself to take you out of the picture, Danny," Agent Snuggles reported as he sat by his desk. "You've done good work, but he doesn't want the public to know how involved you were with COINTELPRO. So here are your documents for name change, etc. You and your family will be relocated to another part of Ohio. We don't want you testifying in this case."

"What about my partner, Don Klapper?"

"Oh, yes, we're relocating him as well. He's going to the Ohio State Highway Patrol. Seems he did good work after you left. Apparently he and a friend visited Krystal Kruczyinski one night. She never filed a rape report with the local police. Only thing though we found out that she was taken to the campus health center by that street punk friend of hers, the one you were checking into. What was his name?"

"Joe Barnes."

"Well, he got her there in time to get her a prescription for penicillin. Too bad the gonorrhea Don gave her was treated so soon. We were hoping it would have had more detrimental effects on her."

Danny left the Cleveland office to prepare his move to Burning Bridges. As soon as he closed the office door, Damian Madden walked in and stood across from Agent Snuggles's desk.

"Well, you've put me off long enough. I need that file on the Kruczyinski family. I've been working with the CIA on obtaining a well they own and I need this information now!" He demanded pounding his fist on the desk.

Agent Snuggles just stared at Damian noting the force by which he spoke.

Damian leaned forward and more emphatically stated, "You're a Republican! I don't think you want it getting around that you don't support President Nixon, do you? I have friends in the CIA that can cause a lot of problems for you - you know, all of a sudden you disappear?"

Agent Snuggles reluctantly handed over the files that Damian wanted. Damian beaming with delight departed with a cache of not only written documents, but surveillance tapes as well. Once at his office he shared with Elliott all he had. Elliott in turn provided Damian with sophisticated bugging devices, electronic equipment and various transmitters and radios that the CIA had perfected in their use.

"You know," Damian surmised, "We can dub in images and make phony tapes with this."

Elliott agreed and then said, "I'm going to leave that up to you. You're free to use these equipment any way you wish to accomplish our goal."

Krystal decided that her lifestyle need a change. After her binge the one night and the resultant encounter with the two males, she stayed at her house in the evenings. She contemplated returning to the Catholic Church on campus, and so went one afternoon and had a lengthy confession with one priest. He was very understanding of her, telling her she was not totally lost and that there was always hope. For some time she attended church and stayed away from any intimate relationships.

She felt better about herself until Grandma Kruczyinski died in 1971. Soon after the funeral while Krystal was spending a few days at her parents' home, a State Trooper with rusty-colored hair knocked on the door. Henry answered it and walked out onto the front porch to talk. Krystal was sitting on the couch and could hear parts of the conversation, although they spoke quite softly.

"You know," Trooper Otto Hartsel began quietly, "Nixon's really keeping your family under a pretty heavy watch with you sending all those packages to Poland. Now that your mother's gone, we think it would be best if you didn't send any more now."

"Well," Henry stated, "there was only a distant aunt that was left of the immediate family. So that shouldn't be a problem. She had tried to help the remaining family. I only mailed them for her as, well you know, she was my mother, and I respected her wishes. But you're right, now that she's gone the packages can stop."

"What I mean is that Nixon is really trying hard to find something here. We've heard bits and pieces that he was hoping to have your daughter shot at Kent State."

Krystal choked when she heard that, and Trooper Hartsel realized that Krystal had been sitting inside close to the door all that time. He abruptly ended the conversation and told Henry not to mention what he was just told.

When Henry came back in he said nothing to anyone. Krystal returned to Kent later that day. As she listened to the radio, she vaguely heard some statement about a search for a "well." For days afterwards she looked through the newspaper and listened for anything else about this, but came up totally empty-handed.

CHAPTER 5

K rystal watched as the tray of various pills began to circulate around the living room. *This is not good,* she thought. She still remembered being taken advantage of when she had too much to drink. She could not file charges then because she had let them in and she was too lethargic to resist. Now as she sat in a so-called friend's apartment, she could not help but think of similar ill consequences. *I could just not participate, but if I should drink anything here, who's to stop someone from putting something in that? I could be raped like before.* After Krystal passed the tray on, not partaking of any of its contents, she immediately got up and ran out the front door.

"This isn't the party I wanted to come to!" Krystal vehemently claimed as she shook off Grant's hold of her arm.

"Where are you going?" I really didn't know they were going to do this," he claimed trying to hide his true intentions. "Don't leave yet."

"No! If you want to burn your brain out, that's your business, but I happen to like mine the way it is. No, I'm leaving." Krystal stomped off towards her house.

"Just don't go to the police!" he yelled after her and then returned inside.

As she walked along Krystal thought about their relationship. She had met Grant in the recreation room at the campus church. After she had talked to the priest, he had invited her to meet some other people that frequented the room there. Grant had introduced himself the first time she entered the room. Several people were playing cards, others were playing board games and watching TV. He seemed genuinely interested in her and so the two had struck up a close relationship. Yet there was something about Grant that Krystal was not sure about. He was quite insistent that they arrange to marry later, but open a joint savings account now. Krystal had saved a fair amount of money, but something about his eagerness of this set-up bothered her. She had put off his request for now. He then invited her to this party at his friend's house. She knew there were plenty of drugs on campus, especially now that the shootings had occurred, the public outcry demanded an investigation, and the hearings lingered slowly onward. Apathy had set in, and many resolved to find an escape somewhere. Yet Krystal was prone to drown her discouragement in some alcohol - just enough to dull the pain. She really had no interest in the drug scene. And up until now Grant had not shown any interest in drugs, at least not that Krystal knew about.

Her previous near-rape episode had left her somewhat anxious about meeting others in the bars downtown. Coupled with her inability to unearth anything about the Nixon rumor and the shootings and the supposed well, Krystal returned to the health center on campus to seek help for a nervous stomach. She was given a prescription for tranquilizers. She disliked taking them and after she noted how sluggish it made her feel, she stopped the prescription. That is when she thought she would give the church another try, and there is where she met Grant.

Krystal angrily walked back to her house from this party. While walking she thought to herself, *I think I've been playing the wrong card. I keep trying to play the Ace of Hearts and I lose it. Now I'm going to start playing a different ace. Maybe this time it will be the Ace of Clubs!* She walked inside resolved that she had done the right thing and went to bed.

Grant showed up at her house a few days later. He was trying to smooth things over when there was a knock on the door. A bearded young man with shoulder-length stringy hair wanted to speak with Grant. Krystal let him in and followed him to where Grant was.

"I need to talk to you!" the man demanded, "alone!" He turned and scowled at Krystal as he spoke.

Krystal reached around the corner, quickly grabbed a drinking glass and entered the bedroom behind where Grant was. She shut the door and waited for the conversation to begin. Soundlessly she placed the glass up against the wall. *I've heard this works, if you do it right,* she thought as she placed her ear up against the bottom of the glass.

"You're getting behind on payments, Grant. I need the money today!" He spoke softly, but was forceful.

"I'll get it for you; it's just that I don't have it now – tomorrow for sure!" Grant nervously responded.

Krystal pulled away from the glass. Now it was making sense why Grant was insisting on a joint account. He needed drug money and he was going to use her own funds, money she had worked hard to save. She waited until the man left. When she opened the door to where Grant was sitting, she began asking questions.

"You wouldn't happen to be dealing drugs, would you?" He hesitated and tried to circumvent the conversation, but Krystal was insistent. After a few minutes of direct confrontation on Krystal's part, Grant reluctantly admitted that he was dealing.

Krystal stared at him with a stone-cold face and said, "Get out! You have an hour to take whatever belongs to you here and get out!" When he obliged, Krystal felt that this time she had played the right ace. Her hard-nosed approach to what she viewed could have been a disastrous outcome gave her some confidence. Maybe what she needed to develop was a more up-front approach in her dealings with the unknown, especially with all the questions she had about Nixon, Hoover, and their rationale behind the shootings, and the like.

A few days later, a Kent city policeman stopped by Krystal's house and began asking questions about Grant's activities.

"I don't really know much about who his friends are," she told him. "I just found out he was into dealing drugs, and it was then that I threw him out. There were times, though, where I did feel like I was followed to his house, but then maybe that was just my imagination."

"You were being followed," the officer claimed, "but we knew you didn't do any drugs."

After the officer left Krystal felt more assured of herself. From that point on, she no longer viewed herself as gullible, but more wary of others' intentions, and began to scrutinize motives by asking plenty of questions.

This attitude began to spill over into her classroom studies. With all the courses that Krystal took in geology, including several related to groundwater sources, she never encountered anything unusual about the geology of Ohio. She found no cause for speculation that the spring on the Kruczyinski property was anything more than just groundwater that surfaced there. There was no indication whatsoever that it held any special significance in relation to supplying a last source of water for anyone. With these ideas in mind, and having heard no more about a supposed well of importance, she put aside any thoughts about what importance the government might hold on it.

At about this time Don McLean released a song entitled, "American Pie." Krystal listened to it several times recognizing that the song held a lot of different meanings. Finally she watched a news release on TV in which the writer was asked about the significance of the song and its lyrics. He just shook his head and would not give any details to the meaning. Krystal listened to it over and over. There were certainly lyrics that could have applied to the encounter and shootings on the Kent State campus. Yet it was the chorus that Krystal wondered the most about.

"Bye, bye Miss American Pie...this will be the day that I die."

Was this in relationship to the idea that Nixon wanted a female student shot May 4, 1970? she pondered, or was she just reading into the lyrics. She was not sure, yet coupled with another song released by Crosby, Stills, Nash and Young, entitled, "Ohio," she speculated on some lyrics as well.

"What if you knew her and found her dead on the ground? How can you run when you know?"

To a certain extent Krystal felt that she was running when she did know. She certainly was quite cognizant that Sandy Scheuer was not promiscuous, but Krystal was. Other than publicly revealing this fact via newspapers or other media, there was no proper way to inform others of her revelation. The closed hearings on the Kent State shootings prohibited her from entering these facts into the court room. And she was not sure she was strong enough to tolerate the interrogation that her actions would have brought about upon herself. She maintained her silence, though she filed these thoughts in the back of her mind. She had no easy answers to give anyone.

Then things began to take shape in Krystal's life. In April 1972, when J. Edgar Hoover died, she shed no tears. When she had heard the statement that Hoover made a few years earlier as he bought his cemetery plot that 'he would only need it for three days,' she waited intently for the grand resurrection to occur. *I guess he thought he was God, so he might as well try to be raised from the dead!* she mused as time passed and the grave maintained a paralyzing silence about it.

As graduation in June neared, she was prepared to seek employment in a field that would engage both of her majors, biology and geology. This was in environmental science and an out-of-state company wanted to hire her. They promised employment as long as she took a few courses in shorthand so that her note-taking skills would compliment her job duties. During her coursework she learned that the FBI had graduated their first female agent. *That could have been me, had I pursued that line of work,* she concluded. Then she wondered, *did it take Hoover's death to make that possible?* Then second guessing her realization she surmised, *I could have been that agent, but, then again maybe not.* With all that had transpired and if the rumor about Nixon was true, she would have had a lot more roadblocks placed before her, she surmised.

In the fall of 1972 a strong effort was made to re-elect President Nixon. He still had not ended the Vietnam War as he claimed he was trying to do, and the controversy revolving the Kent State shootings was a dilemma for him. He strove to win over the general public with lots of rhetoric on "law and order" with many reference to anti-war demonstrators as nothing, but "bums." His democratic opponent was Senator George McGovern.

Krystal went back home to vote. Darlene had left Kent State a year and a half earlier and was making plans to marry and then take a teaching job out west for a year. Krystal had not seen much of Darlene since that time. As the two of them neared the door of the town hall to vote, a man pulled Darlene aside to talk with her.

She was gone only a few minutes and when she returned to Krystal's side, she stated in a low tone, "We have to vote for Nixon."

As the two stood in line with Krystal being in front of Darlene, she whispered back, "Why?"

"Just do it!" Darlene spoke through tight lips. "He threatened me and told me to make sure you vote for Nixon."

Krystal turned back around contemplating these words. She knew from her high school government class, no one had the right to tell you who to vote for, and certainly no one had a right to threaten you. Yet Krystal was concerned about the actions that such a vicious President might take. Even though Hoover was dead, and both he and Nixon had seemed to be a deadly force when they were united together, Krystal was deeply disturbed by what Nixon himself might do.

She stared at the ballot. As she moved her hand to pull the lever for whom she would chose as President, she paused by Richard Nixon's name. *I played the Ace of Clubs once before. I'm going to play it again.* A thought came over her as she rationalized it was possible that the town hall was bugged with cameras and whoever might be watching what she would do. *I don't care. They can't tell me who to vote for!* With that determination in mind, she moved her hand away from the lever and grasping the one next to George McGovern's name she pulled it down forcefully as she bit her lip.

When she emerged from the voting booth, Darlene was waiting for her. "Did you do it?" she asked Krystal.

"Tell that man, I voted for Nixon," she replied confidently.

Then she watched as Darlene approached the man again. Krystal stared at him intently trying to take in everything about his appearance. As it was a snowy November day, he had a hat pulled low across his face and coat collar turned up closely around his neck. Yet she was able to make out that he had black curly hair, was somewhat stocky and for a minute almost reminded her of Danny. When he saw Krystal was staring at him he immediately turned away from Darlene and disappeared into the crowd.

When Election Day was over, Richard Nixon had declared a

landslide victory over his opponent. Krystal wondered, *And how many others did you threaten to get that victory? Well, you think you got my vote, but you didn't!*

This was not the only thing Nixon lost at in the Kruczyinski family. Since her brother had volunteered to serve in Vietnam and Krystal had not participated in anti-war rallies, Nixon could not claim that the family was anti-war. Matt had proved himself to be an asset to the Air Force serving in the capacity of aircraft engine mechanics and maintenance, and there were various honors and commendation medals awarded to him for his diligence in his work.

Perhaps Nixon played a part in keeping Matt from obtaining an early out though. He was allowed an early out to continue college education that he started while in service. However, there was quite a delay before it was granted to him. Perhaps Nixon wanted to keep him in Vietnam hoping that another Kruczyinski family member would lose their life. If that were true, the cards were played against that idea, as Matt later safely returned home and was able to enroll in college.

Yet, Krystal surmised, maybe Nixon won something there. Matt, she noted, had taken on a change of attitude when he arrived home. She understood that many veterans returning from Vietnam were having a difficult transition time adapting back to civilian life. In Matt's case, Krystal was not so sure he completed the transition. The first few weeks at home were awkward. Matt would rapidly crawl under the bed when he heard any airplanes overhead. Fearing that bombs would start dropping, he claimed that he felt he was still at the air base at Phu Cat, Vietnam.

He seemed to do much better in Kent living with Krystal as there were no airports nearby.

The other adjustment was that Matt had gotten into drugs overseas. When his fears of still being under attack weighted heavily on his mind, he sought temporary refuge by tripping out. This began affecting his grades and he soon lost interest in pursuing coursework.

One night he borrowed Krystal's car to go to a party. When he caused a near accident and fled the scene fearing he would be caught under the influence, Krystal presented a strong front and blatantly told him that he could no longer drive her car until he proved that he could stay away from drugs. For some time he did well, but then slipped back into sampling various drugs again.

By the time Krystal was ready to leave Kent State for good, Matt left as well. He finally had to admit that he was hooked on drugs. Eventually he reentered the Air Force and was stationed in Arizona. While there he entered a drug treatment program, eventually getting off all drugs and trying to start a sable life for himself.

Krystal was just about ready to take her job offer out-of-state when Nixon was reelected and put a hold on any environment fund spending. The company informed Krystal that this basically prevented them from hiring her as a cost measure. It was almost as if Nixon knew that this is what Krystal wanted for a job. Undeterred she did find work locally at a chemical research facility. At least she had a bachelor's degree with a good background in the sciences, and research was what she wanted to get into.

This back-and-forth game of who was winning, Nixon or the Kruczyinski family, finally came to a head when the news of Watergate surfaced in 1974. Nixon had used various employees of his campaign group (CREEP - Citizens to Reelect the President) and CIA agents to bug the Democratic political offices of many candidates. Nixon had tried to stop the investigation into the cover-up, but with Hoover now gone, he began losing a lot of support not only in the government agencies, but in the public eye as well. If Krystal had the funds at the time, she would have joined several thousands who lined the gate surrounding the White House demanding either the resignation or impeachment of President Nixon. *Had Jeanne Dixon's prediction about a president ruining the office come true?* Krystal thought so!

Not only did you not get my vote, you lost the Presidency! she claimed when he finally resigned. For a short time she was elated that such an underhanded person would no longer be President, but that feeling was cut short. She was bothered by the presidential pardon given to Nixon by his successor Gerald Ford. Perhaps had President Ford not done so, the investigation would have opened such a crater in public distrust that the fabric of democracy would no longer hold the country together.

As the dominos began falling, senators started inquiries into the activities of the CIA, FBI and other governmental agencies. At the forefront were Senator James William Fulbright and Senator Frank Church. It was here that Krystal became aware that the CIA had illegally spied on American citizens, that the FBI had utilized COINTELPRO on college campuses, and both organizations had participated in underhanded activities resulting in detrimental effects on innocent citizens.

Krystal sat for a long time combing over the news releases each day. As more revelations were brought to surface, Krystal began to wonder about Danny. *Had he been a part of COINTELPRO, and had he supplied the FBI with information about Krystal's promiscuous activities? Is this where Hoover got his information to use in defense of the shooting of Sandy Scheuer?* These answers did not readily surface anywhere.

As the various agencies were scrutinized on Capital Hill, it became apparent that the CIA not only participated in assassinations of foreign leaders, but provided monetary and weapon support for ruthless leaders who they felt would deter Communism. It was uncovered that many leaders in Iran, Iraq and the Middle East as well as in South American and Africa had been put in office by the CIA. Delving into more documentary evidence hit a snag when it was reported that the CIA had destroyed a lot of their documents in the 1960s. In 1975 the director of the CIA, William Colby, publicly revealed that the CIA had indeed been involved in domestic espionage on U.S. citizens. This was in direct violation of the CIA's legislative charter. He also revealed that Operation MK-ULTRA was a mind controlling experiment of the CIA's using LSD on unsuspecting American citizens. As a result Congress began demanding more accountability of the CIA's activities.

The Vietnam War was finally over in 1975, although it was really unclear if the U.S. had won. Over 58,000 soldiers had lost their lives, and many of those soldiers who returned to a country divided not only about the war, but about the governmental corruption that had taken place, and were left disillusioned. As time passed more and more veterans entered Veterans Administration hospitals being unable to return from a war they could not stop fighting inside. Many others turned to drugs and alcohol to cope. Still others threw their medals away and moved to Canada. When Matt saw no welcoming home from the American public for these soldiers, and the effects of the war on them, he filed as a conscious objector and left the Air Force. Not wishing to get back into drugs and disgusted with the government cover-ups, he made his way to Canada as well to begin a new life.

Damian Madden sat in his office in Burning Bridges reading his newspaper intensely. The resignation of President Nixon and the uncovering the CIA's illegal activities had been a shocking loss to Damian. Coupled with this news was the fact that Elliott had gone undercover for quite some time not wishing to be implicated as the falling dominos were crashing around him. So Damian had no contact with Elliott for a long time. With Nixon out of the White House, there was no push to secure the "well" from the Kruczyinski property. Furthermore, the CIA had destroyed many documents to avoid leaving a paper trail that would have incriminated the agency's tactics in securing the well. Also gone was some of the evidence with regards to the CIA's mind control experiments. Damian was saddened by this news, hoping to have gained more information about such projects. Yet he was aware that Nixon had settled down to his house in California and continued his life there, keeping out of the public eye. Damian still was plagued from time to time with nightmares about Agent Mark Mullins and the prediction made concerning Krystal destroying Damian. His attention was directed toward circumventing such events.

His thoughts were interrupted as the next patient entered the office. A black-haired, 35-year-old State Highway Patrolman sat down in the chair across from Damian. Ernie Wilson relayed that he had been referred for help from the post because of family problems he was having.

Damian sat and listened for a while, not really paying much attention to what the patient said. Yet he did ascertain that Ernie and Lily, his wife, had been having arguments ever since they first married.

"She spends a lot of time at church with activities and everything. Then when I come home she has no time for my needs, you know," stated Ernie.

"I take it you're not into church activities?"

"Not really. - Well, I used to be, that is, before I was married, but not now."

"What church?"

"Seventh-day Adventist."

"I'm not familiar with that one."

Ernie repeated it, and then reiterated that he was not much involved in church activities. "Lily thinks I have a demon inside me."

Damian, who had propped his feet up on the desk, was leaning back in his chair staring at the ceiling. As Ernie mentioned about having a demon, Damian began to smile.

"Well, that's just religious jargon. There's no such things as demons. You see, in psychology there's no room for good or evil. No right or wrong. No black or white. There's just gray. You have needs and she isn't providing them. Why not buy her a mink coat or a diamond ring? You see, my wife and I have a very open relationship. She's out of town a lot and so we have an understanding that I can see that my needs are satisfied wherever I can." He looked over at Ernie who by now had a wrinkled brow and perplexed look. Then Damian asked, "Well, what about having an affair, then?"

Ernie did not answer right away. Then he said, "Well, there was someone who I liked a lot before I got married. I'm not sure I want to have an affair, though."

Nonchalantly, Damian replied, "Well, why not go to see her. Look her up and see if there is anything still between you two."

After some discussion Ernie left the office resolved to visit this long lost friend one more time.

Once gone Damian began going through the surveillance tapes he had on the Kruczyinski family wondering what he should do with them. After having seen what Krystal looked like at Kent State, he was not attracted to her in any way. Contemplating his next move as he fingered across the box of tapes, he came across some tapes when Krystal was a little girl. *If only I could have changed this child, raised her how I wanted her to be...* Then he came across the surveillance tape where Krystal was presented the clown doll. Damian took note that Agent Skip Clarabelle clearly stated that she was to be a sacrifice. He stopped for a moment and thought, *if she would be my child, Krystal, she wouldn't be a sacrifice. She would be...*

As the tape deck began to clatter having reached the end of the film, Damian was shaken back into present time. He removed that tape and replaced it with another one. This tape was when Krystal was older, perhaps 10 or 11. It revealed Krystal and Ernie Wilson conversing outside at St. Michael's Catholic Church. Ernie was telling Krystal that he had to get married because his girlfriend was pregnant. Damian stopped the tape starting intently at the figure. He immediately recognized that this was the same person who had just been in his office.

Maybe I'm not ready to dispose of this material yet, he contemplated. Then he gathered up some of his surveillance equipment and left the office for the day.

Krystal had enjoyed working at the chemical research lab for the past two years, although sometimes her job seemed tedious. She worked around a lot of chemicals that questionably were related to producing cancer. From time to time she wondered if that would affect her, so she abided by all safety precautions. She did, however, make some new friends there and began dating Wilbur, another employee. Although 10 years older than her and having never married before, they seemed to hit it off pretty well. They enjoyed the outdoors like taking hikes and camping and were frugal with their money. When their dating became more serious, Krystal held nothing back in revealing her past activities. He was well aware that should they marry, he would be getting "used merchandise." Yet Krystal said nothing about her suspicions about Nixon, Hoover or the supposed well. Krystal had pretty much resolved to the fact that if there was a God, He was not very active in her life – not with all that had transpired in the past five years. Wilbur, too, felt that God had dealt him a broken home and strained feelings between he and his father. So the relationship began with no interest in God on either part.

A month following their wedding Krystal suspected she was pregnant having not used any birth control measures. Approaching Wilbur with the news produced a reaction that she had not anticipated. Angrily he expressed that he had grown up taking care of his brothers and sisters as well as half-brothers and half-sisters, and he did not want to be saddled with taking care of a child at this time. If that were not enough, the chemicals that Krystal had tried to be careful around were starting to make her ill.

Locating an industrial physician who specialized in chemical allergies, she sought to be tested by him. When all the test results were in, he confirmed that she had definitely developed sensitive reactions to what she had been working with.

He made the comment, "I hope you're not planning on getting pregnant right now."

When she questioned him about that, he explained that even though she had been absorbing chemicals through the skin, they could easily have been transported to an unborn fetus with disturbing results. When the pregnancy test confirmed Krystal's suspicions, Krystal faced a dilemma as to what to do. Arriving home distressed over her next step she should take, she approached Wilbur. Since neither had a belief in God at this time, they sought no spiritual answers for advice. Ultimately, they agreed that they were not ready for children just yet. Krystal was increasingly concerned about what damage the chemicals would have on her pregnancy.

"What if the baby is harmed by these chemicals? What if he or she is retarded or has some major problem? Are you willing to take care of a disabled child?" she asked him.

"Are you?" he shot back. "I don't think I want to handle taking care of any child right now."

Though not saying no, he left Krystal with the responsibility of resolving the issue. After several days of contemplation and the conversation between the two not resulting in any conclusion, Krystal took it upon herself to get an abortion.

Once the procedure had been performed at a nearby hospital, Krystal returned home. As weeks began to lapse by Krystal began feeling remorse.

Turning to Wilbur one night she exclaimed, "I'll never go through that again! If I ever get pregnant again, I will go through with the pregnancy. I did a terrible thing by having an abortion, and I'll never do it again!"

He leaned over to comfort her somewhat, although not saying

anything. Krystal finally cried herself to sleep. When she awakened in the morning, she did not really feel refreshed from her sleep.

For the next several days her performance at work began to falter. As the company was struggling with cut-backs Krystal was finally informed that she would be laid off. This left her with more time to hopefully regain some composure. As she sat alone in the house one day after Wilbur had gone to work, she stared across the room to a box that she had brought back from her home. Something enticed her to look through the box. As she pulled out various pictures and knickknacks, she pulled out a Catholic Bible that she had kept. She fingered through the pages stopping at one of the inserts. This one was a painting so well done it appeared to be almost a photograph. Christ appeared in the center looking very direct at the viewer with His arms outstretched to either side. His eyes displayed a determined look, yet also expressed a gentleness. Under both outstretched arms, kneeling at His feet, were two men. One was perhaps blind or ill seeking healing. The other was younger, but his facial expression evoked a sense of desiring truth from someone who would know. Both men looked up to Christ earnestly conveying a desire for forgiveness. Underneath the painting was the verse from Matthew 11:28 "Come to Me all you who are labored and heavy-burdened, and I will give you rest."

Krystal looked up from the painting as she stared out the window across the grassy field. *I certainly am heavy-laden. Is there any room for forgiveness for me?* She sat back down in her chair with tears streaming down her face.

Staring at the painting once more, she asked Christ, "Can You forgive me?" Then she began to shake as she sobbed heavily.

A voice from within seemed to say, *Read the book!* From that point on she would read a portion every night before retiring to sleep.

Coupled with her new-found interest, she began to wonder about this man named Christ. When the movie, "Jesus Christ, Superstar," circulated in the theaters she viewed it alone as Wilbur had no interest in it. The movie definitely took on a radical approach to the life of Christ, something far different than the conservative Catholic Church she had been raised in. Yet Mary Magdeline had found forgiveness in Christ.

When she returned home she read in Romans 5:8 "But God

demonstrated His own love towards us, in that while we were still sinners, Christ died for us." She definitely was a sinner, having now committed murder by the abortion. Yet she read that when Christ was crucified, he was flanked by a robber and a murderer. And He forgave them. *He could forgive me, too, can't He?* she asked herself. Then her thoughts turned to her previous promiscuous behavior at Kent State. She contemplated 'yet while we were still sinners, Christ died for us.' She thought back how she had not attended the rally on May 4th, how a voice welled up inside her and told her not to go up there. *Had I been warned, yet while a sinner? Did Christ love me then, even though I had no knowledge that He could? Was there a reason that I was warned? Is there a bigger picture I don't see?*

Finally she walked into the bathroom and staring at herself in the mirror she asked, *Can you accept the fact that you are a murderer?* For a long time she stood there not saying anything as she looked into her own eyes in the reflection. When a calm felling came over her, she left the room resolving once more to try returning to church activities. She had not been in the confessional since she was 17. Now at 25 she began to tell the priest where she had erred in her life. When she finally told him that she had an abortion, he asked that she speak to him face-to-face. Reluctantly she did so. He advised her to start attending church services. For several weeks she did so, feeling much better about herself.

Everything would have been fine, until one Sunday a visiting priest came to offer a sermon. He claimed as he shouted from the pulpit, "Anyone who has ever had an abortion can NEVER be forgiven!"

He continued reiterating that theme, coupled with the idea that a person such as this would burn in Hell forever. His forceful words and harsh statements began to rile Krystal as she sat in the service. She could feel her face getting red and hot, and she started breathing rapidly. She jerked at one point seriously contemplating walking out. *If I do, everyone will know that I am guilty.* She swallowed hard, stared at the floor and tried to regain a calmer composure. When at last his sermon was over, Krystal walked away, closing the door on Catholicism forever.

At that time the CIA had worked with the Catholic Church, especially in South America where they had used nuns to their advantage. Krystal thought, *Was it possible that the CIA purposely had this priest come to the church at this time?*

She continued to read from the Bible, wondering why the church did not seem to match Christianity portrayed by the founder Himself. He forgave simmers, murders. He ate with people of ill repute. *Why was the church not demonstrating what He said?* She had no easy answer for this dilemma, but continued reading.

As she laid in bed one snowy night with Wilbur sound asleep by her side, she thought she heard some banging outside. She woke up Wilbur.

"I think someone's trying to get into the storage building," she claimed. When he claimed he did not hear it, she insisted that he get up and look around. Finally gathering up a flashlight and rifle he proceeded to circle around the house and the adjoining store/workshop. Confident that the doors were locked securely he returned claiming that he had seen nothing.

In the morning when a friend stopped by, he called out to Wilbur.

"Hey! There's broken glass over here!" Upon inspection, the two of them discovered that someone indeed had broken a window on the side of the store/workshop. They then followed some tracks which stopped outside the house, as if the person had stopped and stood there awhile. They followed the trackes to the road where they disappeared. As the two stood outside puzzled by this, the loose barn roof flapped and banged somewhat in the breeze.

Ernie had wondered about what Damian Madden had said to him. Feeling somewhat confused, he had bought his wife some flowers hoping that would soothe things over between the two. The warm feeling the gesture evoked quickly faded as the two began to argue over how the children were not behaving like either wanted. Both blamed each other and when Ernie got tired of arguing he decided to take a drive.

Stopping at Krystal's house, hoping that she would now be finished at Kent State, he approached Martha who did not remember him from before.

"Well, she no longer lives here. She's married."

"She was supposed to marry me!" he began to shout. "She was

supposed to wait for me. She promised, and now she's broken her promise." He began to rant and rave wildly.

Martha was beside herself as to what to do. When Ernie finally left, Martha decided not to say anything to Krystal until she came to visit the next time.

Ernie stopped at a bar just up the road from where Krystal now lived, having looked up her new address. He sat in the corner downing several shots of whiskey and listening to the honky-tonk music wail out about 'how somebody had done somebody wrong' song. Angered by it all he stormed out of the bar to where Wilbur and Krystal lived. Having no real plan, just feeling spurned and rejected by his wife, the troubles at home, and a notion that he could rebuild a relationship abandoned years ago, he finally took a hoe handle resting idly against the store/workshop and began breaking the window. That seemed to take the edge off the outburst, yet still not knowing how to contend with his feelings, he walked over to the house and stood outside the bedroom window contemplating his next move. As the loose barn roof began to bang in the wind, he suddenly thought, *what am I doing?* Then he turned and left.

For the next few weeks Krystal was not comfortable with the feeling that someone had stood so close to the house. Not knowing who that was only made her more uneasy. As she and Wilbur discussed what had transpired at his work one evening, he related that someone had come in to pay for some items with a check.

"The top part said 'Army Intelligence.' I thought it was because I had been in the National Guard that was the reason he approached me."

"That's right. You were in the Ohio National Guard and got out right before the Kent State shootings."

"Yes, I was in the Guard in 1968 when the Cleveland riots took place. Then we ended up on the trucker strike. It was right after that I got out." The conversation began to drift off into talk of military duty in the Guard.

Krystal brought the conversation back to present day when she said, "So did you know this guy from Army Intelligence?"

"No, I didn't know him, but I thought it was kind of funny with all that you hear about the CIA and their bungled jobs," Wilbur relayed.

"Army Intelligence? Kind of sounds like you found Colonel Flagg from MASH!" Krystal laughed. Then both began to laugh as they recalled the character of Colonel Flagg from the MASH TV series and how unintelligent he was depicted as.

In the next few days she began to think about the CIA as she read a newspaper article which stated that the 100th Military Intelligence Group had monitored disturbances in northeast Ohio during the 1960s and 1970s. She wondered if that person displaying the check had done so for her benefit. *Did he personally hand it to Wilbur, knowing that he would see it and say something to Krystal? Was someone still following her around?* She was not sure. Coupled with the breaking of the window earlier and the ill feelings she had, she urged Wilbur to begin looking for another home, further away.

When at last they found an old farmhouse in a nearby county, they decided to move. In May 1976 they settled on five acres. It was a very peaceful setting for Krystal and she hoped the future would be less stressful. She decided to seek work other than in research and so took more coursework along medical secretarial lines. She attending the local business college and received a diploma in Medical Assisting, which included both administrative as well as nursing aspects of being able to draw blood and give injections.

After several part-time jobs, she finally landed a full-time job in medical records at a psychiatric hospital in 1977. It was a little bit of a drive to Burning Bridges where the hospital was, but she did not mind it. As she drove back and forth she contemplated finding another church to attend.

When the "Jesus" movie was released in 1979 by Campus Crusade for Christ, Krystal found a Methodist church who was hosting a showing of it and so attended once again by herself, Wilbur not wishing to participate. She enjoyed watching the movie noting that the entire story had been taken directly from the book of Luke. It was quite detailed about specific points in Christ's life, but what interested Krystal most was the part where a father presented his demon-possessed son to Jesus. The son was thrashing about, but once Jesus touched him, the demon then left, and the son calmed down, being made whole again.

CHAPTER
6

"You've been gone quite a while. Where were you?" asked Damian anxiously as a tired-appearing Elliott sat down in Damian's house.

"I've been trying to close up some loose ends. We were afraid once Colby spoke out that the whole CIA structure was going to collapse, so we had to take care of some of our operators who might have jeopardized our purpose. You remember the tape we showed you when we first met in Cleveland, the one where we had our Soviet operative in a hospital?"

"Yes, I recall that."

"Well, he recovered all right, but later on he changed somewhat - wanted out - wanted nothing to do with CIA operations. Once Colby had begun opening up about some of our illegal activities, we were concerned that this operative would have spoken out as well."

"So what happened?" Damian motioned to Elliott inviting him to partake of the scotch he had just poured. He handed Elliott the glass and sat down with his.

"We turned him in, and the KGB kept him in a mental hospital there for a long time, that is, until he finally died. You know how the KGB handled opposition."

"I know of some of their methods, the high dose injections of psychotic drugs. I hear they literally drove sane people crazy."

"Yeah, well, they did it a lot better than we did. I guess this operative eventually killed himself."

Damian leaned back against the couch sipping his scotch. His eyes began to brighten as he listened to Elliott's description. "So they gave him a potent trial of drugs. I'd like to find out more about this." Perceiving how he could use such ideas to his advantage, he surmised watching someone be destroyed by instilling something either in their body or their mind. Damian had other people in the agencies who at times would "blackmail" him in various forms, and he contemplated how he could "pay them back."

"Well, that's not all I need to tell you," Elliott said, shaking Damian out of his thoughts. "Of course, Nixon is out of office, but we have kept an almost daily correspondence with him in California. He really wants the CIA to keep him advised of what's going on. He still thinks the well is something we can use now that the Middle East is heating back up again. We need that bargaining chip, the well on the Kruczyinski property. You've got a world map anywhere?" asked Elliott.

Damian at first was at a loss, but began frantically searching through some book shelves. At last for lack of anything better, he pulled out the box holding a "Risk" game. Grabbing the game board, he opened it on the coffee table placing it between the two of them. The Elliott began using the game pieces showing Damian which countries the Soviets were supporting and which countries the United States was supporting.

As the pieces were placed across the entire map, Damian asked, "What happens if the Soviets support a dictator, and the U.S. supports the same dictator in an offense against a third country? Let's just say, that a country such as Iraq begins fighting with Iran. If the Soviets send arms to Iraq and the U.S. sends arms to Iraq, then this would make this dictator pretty powerful, would it not?"

"Then we would probably send arms to the other country, as in your example of Iran and try to win them over. The U.S. and the Soviets are two superpowers. I don't think we'd want someone to try to get the upper hand in this game. That's why we need to have the assurance of that well. That way we have a bargaining chip that we can hold to keep such a dictator at bay." Elliott glanced down at his watch. Then added, "I'll be in touch. See what you can do to get the well."

"One thing before you leave. I'm applying for a staff psychologist position at a local hospital. I need some documents for my dossier; something to make it look good and accentuates my accomplishments. I think I have some ideas on how I can get you that well, but of course, I need something in return."

"No problem. I'll have something for you tomorrow."

After Elliott had left, Damian looked at the game board still positioned on the coffee table. Slowly pacing the floor around the table, he thought, *if I orchestrate this just right, I can make my way up into the CIA in a secure position. Then won't the FBI be surprised. – In fact, if I do this just right, I can have the advantage over them.* With those thoughts in mind, he grabbed his jacket and drove his car to introduce himself to the local police and county sheriffs.

Krystal had been searching for months debating what church she might be interested in attending. She did not come into town, but once a week, staying mostly at her country home when she was not working. Her experience with the Catholic Church left her not as trusting in religious institutions. It was quite one thing to have attended the church on campus looking for a different life, only to find a drug dealer there. Then the other thing was to be condemned in a church pew. Cautiously she attended various Protestant churches in the area. She tried the Lutheran church. It was okay, but there was a lot of overlapping traditions too similar to the Catholic Church and nothing that really inspired her there. Then she moved onto the Methodist church. She stayed quite a while here, until the pastor was insistent on getting her husband to attend. She backed away because the search was not for Wilbur, who had no interest, but was for her. So she attended for a while and then moved on in her spiritual quest for straightforward biblical truth.

Running the gamut of various denominations, she stumbled across an Adventist Church one Saturday morning. She knew nothing about them. As she entered the building she heard beautiful singing, so harmonious that she thought at first it was a professional choir. When she stepped inside the sanctuary, she found no choir, but the singing was coming from the members in the church pews. Krystal had always liked singing and music and was impressed that they sounded so well-orchestrated.

When the service was over, she began to talk with Pastor Jack. She reiterated mostly about her discrepancy with various church doctrines in the past, though she admitted that she was quite unfamiliar with Adventists. When Pastor Jack replied that they were Bible-believing Christians whose doctrines were based on biblical principles, Krystal thought she would give this church a definite try. For the next several months she spent attending services and engaging in an in-depth Bible study. Yet she scrutinized everything she came across testing the validity of the statements.

When she wasn't working or doing Bible studies, both she and Wilbur enjoyed reading Tolkien's Lord of the Rings trilogy. The stories intrigued her and found them enjoyable as well as meaningful. Wilbur had even purchased an actual recording of J.R.R. Tolkien reading various passages from the book. It seemed to add something more to the reading of the trilogy. In their free time mostly on weekends, Wilbur taught Krystal target shooting. It was mostly just local competition that they participated in, but Krystal enjoyed the sport. There were, however, times when male competitors did not appreciate having a woman shoot next to them. Krystal would just move on to another round of competition, not saying anything to them.

She continued to work at the hospital, when one day a state trooper donned in his gray uniform and hat was suddenly standing by her desk.

"What do you think you're doing here?" he demanded in a subdued yet threatening voice.

"I work here. Is there something I can do for you?" she replied politely.

"I'm gonna get you for what you did to me!" he growled, squinting his pale blue eyes behind the gold-framed glasses and contorting his face as he spoke.

"I think you have mistaken me for someone else. I don't know what you're talking about."

"No, I haven't mistaken you for anyone else. You're the one I want! You know what you did!" he stated emphatically, paused and then added vehemently, "I'm gonna pay you back for what you did to me!"

Krystal decided that she needed to seek help on this matter, and as her coworker, Margaret, entered the room, she turned to her and said, "Would you get Dr. Klone for me? It's urgent." Having heard a little of the conversation, her coworker wasted no time in fulfilling the request.

Krystal watched the man noting that even though he had threatened her, he made no real attempt to advance in her direction. She wondered what was keeping him at bay. Perhaps he was just bluffing or waiting for a frightened response from her, but she did her best to display a calm appearance. Realizing that she was short and this man was not only taller than her, but more than likely physically stronger than her, she felt she would not have been a match for him. She said nothing to the man until Dr. Klone entered the office.

"This gentleman is trying to threaten me," she stated. Dr. Klone was startled by the statements and spun around on his heels to look at the father of a patient of his, now somewhat slumped over with head bent down.

"Why don't we go somewhere else and have a talk, Ernie?" Dr. Klone calmly suggested to the trooper. He extended his arm and gently cradled Ernie's shoulder as the two advanced out the doorway and down the corridor.

Krystal was relieved that the situation had easily defused itself. Turning to her coworker who had returned to the room, she asked, "Who was that?" She then handed Krystal a report on Scott Wilson, a five-year-old patient who had just arrived the previous day at the facility. Krystal scanned through the pages hoping to find some clues as to why the father would threaten her. There was not too much to go on, but she read that the family were Adventists and attended the local church, a neighboring congregation to Krystal's. She wondered what crisis would have brought about an admission for a five-year-old. The names, circumstances and faces did not evoke anything in her memory at this time. She put the report aside and continued her work hoping that Dr. Klone would return to talk to her.

Dr. Klone and Krystal had struck up a good friendship ever since

Krystal had come to work at the hospital. The two just seemed to "hit it off from day one," as Krystal would say. She enjoyed having intellectual conversations with him as well as trading humorous anecdotes that both had shared about their lives. The trust formed in this relationship cemented a very strong bond between the two of them. So she had no qualms when Dr. Klone later returned to Krystal and asked for her address.

"Why," she responded with a chuckle, "are we going on a date?"

Both laughing understanding that both were married and had no need for an outside relationship. Then Dr. Klone said, "Well, there's a friend of mine that needs someone to talk to, and I think you'd be the best person to talk to him. He's really a nice guy!" As Krystal handed him the paper with her address and phone number on it, she noted the same trooper peering around the doorway.

Dr. Klone, noticing that she was looking at someone else, turned around to see Ernie standing there. Facing Krystal again he asked, "By the way, do you know this man? He seems to know who you are."

As Krystal looked over the trooper, there was nothing about his appearance or even his name that brought anything immediately to mind and she replied, "No." Yet she could not help, but notice that as the trooper took the paper from Dr. Klone's hand, he almost sneered at her. Immediately she pictured him as clutching a "sought-after-prize." The trooper grinned back at Krystal and quickly left the building.

Pondering on what she had just witnessed, Dr. Klone interrupted her thoughts by saying, "Why not just have a talk with him? He's really harmless. He's got a lot going on in his life. I'm sure it was said more out of frustration than anything else. My mother always said to me that you never really know another person until you walk a mile in his moccasins."

"That's an American Indian saying, and one that I like. Well, we'll just see what happens here." Krystal replied, though not knowing what would transpire next.

The following day, Krystal began to transcribe dictation that Margaret handed Krystal some tapes from the tape deck recording unit. At the beginning of the tape was a poem that Dr. Klone had left specifically for Krystal with a note attached. The note said that the tape was to be transcribed by Krystal and no one else. The tape began with Dr. Klone reading a poem, something his own mother had shared with him years before.

"Teach me to feel another's woe,
To hide the fault I see.
That mercy I to other show,
That mercy show to me.

Hope for a world grown cynically cold,
Hungry for power, greedy for gold.
Faith to believe that within and without,
There's a nameless fear in a world of doubt.

Love that is bigger than race or creed,
To cover the world
And fulfill each need.

I do not ask for any crown,
But that which all may win,
Nor try to conquer any world,
Except the one within.

Be Thou my guide until I find
Led a tender hand,
The happy kingdom in myself,
And there to take command."

Sitting down at her desk still rereading the poem that she transcribed separately, Dr. Klone entered the office.

"I really like this!" She said to him. He sat down in a chair across from her desk paging through some unfinished charts and smiling back at her.

When he was finished, he turned to Krystal and said, "I have a problem here and I was hoping you might help me out with this. I can't find anything wrong with this five-year-old boy. I was hoping you might add some insight into some family dynamics here. Haven't you been attending an Adventist church lately?"

"Well, yes, but this family goes to a different congregation."

"I'm not that familiar with their church beliefs, and I was hoping you might be able to see something there that I'm missing."

"What is the son here for anyway?"

"His father claims that he was going around the house saying he was God, yet I find nothing about him to indicate that he was doing this."

"Maybe it's the father that's the problem and not the son."

Dr. Klone contemplated that statement, looking at Krystal and recalling the previous day's events. "Maybe you're right," he said as he got up to leave. Suddenly there was a commotion out in the hallway. Ernie was frantically pacing back and forth in the lobby, ranting and raving to the nurses who were cautiously standing by. Krystal could hear a heated discussion ensuing for several minutes. Then she saw Dr. Klone firmly grasping the trooper's arm as the two passed by to the admitting office.

Finally, the admitting clerk entered the medical records room. In a loud whisper she said, "Whew! I just admitted a very agitated man!" Two muscularly-built black ward attendants passed by the doorway as she spoke, holding the trooper between them as they entered the ward.

When Dr. Klone later dictated a mental status exam and treatment plan for the patient, Krystal read through the paragraphs. It stated that the patient, Ernie Wilson, had been drinking a lot and that he thought the FBI was chasing him. At the end Dr. Klone put a diagnosis of "chronic alcoholism and a broken heart."

She paused and looked up from the report. Then she asked Margaret, her coworker, "Isn't that odd that he would put a diagnosis of a broken heart in there?" She just replied that it must be there for a reason. Krystal contemplated this for a while and then decided to ask Dr. Klone about it.

When she located him at the nurse's station, she inquired what he meant by that statement. He was busy being saddled with other requests from both patients and nurses at the same time, and so quickly responded, "Well, you ought to know how he got it!"

Krystal looking dismayed at this snappy remark, decided perhaps it was not the best time to ask him about this, and so turned to leave the ward. As she walked out, the trooper, now dressed in hospital gown, only growled as she passed by.

For several days she heard nothing from Dr. Klone until the day the trooper was released. Dr. Klone entered the office and said to Krystal, "I can't find anything wrong with him other than he needs Alcoholics Anonymous." Then he added, "He sure is a nice guy! Are you sure you don't remember him?"

For a time Krystal stared at the trooper who was now befitted and well-groomed in his uniform and hat, yet he still remained somewhat thin-skinned and pale. Yet for a second she caught a glimmer of something like a youthful appearance from him. She tried to focus in on this, but when Ernie became aware of her staring at him, he quickly turned his head shielding his face. There was something foggy that Krystal could not quite recognize about him, but something inside her made her ponder just where she possibly might know him from. As she could evoke nothing specific, she dismissed the idea.

Dr. Klone then affirmed, "He says he knew you in high school."

"I don't remember anyone like him from my high school," she replied as she got busy with her work. Dr. Klone then left the room accompanying Ernie to the front door.

A few days passed and as Krystal was busy with her work, another man approached her desk. He had short brown hair and blue eyes, was of medium build and height. He handed her what appeared to be a resume of some sort.

"Hello, I'm the new staff psychologist. Here's my card!" He handed her an exquisitely embossed business card as well which read, 'Damian L. Madden, Ph.D., Psychologist.' Krystal said hello and was about to start reading from the papers he had handed her when Margaret requested that the papers be given to her.

"I was told to drop off those papers before I started working here. I'm sorry I had to bring them my first day here and that they are so late." As Krystal handed off the papers he frantically began searching his pants pockets for something else.

Amused by the scene Krystal reverberated a phrase of Gollum's in regards to Bilbo Baggins from Lord of the Rings, "What has it gots in its pockets? Yes, Precious!"

Damian quickly replied with another phrase from the Tolkien trilogy as he finally located a dictation mini-tape. Chuckling together, the two of them began a light-hearted conversation about the Tolkien stories.

After a short time he then stated, "You seem to be of some breeding and learning. What's a nice girl –"

Krystal finished the statement as if she could read his mind, "What's a nice girl like you doing in a place like this?" He appeared to be charmed by this.

Then Krystal went on to describe getting a degree from Kent State University, only to encounter unfortunate circumstances in the working world, especially in research chemistry and her lay-off and how she ended up working at the hospital. They continued engaging in talk about college life, her love for folk music, particularly Peter, Paul and Mary, and other interests of hers. He would interject here and there with miscellaneous elements of their experiences that they had in common. Krystal was captivated by how similar their interests appeared to be. His pleasant sounding voice, his wit, his display of knowledge on a vast array of subjects intrigued her.

She watched as his eyes scanned about her face. It was a very soothing feeling that he projected towards her as he did so and commented, "You're very pretty." He continued to flatter her with comments about her intelligence and talents, and how happy he was to have found someone that he could relate to as well. At last, Dr. Madden said he had to see some patients, but would like to come back and resume the conversation.

Later on as Krystal was putting the medical charts together for filing, she came across some of Dr. Madden's transcribed reports. They seemed to be very thorough, as if he had a lot of insight into a person's thoughts and motives. The details described therein prompted Krystal to wonder how well did he really get to know these patients. She concluded that he probably was pretty good at what he did and left it at that.

Two days later Dr. Madden approached Krystal to pick up where he had left off. He did not notice that someone else in the next room was listening to him. As the conversation continued to be light-hearted, he invited Krystal to go out and have a drink with him sometime after work. Having previously had much complimentary attention poured over herself by his charming support, she found herself curious about the proposition. He seemed so self-assured, so knowledgeable, so humorous, and yet so gentle in his approach, that had she not been satisfied in her marriage, she might have been tempted by his offer. Yet she rarely had a drink, and was not that thrilled about returning to drinking, nor wanting to jeopardize her marriage, she politely told him she would think about it.

When he left the room, Margaret, came around the doorway and speaking in a low tone emphatically stated, "Don't you dare! He tried that same play with a very close friend of mine. All he wants to do is go out and have a good time. He's known for doing that with several women. And he always seems to go after married women."

Margaret then went on to describe how her friend had been having a rough time in her marriage. She went to Dr. Madden for counseling. Then Margaret described that he made plenty of advances towards her friend, stating that he needed to get to know her much better to help her. He persuaded her to have sex with him, saying that it would strengthen their marriage if she knew how to properly make love to a man. When she finally obliged with his requests, he ended up making her feel guilty about it all.

"She almost lost her husband over the entire matter," Margaret stated emphatically. "He's just very manipulative with women! You let him in your life, and your whole household gets upset."

"What do you mean?" Krystal encouraged Margaret to continue.

"He just gets everyone irritated. Her husband got very violent with her, even though she was no longer seeing Dr. Madden. Eventually, her husband got so abusive, they got divorced. I think that happened all because Dr. Madden interfered in their marriage."

Krystal sat somewhat stunned as she listened to what Margaret was saying. She certainly did not want anything upsetting her marriage. She recalled how Wilbur reacted before she had the abortion, and she did not want a replay of the anger she saw in him. She was glad that she had not revealed to Dr. Madden anything really about her feelings at Kent State, the shootings, the FBI visiting her, her promiscuous activity, or her encounter with the drug dealer. She felt had she succumbed to what seemed like an innocent invitation by Dr. Madden would have only opened a door to some devastation she could not even have imagined.

The following day Dr. Madden returned to talk with Krystal. Once again Margaret was around the corner where he could not see her. Krystal decided to use a straightforward approach much like when she played the Ace of Clubs at Kent.

"I hear you like to take our married women. Is that so?"

Immediately his upper lip tightened and he blurted out sternly and defensively, "Do you have 'God' written on your driver's license?"

His irritated and infuriated behavior manifested in both his eyes as well as his clenched fists at his sides took Krystal somewhat by surprise. This was such a switch in his character from what he had displayed before, and it shocked her. So she backed down a bit claiming that no, she was not God. He then immediately stormed out of the room.

Margaret then appeared from behind. "Why did you ask him that?"

"Because I wanted to know," affirmed Krystal, "but I guess that's not the way to find out!"

Weeks then passed and neither Dr. Madden nor Krystal spoke to each other. Krystal was dismayed immensely because their discourse, which had sounded so enlightening in the beginning, had quickly been reduced to rubble. He particularly avoided coming near the medical records room and would turn and walk another way if he saw Margaret anywhere in the hall.

Then at last he made a final stop by Krystal and said, "Well, you can be happy now! I won't bother you anymore. I'm leaving my position here!" Krystal was still regretting how her question had turned him so suddenly away, and tried to apologize, but it was to no avail.

Damian stomped off and drove frantically to his office. Once inside he retrieved the tapes of Krystal that he had procured and began scanning through several of them as if looking for something. Yet he knew he could not spend too much time with this. His secretary had laid several unpaid bills on his desk as well as overdrawn bank statements. He had to resolve his financial crisis somehow. At last he gathered up his papers and drove to a nearby counseling center and put in an application there.

Within weeks he had secured a position at the counseling center and his money problems eased off. He was careful about his love affairs at first, not wishing to lose his job right away.

Elliott showed up again at Damian's house one evening, stating that hostages had been taken at the American embassy in Iran. Pacing the floor and smoking cigarette and cigarette, Elliott expressed his concerns.

"We're trying to negotiate a deal, but they won't give in. We've been selling them some arms, but the black market is trying to undersell us. We need something extra to go along with these arms. I have to introduce you to one of our other operatives. We call him "The Gatekeeper." He channels children in an underground network for sale overseas. He's been getting mostly runaways, but lately his contacts are wanting for fresher, virgin material, if you get my drift!"

"Yes, I understand. So what do I have to do?"

"We need you to start targeting some for us."

"What about the police? Won't they get involved in a search?"

"Sure, but we can fix that, too! You know politics and money go a long way! Have you scouted out any of the local cops yet?"

"Yes, I've talked with them offering myself to their services as a criminal psychologist."

"Any you think might help us out?"

"Well, there's a few that think might. County Sheriff Cory Dumas is one. I think if I work it right I can get his help on this matter. He has contacts as well in the surrounding sheriff's departments."

"Good. Keep up the good work. I'll be back in a few days to know how you made out. – This is really important."

"I'm sure it is. This won't look good for President Carter, the holy-roller preacher son, will it? In fact, this would be one way to get the Democrats out of the White House and let the Republicans back in charge. I'm sure Mr. Nixon wants that so he can continue his contacts and advice. And I'm sure there's a lot of cabinet members that would like their jobs back."

Krystal had read about the hostages in Iran and wondered what was going to happen. Although she wondered if there was any underhandedness by the CIA in the workings, she had nothing to really go on. Certainly nothing was coming forward in the newspapers of such. Yet she remembered reading that the CIA had closely aligned itself with the Catholic Church using their operatives in churches in foreign countries as nuns and priests. *I don't think they'll be using many nuns and priests over there, though, not with all the Muslins that are there,* she concluded.

She continued to study with Pastor Jack and finally in the spring of 1980 after she had meticulously studied through the Bible-based beliefs of the church, she chose to be baptized at a local lake. When she emerged from her new birth, the congregation on shore sang "Amazing Grace" with such clarity and harmony even better than she had heard them sing before.

Pastor Jack cautioned her. "Now that you've taken this step, know that the devil will put greater temptations in front of you."

"I understand what you're saying. I certainly will trust in Christ for His guidance now."

Several weeks after the ceremony she was hanging laundry in her backyard. It was a balmy summer day, with just enough breeze and temperature in the 80's. Krystal just wanted to soak it all up, and so she dressed appropriately in a T-shirt and shorts. As the clothes dried very fast, after a few hours she began taking down the sheets and folding them into a basket at her feet. She did not see the state trooper come around the corner of her house, and when he spoke he startled her. Krystal's Rottweiler came forward from the wooded area ran barking at him, and Krystal ran to catch her and put her inside so that the two of them could talk.

He began, "A friend told me that you could help me." Krystal appeared confused, not remembering her conversation with Dr. Klone over a year ago or any of the circumstances, but she encouraged him to continue.

"Don't you remember me? I'm Ernie Wilson.

Krystal stared at him for a long time before speaking and then said, "The name just doesn't seem to ring a bell. Where would I know you from?"

"You were going to marry me, remember?" he blurted out.

"We were going to get married? I'd think I'd remember that! Did we date?"

"No," he replied softly as he looked down and away from her. "You promised you weren't going to date in high school and that you were gonna wait for me."

Again, Krystal struggled to remember the details of what he was describing, but she was trying to remember Ernie from high school and there was no such person at her school that came to mind at this time. Had he mentioned Chrysha or some of the two girls' projects, such as their "church" they built for dogs, she might have remembered him, but he did not. His facial features had long lost any youthful appearance to them, and Krystal saw no resemblance to anything that she could recall.

He tried to use some of the suggestions that Dr. Madden had offered him in several counseling sessions and varying on Dr. Madden's technique for attracting women to view him in a better light, he moved closer to Krystal. She, however, could smell alcohol on his breath and backed away. It was at this point that Krystal's dog began barking at the window at Ernie. When Krystal looked at Ernie's face, it seemed as if a black shadow had covered over it for a second or two and then disappeared.

"Well, I'm married now," she claimed as she quieted her dog.

He shrieked, "When did you get married? You were supposed to marry me!" He shouted at her his voice cracking with the words.

Krystal began to explain when she married and that at this point they had not had any children, not mentioning any other details.

Ernie was silent and then began to defensively stated, "Well, we know all about you! We know everything you did at Kent State!"

Krystal was taken back. She had tried to put Kent State out of her memory for the time being. She was struggling to find herself, to gain a hold on her marriage and now to get a good grip on her spiritual life, and his statement brought some of these hidden feelings to the surface.

"Yeah, we know all about you!" She wondered if he meant he knew about her visit by the FBI, the Nixon rumor and all that the shootings entailed, but then he would also know about her inappropriate behavior. Other than letting Wilbur know about her promiscuous behavior, the rest she had not shared with anyone else.

He continued the attack. "Yeah, we know everything you did back then, and I'm gonna tell it all to your husband!"

"Go ahead," she retorted. "He knows about my activities." She hoped that a little aggressiveness on her part would overthrow his defiance. So she used an Ace of Spaces, but instead of stopping his tactics, it only challenged them.

"Well, I know every little thing you did!" He took one step towards her in a more menacing way, and then stopped. "And I'm gonna get you for it!"

She cried out and then grabbing her basket she ran inside the house. Flustered she sat down on a chair and began to sob. *Why did all of this have to come back to me? Why couldn't I just forget about it? Oh, God, why did this have to happen to me?*

After about 10 minutes she wiped the tears from her face and went back outside to retrieve more dried laundry. As she emerged from the back door, she noticed Ernie was still there, but he had been tearful as well. She was struck by what she saw, and wondered why he had not followed her into the house, if his true intention was payback.

"I didn't really mean it!" he sobbed. "I would never have hurt you. I just didn't know what to say. – I was trying to do what he told me to say, and I just didn't do it right."

"Who told you to say this?" she inquired struggling to comprehend it all.

"That guy – the counselor. I have to see him as part of my therapy. He's at the counseling center." Krystal had not seen Dr. Madden since the day he quit working at the hospital, and so was not sure who the counselor was, and Ernie could not remember his name. Ernie was speaking much more calmly now and Krystal considered his threat to have been merely words of anger and frustration with no substance behind them. They spoke at length about Ernie's marriage, how unhappy he was and wished he could make it better. Krystal tried to encourage him to love his wife more. He genuinely seemed to appreciate what Krystal was saying to him, but when he tried to jog her memory about wanting to marry her so long ago, she still drew a blank.

When Ernie made one final attempt to play up to Krystal's emotions, she replied, "You know I could turn you in for threatening me."

As she did so, Ernie's face became contorted and he genuinely appeared to be afraid. "Please don't. This is the only job I have."

Krystal noted his reaction and felt his gesture was superficial, that perhaps something was buried inside that he wished not to discuss or bring out. She then told him that she would not report him, but that she wanted him to never threaten her like that again.

As he left the yard, Krystal tried to replay the entire scenario in her mind, but just shook her head to dismiss the incident as just a quirk. Yet, she continued to focus on the part where Ernie's faced turned darker. She wondered if what she had seen was something more spiritual in nature. She was not unfamiliar with what she called "the dark side." There had been patients at the hospital who came in from time to time describing odd circumstances involving "evil spirits." As Krystal placed reports on the charts of the floors, she would many times engage in conversations with the ward attendants. Of course, a lot of people had their own theories about it. Some did not believe that evil spirits existed at all. Others had more detailed stories of supposed encounters by friends of theirs. There was one black orderly, though, who had described more odd occurrences when evil spirits were successfully cast out. He told her that there were times when it appeared the cast-out spirit would "shake up the room" with objects being thrown about. Other staff members described that the Catholic Church was the only ones knowledgeable about these episodes. They claimed that it was an involved and complicated process to dispel the hold of such spirits on individuals. As a result there was an entire service performed involving much chanting of litanies by the priest. Though Krystal had been a Catholic, she had never heard about those ceremonies.

She pondered, *could this trooper somehow he possessed by an evil spirit? Was this what Pastor Jack was referring to when she got baptized, about the devil placing more temptations in front of her? If that was true, then he certainly did place something right in front of her.* She decided to seek Pastor Jack's advice.

After church service the following Saturday, Krystal was invited to Pastor Jack's house for a meal. Also present were some new-found friends of Krystal's, Melody Gable and her nine-year-old daughter,

Brittany. When the meal was finished and the Gable's had departed, Krystal began questioning Pastor Jack.

"Remember what you said to me about being tempted more now that I've been baptized?"

"Yes, I do." He began to look at Krystal curiously and then asked, "So what is happening?"

"Well, I'm not sure. I had an odd experience with someone that I think may be possessed by a demon."

With a half-smile he responded, "I know it happens. I know others that have dealt with this phenomenon, but I personally have not." He eyed her in a friendly manner as he spoke.

"Hmm," she stated somewhat disappointed, "I was hoping that you might be able to help me with this. I don't think this will be the last time I encounter it, and I'd like to know what to do the next time I come head-to-head with something so strange. You see I think God has a strange way of working with me, just from the way I felt He led me to the truth in the Bible. I don't know much at all about demon possession, let alone how to counteract it. Is there anything you can give me to show me what to do?"

"Like I said, I've never had to deal directly with this," he stated as he ran his fingers down the book shelves jammed with various paperbacks. "I can't really say there is a manual on how to cast out demons. In fact, Ellen White only refers to such occurrences now and then in some of her letters." He pulled out a smaller book and handed it to Krystal. "Why not take this with you and see if these will help? In the meantime, I would certainly pray for this other person. If it's true that he is possessed, he may be seeking a way to be released from the hold that's on him. You could be an asset to bringing him closer to Christ."

Krystal thanked him for his support and drove home to read what he had given her. Perhaps Pastor Jack was right. Maybe this trooper was seeking a way of help and maybe God was intervening to bring someone out of a spiritual bondage. She decided to wait and see what would happen next, yet began searching for more about the subject. She chose not to see "The Exorcist" as she knew that the story involved a Catholic priest and the ceremony that had to take place. Krystal had no intention of returning to a church and their traditions, when she had questioned so many of them. Now that she had found a Bible-centered church, she had discovered a lot of fallacies that the Catholic Church held up as having been directed by Christ. These, in fact, had been incorporated from the Roman army as well as Roman culture after Christians had been persecuted – after Christ had died and ascended into heaven, and were not directly orchestrated by Christ's instructions.

She sat down and paged through the Bible. *Surely, if God wants me to perform such a feat, a feat that the apostles themselves carried out, He will have to give me more information and confidence.* She read through the passage in Matthew chapter 17 where the apostles were unable to exorcise one particular demon, and that Christ Himself had to do it for them. They verbalized that they could not understand why they were unable to cast the demon out. Yet Christ replied to them, "It was because of the littleness of your faith, for truly I say to you, if you have faith as a mustard seed you shall say to this mountain, 'Move from here to there,' and it shall move, and nothing shall be impossible to you." Pondering over this passage, Krystal decided to undertake an in-depth search not only about demon possession, but about having enough faith. She opened the book that Pastor Jack gave her and began reading through various letters. As she did so, she did not notice the county sheriff's cruiser drive slowly past her house and down the road.

Cory Dumas, dressed in his sheriff's uniform walked into Dr. Madden's office and sat down, placing a video tape in front of Damian. "It seemed that Krystal's some kind of Bible reader, and from what I gathered it seems that Ernie Wilson think she's gonna help him."

Damian immediately put the tape in and viewed it. After several minutes had passed by and the tape was finished, he commented. "Maybe we can throw something really interesting in here. I'm not a Bible reader, but there is mention of two witnesses. What would happen if we fix things so that these two witnesses work against each other?" He smiled as he mused over what possibilities could result. Then he immediately began looking over his schedule. "Ernie's due to come in for his appointment today. This will be great!" As Cory got up to leave, Damian thanked him and stated, "Keep up the surveillance on that house of hers. Let's see what happens here. I'll take care of the surveillance on Ernie's house."

CHAPTER
7

Krystal continued with her Bible studies and attendance at the Adventist Church. Her deeping friendship with the Gable family led to weekly home meetings. Wilbur enjoyed their family also, and so a closer bond began to form between Krystal and Wilbur as well.

One day Krystal talked over with Wilbur about having children once again. "You know I'm 30 now. It won't be much longer before I won't be able to have children. Couldn't we just have one child?"

After several months of talking it over, Wilbur agreed and so in later summer of 1980, it was confirmed that Krystal was pregnant. When she broke the exciting news to Dr. Klone, he was just as ecstatic. For the next several months, Krystal concentrated on preparing room in the house for the new family member with Dr. Klone offering a bassinet for the baby's use until the nursery was finished. Krystal commented several times that she felt the baby would be a boy, "because he's so active and kicks so much."

For the most part the pregnancy was going along fine. Now in late fall she was beginning to show quite a bit and with her short stature, her pregnant state somewhat accentuated this. As she sat at her desk at the hospital busy with many duties, she heard a scuffle in the hallway. A black-haired state trooper was being whisked back to the ward. Shortly afterwards Dr. Klone had typed reports completed explaining to the insurance company why the patient needed admission at this time.

The report was much more in depth than Krystal usually found on Dr. Klone's patients. It described Ernie's condition greatly exacerbated with extreme agitation at home. Several times his wife found him drinking heavily and in an irrational state. At times he would rant and rave "claiming he was God," and other times would quote from the Bible and begin condemning various family members, claiming that none of his children were his own. As a result Dr. Klone diagnosed him with paranoid schizophrenia.

Krystal began to get more interested in this case, and two days later other department reports appeared on the chart that Krystal needed to pass on to the insurance provider as well. As she read the social service assessment, things began to come together for her. She read that Ernie knew a young girl named Krystal, who years ago had lived near Cleveland, and that from time to time, he would try to visit her. The report went on to describe how Ernie watched this young girl play an instrument in the town band at various civic functions and other detailed activities. Krystal now began to recall these events.

Becoming somewhat distressed, she now remembered parts of the conversation between Ernie and her in her backyard well over a year ago. As she recounted that he had verbally threatened her several times, she instantly got up from her desk and sought out Dr. Klone on the ward.

"This is me in this report! I know this man!" she soundly claimed as she pointed to parts of the report.

Dr. Klone only shook his head negatively. "You don't understand. This man is so out of touch with reality, we can't believe anything he says."

"But it's you who doesn't understand! What he is saying here is true! My name is Krystal, and I grew up near Cleveland! I did play an instrument in the town band! You have to believe me this is all true!" she pleaded with her voice straining and cracking. Frustrated that he would not agree with her, Krystal stomped out of the closed-in nurses' station and returned to her desk.

Meanwhile at his office, Dr. Madden reviewed the surveillance tapes he had made of the Wilson household. *Wait until I see Elliott again!* he surmised. *The CIA will think very highly of me now – I've found a new mind control method.* He then played back the audio tape he had made. The whispered suggestions he had recorded had worked in the minutely-hidden microphones Elliott had given him some time back. Strategically placed in Ernie's home, the microphones provided a means similar to that of subliminal messaging, which the CIA was known for using in the past. Ernie believed everything that these "voices" told him. Dr. Madden sat back and began to laugh. *To have such control over such a simple mind and I can have such power over someone. I am like God!*

Dr. Madden then began to report how Ernie claimed he had heard "voices coming from the radio and TV" telling him that his wife had been cheating on him, and that his children were not his. Dr. Madden put his pen down as he smiled. He contemplated at his ingenuity of introducing the thought that Krystal was mentally torturing Ernie by reminding him of what he lost by marrying Lily. Then picking up his pen again, he asserted in his assessment of Ernie that he was an unstable and unpredictable person who might commit murder at some point, thoroughly describing someone who would be in a deep state of psychosis and paranoia. When Dr. Madden was finished, he asked his secretary to type up the report. Then he grabbed the finished report as he made his way over to the hospital. He was careful not to disclose his methods.

Krystal had just finished taking reports to the floors and was still standing beside her desk when Dr. Madden rounded the corner and handed her the report on Ernie. He could not help but notice her pregnant state.

"So your husband gave you the only thing that I couldn't," Dr. Madden blurted out. "I had a vasectomy, but you stayed with your husband so you could have a child?"

Having not seen Dr. Madden for well over a year, Krystal had other thoughts presently on her mind than their last encounter. Yet after a few moments she joked that she had eaten too many watermelon seeds and her pregnant-looking abdomen was the result. Then more seriously she began to apologize to him, but was cut short by his remarks.

Brushing off her attempt he stated, "It is I who should be apologizing. I put you in a rather difficult position and it wasn't fair to you. I hope we can still maintain a friendship in spite of it all."

Preoccupied with her future role as a mother and having a new outlook on life, she smiled at him and claimed that she held no grudges against him. When he had left the room, she sat down and began reading the report on Ernie.

The report was even more detailed than she had read before, describing exactly what the voices were telling Ernie to do. There was more delving into Ernie's past in relationship to knowing a "bully" who made idle threats to Krystal when she was young. At that point Krystal sat back staring off into space. *There was a bully who had threatened me. That's when I felt a hand placed on my shoulder!*

Krystal, engrossed in her thoughts, would not have noticed Ernie standing outside the door, except for the fact that Dr. Klone began to speak to Ernie.

"What do you want here?" he asked Ernie.

"I wanted to know what she was reading about me."

Dr. Klone gently put his arm around Ernie's shoulder and slowly walked him back to the ward. "Do you really know Krystal?" he inquired.

Ernie hung his head down, "Yes – I was going to marry her. She was the one I wanted, not my wife." Ernie began to sob heavily as he related the events of 20 years ago between Krystal and himself.

"Then why didn't you marry her?" posed Dr. Klone.

"I had to get married. You know what I mean."

"In other words, you got your wife, Lily, pregnant."

"Yes – I mean, no! I mean – well, I'm not sure the kids are mine!" stammered Ernie uncertain as to what he should say. Then he continued, "But Krystal spurned my love, so I went to someone else. She was supposed to wait for me. I was going to come back for her. And now she broke my heart!"

Dr. Klone motioned for Ernie to wait where he was as he went to talk to Krystal.

"You were right. He does remember you. But he claims you broke his heart! He said you spurned his love."

"I spurned his love?" Krystal exclaimed in disbelief. "I don't think so. I think it's the other way around. He went and married someone else."

"Well," commented Dr. Klone, "he had to get married! He got his wife pregnant!"

Krystal stared at the desk with a puzzled look on her face. Vaguely could she recall someone telling her on the steps of St. Michael's Catholic Church that he had to get married. *That was so long ago,* she murmured. *I really don't remember very much about it.*

"So then you did hurt him somehow," affirmed Dr. Klone then returning to Ernie.

Krystal continued to sit with a befuddled look on her face trying to understand everything that was happening. She looked down at Dr. Madden's report and read further into the report. It claimed that Ernie felt the FBI was following him and that they had bugged his house. *There's something strange about this report,* she thought. *I don't know what it is, but this may not be so unusual to have the FBI follow someone. After all, look what I encountered at Kent State! And in my backyard Ernie mentioned knowing all about me at Kent State.* She decided to inquire more from Dr. Klone when he got done speaking with Ernie. *Chickens always come home to roost,* she concluded. *The truth in this matter is going to come out.*

The following day Dr. Klone did indeed come to speak with Krystal. "I think someone's not telling everything that happened here, but it's a matter of who is not telling what."

"Well, I will say this," she began. "This part in the report where he talks about the FBI following him and bugging his house, and so on, that's not so strange."

"There's lots of patients who come in here with persecution complexes that feel someone is after them. It's easy for them to blame the FBI and the CIA. We get that a lot."

"That may be true, but what if it were true? Would you believe someone if they told you that?"

"What do you mean?"

Krystal then went into quite a bit of detail letting Dr. Klone know about the Kruczyinski family sending packages to Communist Poland and the scrutiny that she felt the FBI kept on the family. She also relayed the incidents at Kent State when the FBI agent came to her door and began questioning her about rumors on campus. She reiterated that they followed her to her classes and even sat in on them.

"So it is possible that the FBI could be following him and bugging his house," Krystal concluded.

"But why? He's in law enforcement, too. Why would the FBI want to follow him? They're on the same team, right?"

"Well, I would hope so. What if they were doing some kind of checking on their own for something? Maybe Ernie would sense this. Maybe he's afraid of what they might find – I don't know." Throwing up her hands in exasperation, Krystal was just as perplexed as Dr. Klone was.

At last Dr. Klone spoke, "Still, there's something here that is not being told. I'll be back in a few moments." He exited down the hallway. As he did so Dr. Madden, who had just entered the building, followed him in pursuit of Ernie. They both were engaged in a conversation with Ernie on the ward and Krystal could only see that there was much talking going on between all three of them, although she could not hear their discussion.

When Dr. Klone returned to Krystal, he asked, "You were in high school when he got married, right?"

Krystal looked through the various reports. "It says here he got married in 1962. I wasn't in high school then. I was only 12 years old. It's on my driver's license." She produced her license and pointed out her birth date. "Driver's licenses don't lie!"

Dr. Klone stood speechless for some time and then spoke to Dr. Madden aside in the hallway.

"If she's right, and Ernie is lying about this, how stable is he? Do you think he would seek some retaliation from her?"

Dr. Madden maintaining a professional attitude claimed, "I've been involved in criminal psychology for some time. I've seen this type of personality seek revenge as payback for wrongs made against them, no matter who is at fault. I think he could do something very harmful to Krystal."

Returning once more to Krystal they expressed their sentiments arousing suspicion in Krystal's mind and fears as well. "So what you're saying is I'm safe as long as he's in here, but what happens when he gets out?"

Dr. Madden assuredly said, "There's nothing we can do to keep him here against his will. Until something happens, we just have to wait and see." He stared at Krystal watching her reaction to what he said.

Krystal just put her head in her hands, not knowing what to think. In the meantime, both doctors retreated to the nurse's station where they began to write a discharge plan for Ernie.

"You will see him in follow-up?" inquired Dr. Klone as he wrote.

Dr. Madden smiled dryly, "I would be glad to." He stroked his chin as Dr. Klone continued to write, pondering what would be his next move. When the orders had been completed, Dr. Madden returned to his office.

When Ernie's wife arrived to question Dr. Klone about the discharge, Ernie stopped her in the hallway. She was dressed in her full-length sable-colored mink coat bought by Ernie.

"That's her!" Ernie pointed to the medical records room. "She's sitting in there. – I'm not crazy! I knew her a long time ago and everything I said was true. Her name's Krystal!" Lily rolled her eyes around as she listened to Ernie.

"Go ask her! Go ahead, if you don't believe me!" At last Lily stood in the doorway to medical records and asked if her name was Krystal. When Krystal replied to the affirmative, Lily then asked, "Then you knew Ernie when you lived in your home town?"

"Well, yes – I don't remember everything right now. It was so long ago, but yes, I do remember some things that he has said.

"See! I'm not crazy!" Ernie stated as he emerged from around the corner. "Now take me home!"

When the two had left the building, Krystal wondered, *there's something really strange about this case. Something makes me feel very ill at ease. I just wish I knew what it was.* Krystal left work that day and when she arrived at home both her and Wilbur decided to spend the weekend involved in various activities. Krystal was grateful for this diversion from events at work. They concentrated on putting up drywall for the baby's room and then taking in a movie.

Several weeks passed by and things appeared to be quite calm. Krystal concentrated on her work once again. However, she was once again brought back to consider Ernie's situation when Margaret entered the office and remarked that he had been admitted. Krystal waited for some word from Dr. Klone. When at last a report appeared on the chart, Krystal read it carefully.

"We have reason to believe that this patient, Ernie Wilson, possibly committed murder. Unfortunately, we have no concrete evidence, and the patient is so out of touch with reality that he is unable to effectively communicate with us. We are, therefore, unable to ascertain if he indeed did commit murder."

Krystal placed the report down as both Dr. Klone and Dr. Madden entered the room.

"I guess I should have listened to you. You were afraid that something might happen – I even gave him your address some time back!"

"Yes, I know," Krystal stated matter-of-factly. "He already came to visit me." Krystal sat down calmly in her seat.

"What happened!" both doctors yelled out in unison with anxious faces.

She did not immediately look at either of them, remembering the conversation in her backyard and the uncomfortable feeling she had when Ernie had threatened her. She did not readily speak about the darkening of Ernie's face, but rather serenely stated, "We just talked."

"Nothing else happened?" inquired Dr. Klone astonished.

"No."

"What did you two talk about?" probed Dr. Madden, recalling the tape Sheriff Cory Dumas had provided him. "Did it have anything to do when you were a young girl?"

"Lots of things happened to me when I was a young girl."

"That son-of-a-bitch!" he blurted out attempting to suggest some animosity ought to be harbored.

Krystal corrected his assumption by saying, "I didn't say Ernie did anything to me. – I just said lots of things happened to me when I was a young girl. We talked about him wanting to marry me a long time ago."

Dr. Klone interjected, "Is that all you talked about?"

"No. He talked about some problems he had." Then recalling his darkened face, she asserted, "I promised him I wouldn't reveal any more."

Pressing for more background information, Dr. Madden sternly asked, "Did he make you promise that? Did he threaten you?"

"No, he did not!" Krystal retorted. "I promised on my own accord. He didn't hurt me in any way. He never laid any hands on me."

Surprised both doctors backed off in their interrogation of Krystal. Dr. Klone motioned for Dr. Madden to follow him as they retreated to a private room to assess the situation.

"Everything known about Ernie points to the fact that he should have hurt Krystal, yet apparently he did not," stated Dr. Madden emphatically. "Why do you suppose that is?" he queried eyeing Dr. Klone's reaction.

"I don't know," replied Dr. Klone. "I do know one thing. She somehow means something special to him in some odd way, and maybe more than we think."

"We need to find out what that is!" Dr. Madden asserted as he walked back to talk with Krystal.

"Apparently you made quite an impression on Ernie," he stated.

"What do you mean?"

"He seems, I guess, impressed by your statements and attitude." Hoping to appeal to Krystal's gentler side, Dr. Madden strove to have Krystal relate more. Krystal did not respond right away, but had a curious look on her face trying to understand what Dr. Madden was getting at. "It seems he remembers you relating a story about a victorious saint involved in a battle," he stated.

"Yeah, but so what."

Then shifting his posture and leaning closer to Krystal's desk, he continued. "I've been through that town before. What church did you attend?" At that point Dr. Klone entered the room listening to what was being said.

"Actually it was St. Michael's Church. I do remember telling someone about the story of St. Michael, the archangel." Krystal began to straighten the papers on her desk as she related when she could recall.

"That saint actually depicts Christ and is a reference to the book of Revelation in the Bible where Christ fought the devil." Krystal began to look over at Dr. Madden more closely wondering how he knew about her home town. In all her encounters with people, nobody had ever heard of that town before. *How was it that he was familiar with it?* she pondered.

"He's definitely impressed by something in that story," interjected Dr. Klone. "He thinks you can cast out demons!"

"What? I really don't know anything about demon possession. – I mean, I've read a little bit, but nothing that tells me anything about how to do such a thing!" Then Krystal became silent. She recalled the "Jesus" movie that she had watched, how the father had presented a son who was thrashing about. Jesus walked over to him and the demon was cast out. Yet the book that Pastor Jack had given her only contained two letters that made reference that demon possession did exist, but nothing about how the demon was actually cast out. As Krystal mulled these thoughts over in her mind, the two doctors moved further out into the hallway.

"I think what we have here is some sort of scenario," commented Dr. Madden. "Something we might watch being played out."

"Romeo and Juliet?"

"More like Beauty and the Beast," Dr. Madden exclaimed emphasizing the beast portion. At that moment Ernie emerged from the ward somewhat restless and approached Dr. Klone.

Dr. Klone then returned to Krystal and claimed, "Ernie says he needs to have a demon cast out."

As soon as the statement was made, Ernie not looking at Krystal spoke up. "I don't want her casting the demon out! She's nothing, but a whore!" He then began to scream.

Pointing his finger now in her direction and facing Krystal he continued his accusations against her. Krystal was shocked at this sudden change in his demeanor and felt the vicious impact of the words he was saying. She could no longer keep her emotions pent up and began to shake with tears streaming down her face. Ernie's extreme hostile verbal attack of Krystal even surprised Dr. Klone. Dr. Madden stood by saying nothing.

Ernie continued with his barrage, "It's all your fault! You promised to marry me! You promised to wait for me! You promised never to have any kids!" Then looking at her belly he continued, "And you've gone and broken all those promises! That's why all these horrible things have happened to me! It's because of you! It's all your fault!" Once more eyeing her pregnant state, he blurted out in a half-tearful tone, "That's my son inside her! It's my baby!"

Staring at Ernie through tear-blurred eyes, she defended herself by retorting sharply, "I'm not responsible for all this! You never came back!"

"Oh, yes I did!" claimed Ernie as he moved closer to her desk. At that point Dr. Klone firmly grasped Ernie's arms and turning him around, marched him back to the ward. Dr. Madden continued to remain in the room attentively watching Krystal's reaction.

Krystal repeated her statement as she stared off in shock, "I'm not responsible for all this. I'm not responsible for all this!" She began to shake her head 'no' still portraying a somewhat stunned appearance. Then she began to recall what had happened so long ago. She then postulated, *Could I be responsible? Could I have done something that would have changed all this? Could his life have been entirely different?*

Finally with pleading eyes she turned to Dr. Madden and asked, "Could I really have been to blame for all this?"

His thoughts were jarred by such a direct approach and shifting his eyes away from Krystal's imploring gaze, he nervously searched for something to say that would be more consoling.

At last he more assuredly spoke, "No – no, you're not responsible for all of this." He slowly began to pace back and forth in front of her desk nervously rubbing his chin. Krystal felt a bit of relief at the confirmation that she was not at fault. Aware that Krystal breathed a heavy sigh and sat back in her chair, Dr. Madden suggested, "If you want to talk this over with someone, I have an office here in town. You're welcome to come by and we'll sit down and talk, okay?" Hoping that she would take him up on his offer, he anxiously stared at her awaiting her response.

Krystal looked at his face. She recalled a similar approach when he tried to ask her out for a drink. Not wishing to produce the same reaction she got from him the last time, she courteously replied, "I appreciate the offer. I'll certainly think about it." Yet something about his proposition bothered her, and she decided not to pursue finding out what he might have wanted.

Dr. Madden thinking that he had succeeded in his charming display, departed from the room and approached Dr. Klone in the hallway once more. "She's pretty upset about this! What happens to her if she ever finds out that he did come back to see her, and that her parents never told her about his visits?"

Dr. Klone tightened his lips as he spoke softly, "Let's hope she never finds out!" The two doctors then parted their ways.

Krystal said nothing to Wilbur about her day's events, but after her household chores were finished, she sat down in an overstuffed chair. Picking up the Bible, she prayed for guidance, acknowledging that she did not understand what all was taking place, but that if God had a plan for her surely He would make it known to her. Then she began reading the book of Revelation. After several hours of study, she fell soundly asleep, resting in the assurance that whatever happened would be under God's direction.

The following day both doctors met to discuss Ernie's progress. As Ernie walked down the hallway, he was calmer, not provoked in any way. As a result he was allowed to roam the corridor unescorted. The two doctors then approached Krystal to see how she was doing.

"It's a good thing you didn't marry this guy," began Dr. Klone.

"The man's an ogre!" claimed Dr. Madden once again watching Krystal's response to his words. "He eats children!" Then quickly attempting to clarify what he meant, he stated, "We think that he was working on a case of a runaway girl. We're not sure, but we think he somehow sold out because of his drinking, and the girl somehow got sold into a prostitution ring."

"Is there any way to check into what happened to her?" Krystal asked innocently.

"We're not sure what happened to her. We think she's dead!"

"But somewhere in his social history, he talks about some young girl that he lost. Yet he says she's alive." Krystal responded, yet puzzled by what was being put before her.

"He thinks she's alive, but we have no evidence to indicate that his is true. He's so out of contact with reality, he believes she's still alive and is going to come back someday," asserted Dr. Madden.

Krystal thought for a few moments. Then recalling that Ernie's record stated that he had been an Adventist she finally commented, "I bet he's got some of this somehow tied up with the Second Coming." She recalled her previous night's study. Neither doctor replied to her statement, but as Ernie walked by they began to talk with him in the hallway.

"I'm doing better today. Every time I come in this hospital, the voices stop. They don't wake me up at night here, so I sleep much better here. I still say the FBI is bugging me in my home."

"Now, Ernie," began Dr. Madden not looking directly at the patient.

"No, it's true! They think I know what happened to that girl – that I had something to do with it – and they think by bugging me, I'll tell them something. But I don't know anything!" He walked away from them back to the ward clenching his fists. *If only I could find out for sure. If only I didn't feel so helpless,* he considered retreating to his room. He sat down on his bed and stared at his cupped hands in his lap. *I feel so lost like I'm nine years old and caught in a jungle – a jungle filled with lions ready to devour me and snakes prepared to swallow me whole!* He began to cry into his cupped hands.

As Dr. Klone entered the room he sat down on the bed beside Ernie offering comfort. Relaxing somewhat Ernie began to convey some of these inner fears of his.

Dr. Madden had not pursued Ernie, but remained outside Krystal's door watching Ernie as he walked back to the ward. *So far my plan is working well. I just need some more finishing touches added.* He smiled as he contemplated how much more enjoyment he could get out of this game of his. *Watching this schmuck turn against a person who might help him is heading in the direction I want. All I have to do is create more animosity between these two and he'll eventually destroy her. Then I won't be plagued by these nightmares about Agent Mullins any more. If Ernie destroys her, she can't destroy me.*

When he noticed both Dr. Klone and Ernie returning to him, Dr. Madden was curious as to what would happen next. As soon as Ernie saw Dr. Madden standing close to Krystal's office, his face muscles began to tighten up.

Dr. Klone spoke to Krystal, "He really thinks that you can help him with this demon. He says you would be the only one who could do it. Will you help us?"

Krystal was about to speak when Ernie instantaneously responded once more with his accusations of being a whore and that the baby inside her is his. Krystal was perplexed at the sudden change in his attitude. *Is there something about me when he sees me that makes him do this? Or is it something else?* she pondered.

Then Ernie broke into a new train of thought, "It is prophesized in Revelation that there was a woman with child, and the dragon stood before her to devour the child when it was about to be born. And I'm the dragon, and the dragon is the devil himself!"

Dr. Klone attempted to calm Ernie down, but was interrupted by Krystal. Calmly she rose from her chair and stood alongside her desk. "It is also prophesized that the woman fled into the wilderness where her food was provided and her water was sure!"

Astounded by her response, both doctors stared at her not saying anything. Neither were that familiar with the Biblical passage.

Upon hearing Krystal's response, Ernie screamed, "You know the prophecy!"

"Yes," she sternly replied, "I DO know the prophecy!"

At once Ernie began ranting and raving quickly departing from the doorway. Dr. Klone quickly approached him from behind as a stunned Ernie blurted out, "She really can do it! I know it! She knows about me!" After placing him in his room, Dr. Klone returned to Krystal.

"Yes, I'll cast out this demon," her eyes brightening as she spoke. Dr. Madden noted something different about her bearing – something he was not sure he liked. "But this won't happen until October 26, 1987. Meet me in Friendly's restaurant in Scoria at noon." Then she sat down.

"1987? That's almost seven years from now!" Dr. Klone exclaimed in disbelief.

"I know," continued Krystal calmly and yet appearing somewhat astonished herself at the words that were coming out of her mouth. "That is when I will cast the demon out. There has to be one more murder." Krystal knew that she had prayed earnestly for answers the night before, and she felt whatever was going to happen was not under her direction, but someone more powerful than her. As Dr. Klone balked at what she was saying, she replied, "You see, I'm not the one dealing out the cards. I'm only giving the message."

"Isn't there anyone else who can help us?" spoke Dr. Klone in exasperation.

"If his claim is that I am the only one that can help him, and I do believe that this whole event is being God-directed, then no, there is no one else," she retorted still feeling an indescribable influence hovering over her.

As last Dr. Madden spoke, "I don't believe in things like the devil and the like."

"Maybe not, that remains to be seen." She stared at him in contemplation and continued, "If I know you, and I think I know something about you, you wouldn't miss this for the world!"

He stared back at her as he tightened his clenched fist as his side. *She's right! I would be interested to see if this is possible!*

She then asserted, "You will be responsible for bringing the music."

"But I don't even know if I'll be around this area then."

Smirking a dry smile at him, she commented assuredly, "You'll be there!"

"What kind of music?" he inquired now wide-eyed feeling a bit unnerved by what was happening. "I really don't know much about these sort of events."

"With this situation, I will need music to revive me. From what I've read these events can be pretty straining on the person doing the casting out. I will need to be revived and the music will do that."

He gasped at her as his open jaw hung down lower. *This is so different that what I have planned. – Not what I expected at all,* he contemplated to himself.

"When that day comes," Krystal claimed, "you will go into a music store and whatever you select will be appropriate." She then turned her attention to the paperwork she needed to get busy with on her desk. Dr. Madden remained standing at her desk not saying anything and then finally left the hospital.

Krystal did not understand why the date was picked, but that was what came out of her mouth. When the date did finally arrived seven years later, it all became clear that there definitely was a Higher Power at work here. Krystal would only understand all that was being put into play until much later, and that this meeting in seven years would have much larger ramifications than Krystal could have thought possible.

Upon his return to his office, Dr. Madden sat in his chair with feet propped up on his desk, wondering what to do next. The plan he had contrived in his mind he considered almost fool-proof. Now there was a factor thrown in that he had not anticipated. He had hoped Krystal would have been fearful enough to come to his office whereby he would have planned another scheme to undo her character similar to what he was doing with Ernie. *Yet she said there had to be one more murder. – There's still hope I can pull something off here*, he pondered as he jerked his legs off the desktop and planted them on the floor.

That evening Krystal returned home and resumed her Bible reading. The influence of something more powerful than her in her office, though no longer present, had left her with an eagerness to embark on a more thorough search. She began by reading the passage that Ernie had spoken about. It began in chapter 12 of Revelation with the woman with the child and the dragon. Then it went on to describe Michael and the angels waging war with the dragon. This is the story that Krystal knew from so long ago.

After Krystal read the passage she sat back in her chair. *Well, Ernie's certainly misinterpreted what he quoted to me. Even so, I recognize his misunderstanding. He sees me as the pregnant woman about to give birth, even though that clearly is not me in Scripture.* Dialing Pastor Jack's number they talked over the passage.

"I know that the woman in the wilderness is truth, and that the devil will go to great ends to stop the truth from being known, especially about him," she stated.

"Yes, that's correct. Actually, according to what Ellen White writes, the woman represents the church in the Middle Ages when corrupt church power sought to hide biblical truth. God provided for the truth to endure and be heard," commented the pastor.

"The child is of course Jesus Christ and the offspring of the woman are believers and followers of Christ, right?" she queried.

"That's right."

"Now the part about Michael and the war in heaven – that is actually long before Christ is born on earth, is it not?"

"Yes."

"So then if a third of the fallen angels that were deceived by Satan fall to the earth as well, then there are evil angels on this earth along with guardian angels."

"Okay, but some of those evil angels are bound in an abyss waiting the final judgment."

"So if there is a guardian angel for every person on earth, there has to be a lot of angels in heaven, right?"

"Yeah, and there are not only guardian angels, but recording angels, seraphim and cherubim, and there are so many other duties that good angels do – it's really hard to say how many angels there are, but yes, there are a lot of angels in heaven. John in Revelation talks about ten thousand upon ten thousand angels that he sees in vision – I think he means that there are too many to count."

"Then just for the sake of argument, let's just say if there are six billion people on earth, and there is a guardian angel for everyone, there could conceivably be six billion angels in heaven."

"Okay."

"If a third of these were thrown down to the earth, then presumably there could be two billion evil angels on earth, right?"

"Well – yes, but like I said some are bound in an abyss, so not all of these evil angels would be free to move about on earth."

"Then in a sense there is a battle continuing down here as well."

"True. Paul's letter to the Ephesians tells us that we do need to be on the alert, and to be prepared for a spiritual battle. The armor he describes in the latter half of the sixth chapter, tells us we need to be spiritually grounded in order to resist everything these evil angels can throw our way."

"In other words, we need a lot of faith as well."

"And Paul even points out when he says to take up the shield of faith so that you can extinguish all the flaming missiles of the evil one as well as to pray at all times. Even though the victory over death has been won by Christ, we still need to hold onto Him, as we were confronted by the spiritual battle we fight here on earth."

Krystal thanked him for his reaffirmation of what she had already concluded. She sat back down confidently musing, *God had protected me before in so many ways that I was not aware of. Yet if I trust in Him, He can protect me again.* Putting her study aids aside she got ready for bed. She laid her hand on her belly. She could feel the baby move once again and she was thankful that everything was going well with her pregnancy.

As she felt the baby give her another jab in the ribs, she thought about an incident that happened at the hospital soon after she began to work there two years ago. A coworker had brought their newborn baby in for everyone to see. When Krystal extended her arms in anticipation of holding the infant, an overwhelming feeling came over her at that time. She immediately withdrew her hands as a stern warning came to her. *You murdered something as beautiful as this! – Don't ever do this again!*

Krystal never forgot that incident. It reminded her that there is a Creator and that the creation of another human life is a very sobering and responsible task. Now that she was preparing to be a mother, she did everything she possibly could to ensure that no harm would come to this baby, no matter what.

Three days after Krystal had read the passage from Revelation, she was at work when she noted Ernie bedecked in his uniform pacing the hallway. Every so often he would stop by her door and looked at her. Then with a sorrowful facial expression without saying anything, he would turn away and proceed with his pacing. He repeated this action several times until both Dr. Klone and Dr. Madden arrived to speak with him.

Dr. Madden then approached Krystal as Dr. Klone and Ernie remained in the hallway. "I deal a lot with the police and other law enforcement personnel. We need your help with this matter."

Krystal looked at him and then at Dr. Klone trying to understand what was being asked of her.

"Ernie claims he is on special assignment to discover lost children who are kidnapped by drug lords," asserted Dr. Klone.

"We are hoping you'll help us. After your baby is born, we would like to ask you to help solve this dilemma. He wants to 'borrow' your baby, and see what happens to it. Perhaps that will lead to where the other lost child is," Dr. Madden stated.

Krystal sat there shocked by what she was hearing. "You'll be completely protected and watched!" affirmed Dr. Madden.

Krystal, though, ignored looking at Dr. Madden and turning to Dr. Klone she replied forcefully, "Over my dead body!" Then she went on, "If you believe this story, then you're in just as bad a shape as he's in!" She pointed in Ernie's direction.

Wide-eyed and dismayed, Dr. Madden whispered to her, "But we really need your help with this. Believe me we have it all arranged. Your baby will be safe!"

"The answer is No!" she stated adamantly, "I'm not giving up my baby to anyone!" She recalled the feeling she had three nights ago. "This will probably be the only child I ever have, and I'm not letting him go to anyone!" She felt no matter what they said if she participated in this scheme, she would never see her baby again. She felt there was no way to guarantee protection. "Besides," she continued, "from what I've seen so far, I'm not so sure I trust any of the police or law enforcement." She thought back on how she felt after the shootings at Kent State.

When Dr. Madden persisted with his request, Krystal shouted, "No! Go find somebody else to do your dirty work!" Upon that statement Ernie turned and walked away. Dr. Klone followed along.

Dr. Madden, however, lingered behind still desiring to change Krystal's mind. "We don't really believe his story, but we need help in finding this other child," he insisted.

Exasperated that he would not accept her answer, she replied, "Look, sacrifice your own child if you want to! If I allow you to have my child, I'll never see my child again. The answer is No! – Now leave me alone!" With that Dr. Madden went in pursuit of Dr. Klone.

Irritated by the entire confrontation, Krystal could only sit at her desk and fume over what had transpired. The whole scenario reminded Krystal of when she was a child. Two older boys, much larger than her, had taken a doll of hers and were fighting over who should get it by each pulling on a part of the doll in opposite directions. Krystal was pleading with them to give it back to her before they destroyed it.

Shaking her head to rid herself of those mental pictures, she contemplated her situation now. It did not seem that much different. She wondered that maybe this was not the best notion of having a child when she felt so vulnerable to two men who were bent on finding ways to snatch the child away from her. Yet she definitely wanted this child, wanted to be a good mother and was afraid that her desires would be thwarted by others. She immediately prayed that she had made the correct decision. She felt a calming sensation wash over her. At last she said to herself, *Yes, I have made the right decision. I will step out in faith in God's direction, whatever that may be. I will have an answer somewhere in the future whenever He finds a way to make it clear to me.* She knew though that she needed to really develop this thing called faith, and it was going to take some time to get where she wanted to feel comfortable in her faith.

After work that evening she attended a baby shower given to her by one of the church members. When the gifts had all been opened and she thanked everyone, they all knelt in a circle and prayed. When Krystal's turn came around she prayed for the baby's protection putting the child completely in God's care. *After all,* she thought, *who else could guarantee my safety as well as my child's?*

Two days passed by when both Dr. Klone and Dr. Madden approached her once more. "You're safe," they both tried to reassure her. "Inside here he can't hurt you."

"What happens when he leaves? Can you assure me then that he will not try to harm me?" Neither could give her any concrete answers, and she felt uncertain that either doctor really understood how she felt.

Dr. Madden had been dismayed that she had not taken him up on his offer for the baby's protection. Upon walking out of her office and visiting some of the patients, he found himself unable to concentrate on the tasks at hand. His thoughts would drift off and he had to ask the patients to repeat their last statement to try to get him back to what was being discussed.

While in the process of walking down the hallway after finishing rounds for the day, something overtook him. Krystal looked up from her desk as she heard Dr. Madden yelling in the corridor. She got up to see what the commotion was about and noted that there was no one else visible that he was talking to. He appeared to be involved in some argument. At the end of the long passageway stood several nurses observing the same sight as Krystal was. The nurses then called another psychiatrist present in the lobby who then approached Dr. Madden.

"Get away from me!" Dr. Madden began to scream. "I can't stand it. I can't get rid of his face." He began waving his arms around as if he was trying to push someone aside. "Why can't I get Mark to leave me alone?"

The psychiatrist tried to get Dr. Madden to explain what was happening, but the conversation made no sense at all. Since Dr. Madden seemed to be quite irrational and unable to speak coherently about his situation, the psychiatrist had Dr. Madden admitted as a patient. As the nurses helped to take him to the floor, they passed by Krystal's office. Dr. Madden mumbled something like, "I don't want Krystal to destroy me."

Krystal had no idea what really had transpired, but that he lost touch with reality at that time. For the next several days, Dr. Madden remained in seclusion, although did calm down. When he insisted that he was a psychologist and had no right to be admitted or held at the hospital, he managed to sign himself out and return to his practice. Krystal did not see him again at the hospital up to the time when she took her maternity leave.

CHAPTER 8

D anny Boy thumbed through the open files at the neighboring Scoria's Sheriff's Department. As a private detective, he frequently went to the surrounding law enforcement agencies looking for leads in the cases he was working on. Today, he was looking into a few suspects wanted in a missing person case in the adjoining county. Sheriff Cory Dumas watched him page through the photo log and then approached him.

"Hey, we got word that there might be another murder taking place around here. Wanna know who we suspect?" Dumas sauntered over close to where Danny was and leaned across the countertop.

"Go ahead," replied Danny wondering what Dumas would have to say.

"It seems that one of the patrol's got a real problem. His name's Ernie Wilson."

"So, what's that got to do with me?"

"It seems he had an old girlfriend who knows about him. She was at Kent State, probably one of those anti-war hippie types."

Danny looked up from the photo sheet. His expressionless face concealed any dealings with Kent State. Yet the mention of the college brought back memories he wished not to think about. Trying to display an attitude of indifference, Danny replied, "So I still don't know what that has to do with me."

"Well, I talked to Don Klapper when he stopped in here yesterday, and he mentioned something about Ernie having a former girlfriend. Don said he knew you and that he knew something about her, but didn't say what. I just thought maybe you knew something about her."

"So, does the girlfriend have a name?"

"Yeah, Krystal something. I guess her name would have been different back then before she married. She lives out in the county." Once more Danny looked up from the photos and looked away from Dumas. Danny recalled keeping tabs on Krystal for some time after she left Kent State. However, it was Don Klapper who relayed to Danny about Krystal's marriage. From his infrequent contacts with Don, he knew where Krystal now lived. He was somewhat startled when Dumas continued.

"Do you ever talk with Don Klapper?"

"I've had contact now and then with him," not wishing to divulge any other information about the two's activities.

"Well, he says he knew some of the on-goings at Kent State when they were investigating the shootings, and he remembered hearing something about this Krystal."

Closing the photo book and putting the remaining papers in his briefcase, Danny inquired, "So what does Kent State have to do with a murder case of someone else now? Why are you telling me this?" Danny replied irritated.

"Just thought you'd might want to know, replied Dumas. "You know, something more might come out about Kent State…"

"The case was settled finally in 1978. There's probably nothing more that will surface now," stated Danny emphatically as he made his way to the outside door of the sheriff's department. When he turned the ignition on, he breathed a sigh of relief. He had not wished to delve into his feelings, yet he was irked that Don would have given out some information. He started the car and drove out to the patrol department at Burning Bridges wishing to have a few moments to talk with him.

Don, however, was out on road patrol. Danny left a message for the two to meet at the Rusty Nail that evening. The Rusty Nail was a popular drinking establishment that various police officers frequented. Danny had hoped Don would show up as he frequently did during the week.

Danny sat down at a corner table and just started sipping his beer when Don walked in the door. He was accompanied by Sheriffs Cory Dumas and Keith Munson as well as city policeman Greg Fleuzy. They in turn were followed by Damian Madden. Danny was familiar with Damian having investigated some alleged complaints by various female patients of Damian's. Yet the cases always were incomplete with Damian denouncing any charges made against him by the women. Danny found these cases to be quite frustrating to work on with his clients always walking away empty-handed.

The group approached Danny with Don quickly ordering a round of beers for everyone at the table. Damian sat down across from Danny with Don in between the two on his right and Cory on his left. The conversation began light-hearted exchanging various jokes.

Then Damian posed, "Does anyone know anything specific about Krystal Kruczyinski? I've been trying to get her to cooperate with some investigations related to Ernie Wilson, but she just doesn't seem to want to help me."

Danny quickly spoke up, "You're a psychologist. What investigations are you talking about?"

"True," replied Damian quickly, but then in a low tone and leaning forward, he added, "but I also work for the FBI and CIA."

Danny stared at him. *So you've got some connections to keep you comfy,* he concluded. He then stated that he knew nothing about Krystal.

Don, who was on his second round of beers hastily responded, "Yeah, but you followed the Kent State case, and…"

"And the case was settled in 1978. The four families got a payment. Don't any of you read the newspaper?"

"Do the shootings at Kent State bother you?" inquired the psychologist as he took note of Danny's reactions.

Aware that Danny was being put under a little heat, he breathed a deep sigh and stated, "I'm just reporting the facts. The case was closed.

I never read anything about this Krystal." Then turning quickly to Don he asked, "Did you?"

Feeling rather mellow Don replied that he had not read anything as such, but that he had looked into some of the formal reports where he claimed Krystal's name was mentioned. As the conversation began to deteriorate, Cory turned away and began watching the door. He motioned to Damian as two attractive females entered the establishment.

Later when both Cory and Damian moved to the bar to check them out, Danny leaned over to Don and spoke softly.

"Why don't you just leave this Kent State matter alone? You know Krystal wasn't involved in anything!"

"Hey, I hadn't planned on it, but Damian mentioned her name a few days ago and something about the way he asked I just couldn't help it – it sort of slipped out."

"Well, watch it! You're gonna blow both our covers."

The two females were then joined by two other officers at which time both Damian and Cory returned to the table.

Danny, too, feeling the effects of the beer, blurted out, "What's the matter, Damian? Kind of lost your touch with women?"

If Damian's eyes could have shot arrows, one would have pierced Danny directly between the eyes. Damian glared across the table for several seconds. Then he collected his thoughts and maintaining a more relaxed composure, sat down stating that the women were not his type anyway.

After about an hour Danny decided to leave, having said what he wanted to say to Don. Damian remained making some more comments about Krystal trying to get anything that would help secure the unborn child for his endeavors. Although he said nothing about the child to anyone at the table or what his intentions were, he tried to get Don to reveal whatever he knew. Don, however, noting Danny's irritated attitude, only claimed that he had heard her name mentioned before, and that he really knew nothing about her.

Several days later Damian sat in his office staring at the newly purchased painting which now hung directly behind where his patients would sit on the couch. He had bought it at an auction, not knowing who had painted it or really much about the relevance of what was portrayed. He liked it because of what it depicted. It was painted in a style similar to M.C. Escher's drawings. There were white faces across the top and black faces across the bottom. Separating the two rows was a vast open, almost desolating appearing landscape. In the center of the painting, set off in the distance was a totally black figure, yet the distance discounted any recognizable features of this person. The painting was titled, "Revelation," and Damian liked it because it seemed to portray an ominous attitude that the figure in the center had some power over the faces on the top and bottom of the painting. It gave Damian a sense of power, and he kept the painting over the patients' heads to remind himself that he had that type of power.

For a long time he stared at the painting thinking about various patients that he had, when his thoughts once more centered on Ernie Wilson. Then he thought about Krystal again and decided he needed to find the delivery date for the baby. He drummed his fingers on his desk thinking about their last encounter. He certainly wasn't happy that she had rejected his offer. He recalled Elliott wanted this child supposedly to be traced, but Damian knew better than that. He knew with George H. W. Bush as previous CIA director, there was a lot of underhandedness that took place. Selling children on the black market came as no surprise then to Damian. If it was not for the fact that Damian needed funds to keep afloat financially, he would not have been so obliging with Elliott. But Elliott had connections with George Bush and made sure that Damian was 'persuaded' to comply with the CIA's orders, regardless that there were a few bad apples in the mix.

When Damian thought about his hospital stay, his fists then tightened, *they had no right to put me in there! I'm a psychologist with a Ph.D. Yet, it was something about her that made me mad. – If only the rest of them could see that I am trying to do something here.* He contemplated his situation and then slipped into a conversation almost with himself, claiming that Krystal had to be paid back. Finally he blinked rapidly as he once more thought about the unsure delivery date.

He smiled as he conjectured how he could steal the baby away from her. Something inside him convinced him that it had to be a baby girl, just what he wanted for his plans. He decided to gather up some surveillance equipment. After he checked with Sheriff Cory Dumas, he drove out to her house. Sheriff Dumas had noted that both cars were gone for the day with Krystal having had to take the dog to the vet. As Damian slowly drove by the white clapboard house, he noted where the electric meter was. He then parked his car down the road a bit and walking back into the wooded end of the property he made his way to the back side of the house. Sheriff Cory relayed to Damian that there was a spare key in the garage. Making his way into the house, Damian set up several microphones and hidden cameras.

I still can get that child away from her. Once she delivers and then returns to work, I will get my hands on that child, he thought as he set up his bugging devices throughout the house. Once he was satisfied he had everything covered, he promptly left. Sheriff Cory would operate the taping equipment from a nearby abandoned house trailer. He would stop every day to check on any recorded developments with Krystal's pregnancy.

Krystal returned home that afternoon and laid down to rest for a while. Noting that her due date had come and gone, she wondered if everything was okay. The last time she had a doctor's appointment, he claimed there were no problems. As she lay on the bed, her mind drifted off thinking about all she wanted to do before the child was born. She did not directly recall the conversation between her and Damian concerning the baby.

A week later she gave birth to a healthy baby boy whom she named Joshua. Both she and Wilbur were ecstatic over the birth and spent all of their time doing everything they could for the baby.

After several months had gone by, Krystal knew her maternity leave time was coming to an end. She really enjoyed staying home with Joshua. It was then that the pervading thought about Damian's offer of "using her child" surfaced in Krystal's mind. She was unaware that Damian wanted a baby girl, and that he was disappointed now that she had a boy. She was concerned about her baby's safety. *If I leave him in a day care, suppose someone comes along and steals him?* she queried. For several days she carefully considered her options. Then at last approached Wilbur, stating that she felt uncomfortable returning to work at this time. She then let the hospital know that she would not be coming back.

A very close relationship then began to develop with the Gable family at the Adventist Church in Scoria. Melody and Krystal enjoyed taking care of Joshua while there, as Melody taught the children's division of Sabbath School. Melody's daughter, Brittany, was present there also, but seemed to be quite shy and quiet and did not interact much with Krystal directly.

Unknown to Krystal at that time, several sheriffs who were close to Cory had set up surveillance equipment at the church as well. Distraught that Krystal had given birth to a boy, and not a girl, as Damian had wished for, he strove to find some other means to upset her. As his camera scanned the room he noted the blonde-haired, nine-year-old Brittany sitting by herself. He watched for a long time noting that Krystal made several efforts to include Brittany in activities that were going on, but she seemed to be somewhat hesitate to cooperate with Krystal.

When the church activities were over, he followed the Gable family to their home, noting where they lived. *This gives me a very interesting idea*, he surmised. He planned to return a few days later and found that someone else had placed cameras as well as micro-chip bugging devices in the Gable home.

As weeks went by and Krystal continued to help Melody with the other children at church, she noted that Brittany became more distant. She almost seemed to become more withdrawn and would actually pull away when Krystal approached her. Krystal was taken back by the action and wondered what was going on. As she became more involved with Joshua's needs, she decided not to push the matter with Brittany, but to see what would transpire if she more or less left Brittany alone.

When one Saturday church morning service, Pastor Jack announced that he was transferring to another congregation further away, Krystal was somewhat saddened. She and Melody discussed Pastor Jack's departure, and the new incoming pastor. As Krystal spent a little more time at Melody's house, she noted Brittany did respond to her some, and seemed to be okay. Krystal thought that perhaps Brittany was just a shy child and that she would eventually come out of it alright. She then gave it no more thought.

Cory and others continued to watch the Gable family until Krystal left. When Melody had reported to Brittany that she had to check in on a client of hers at his home she instructed Brittany that she would be back in about one-half hour. They continued to watch Brittany. Then using the microphones hidden in the house, some of them began "whispering" messages that Krystal was a "mean and bad person." They continued with this, even using subliminal messages next to her bed. By Saturday morning when Brittany would look at Krystal in the church classroom, she would retract from Krystal's presence as she neared her. As Cory watched further along from his camera's eye the reactions and when he saw how easily Brittany complied with these 'messages,' he grinned.

After several months with the new pastor established, Krystal could not bring herself to warm up to him very well. At last she decided to visit the church where Pastor Jack had settled at. Finding a very warm atmosphere at that church she quickly transferred her membership there. By doing so, she spent less time with the Gable family.

Damn it! Cory vented. *Now I won't be able to get Brittany to harm Joshua. Why are my plans always going astray? What is it about this Krystal that makes her do opposite of what I want!*

As Krystal made friends with the new congregation, Cory and others decided to move their cameras to that church as well. Hoping to find some other person to coerce into his plan Cory was dismayed by what he saw. Krystal had made friends with Sherita, an outspoken African American woman. The two spent much time together conversing about their lives and laughing over many humorous moments they shared with one another. And when Krystal started up a nurturing group in the church, Sherita opened her house to the weekly meetings.

Jesus! Thought Cory angrily, *this was going along pretty good, and now Krystal's left a congregation I had hoped to turn against her. And now she's got a close friend who I don't like! Guess I'll have to get Keith Munson to help me with this. He hates black people!*

When Cory related to Damian what he and Keith were planning to do, Damian made no comment. Then Damian thought back on the dream about Agent Mullins, and how he wished he could have had the opportunity to "raise a girl child" his way. *Perhaps I can do more damage another way,* he contemplated. He decided to bounce some of his ideas off Elliott the next time he saw him.

Meanwhile Cory and other wayward sheriffs continued nurturing Brittany the way they thought she should progress. "I've got a better idea. Maybe I can have her ready by 1987 to divert whatever may happen then."

So Cory, along with Keith Munson, and Greg Fleuzy embarked on a plan to turn Brittany against Krystal in any way they could. Cory, Keith and Greg were known to abuse their authority as law enforcement officers. At times they made sure fines from tickets were waived so long as the women had sex with these officers. Greg, who taught criminal justice classes at the local college, would offer grade changes so long as the women would comply with his sexual advances. So it would be no surprise to find these officers willing to bargain in some way with Brittany in time.

Damian had relayed what had happened at the psychiatric hospital to Elliott, who in turn relayed information to several others in the CIA. When William Colby, then CIA director, was ousted by President Gerald Ford, George H.W. Bush then became the director. Likewise, Dick Cheney, another of Ford's cabinet advisors, became head of the Department of Defense. Interestingly, George Bush had entered World War II as a pilot near the end of the conflict, having fought in the Pacific and not Europe. Dick Cheney, on the other hand, had several deferments from the military during the Vietnam War and never served in the military, but was a senator and businessman who viewed capitalism as the route to ensure a productive economy. In time, this partnership between George H.W. Bush and Dick Cheney fostered a very close business relationship and later on incorporated Donald Rumsfeld, who was involved in foreign affairs, particularly in the Middle East with Iran and Iraq. Donald Rumsfeld had made his acquaintance with Saddam Hussein and later strove to get the White House administration under President Ronald Reagan to support Iraq in the Iraq/Iran War. Prior to Reagan, President Carter had the unfortunate occurrence of hostages taken by Iran with a failed attempt at rescue, orchestrated mainly by the CIA.

Damian became familiar with these close-knit relationships in the CIA and the Middle East situation and wondered how he could come away from their underhandedness unscathed.

Still seeing Ernie Wilson on a now and then basis, Damian still maintained a watchful eye on him privately. Ernie was once more plagued by these "voices." Not knowing for sure whether Damian had anything to do with them, they did seem to be waking him up from sleep with troubling thoughts about somehow hurting someone else. Disturbed that his sobriety had not lasted like he wanted, and expressing to Dr. Klone that he needed something to help him sleep, Ernie began taking prescriptions for sleep aids, mostly barbiturates. For a while these helped and Ernie would no longer wake up with such thoughts.

Well, I'll have to change that, thought Damian as he viewed the tape of Ernie sleeping. *Perhaps I still can get Ernie irritated that Krystal is doing nothing to help him. Maybe then he'll get rid of her!*

Once again his plan was derailed as he watched Ernie dial Krystal's phone number. Krystal had placed an article in the newspaper concerning self-help from an anonymous group, based on the 12-step program of Alcoholics Anonymous. Confused from the effects of the drugs and conflicting therapy he was getting from Damian, he only identified himself as "George" when he began to ask about the group. Then he proceeded to relay to Krystal contradictory stories about himself.

Krystal had long forgotten about the plans to meet at Friendly's in 1987, and the reason behind that. However, upon hearing this conversation from "George" something vaguely familiar began to surface.

"Is that your child talking in the background?" he then asked.

"Yes," she replied, although she wished Joshua had been quieter at that moment.

"A boy?" he went on.

"Yes," she answered quickly although decided she would say no more.

He paused for a short moment, and then said, "My wife won't come with me to these group meetings."

"That's too bad. Is there anyone that may help convince her to come with you?"

"Can't you come to my house and talk to her? She won't come because of me – she doesn't think there is anything wrong with her."

Krystal felt a sense of uneasiness with his request, but did not say so outright. There was just something about his story that appeared to Krystal to not quite be all true. Also, she was not sure that she wanted to visit someone in their home, not knowing anything about them. *What if this was some sort of joke or trap or something,* she thought. She declined the offer to come to his house, but encouraged him to come to the meetings.

"I guess you can't help me then," he stated and then abruptly hung up.

Krystal stood in the kitchen for a few moments thinking about the conversation when Joshua distracted her. She then was busy entertaining him by chasing him around a little bit, and forgot about the phone call.

The next few days there would be several phone calls, but when Krystal would answer the caller would hang up. When she was almost ready to call the phone company, the calls stopped completely.

When Ernie visited Dr. Madden the next time for his session, he asked about the 12-step program groups and if he recommended them.

"Actually, they are based on a religious belief. – I'm not sure that is what you need to help you, since you said you're not involved much in church activities."

"But Dr. Klone thinks the 12-steps are a good thing," balked Ernie.

"That's the old school of thinking. The new school is that you are your own god. You don't need some abstract god. God is all you make yourself to be."

Discouraged Ernie left the office once more confused by Dr. Madden's so-called therapy sessions. Damian though felt he was winning. *I just need to tweak this just a little more. Then he'll be putty in my hands.*

When Elliott stopped to visit Damian several months later, he was not happy that Damian had not secured "fresh meat" like he had claimed he would. In fact, Elliott paced the room nervously, smoking cigarette after cigarette, as he expressed his dissatisfaction with Damian's overall performance.

"But there's been progress in another way. Take a look at this child, Brittany. The sheriffs pretty much got her to do what they want. And the beautiful thing is that she's starting to lie to her mother, yet her mother believes she's a wonderful child. This has so many possibilities."

Elliott watched various tapes that Damian produced from Cory finally settling down on the couch.

"Alright," he said at last, "This seems a long way around, but it just might work. I can find a few people I know who will help you with this."

"Great! The more people I have, the better this will work. It will almost be like having a child raised by wolves." Damian smiled as he felt his plans were becoming more solidified in place. However, that satisfaction did not last long after Elliott left when Damian recalled how irritated Elliott was with his nonproductive results. *If the CIA becomes dissatisfied with my performance, they may push me away like the FBI did. I must do something else to make some money off this government before that happens.*

Remembering that he had just glanced over a brochure concerning a seminar dealing with Medicare patients, he quickly riffled through this mail on his desk at home. He then made plans to attend along with setting an appointment time alone with the speaker to discuss his ideas. He then drove out to Krystal's house and removed most of the transmitters he had set up. He would only keep the ones so Cory and his crew could keep tabs on her and report to him.

Damian's funds began to dwindle, and with lack of enough patients coming to see him, he knew he needed to do something else. Damian made his way to various surrounding college campuses and persuaded several psychology professors to offer up services from various graduate students. Their compilation of research enabled Damian to begin incorporating several nursing homes to use his corporation's services.

Things would have gone well except that the graduate students began to complain that they were not paid for their services. He had received money from Medicare for some services, yet he had proposed that because his corporation had a contract with the nursing home and that the students were performing the testing, that Medicare owned him additional payments.

Finally, his lawyer went to great depths through Medicare rules and regulations discovering and then relaying to Damian that essentially he was trying to double-bill Medicare. The rules strictly prohibited such, particularly since Damian was not directly participating in the testing of patients himself, but merely available by telephone for consultation by the corporation's graduate students hired for such. His lawyer exasperated by the time spent unearthing the double whammy Damian was trying to place on Medicare, withdrew from being Damian's attorney, sending him a bill for over $12,000 for services rendered.

With the truth surfacing, and various lenders now claiming priority for repayment of their funds, Damian could no longer continue in debt. By this time Karla had decided a divorce was in order. Damian then filed for bankruptcy in 1985, unable to repay his loans. The day after he filed, Cory Dumas came to visit him upon hearing the bad news. Damian had decided to sell several paintings he had at home as well as in his office. Loading them up in Cory's 1978 Ford Fairlaine, they drove to a pawn shop in downtown Burning Bridges. As Cory parked his dull-blue vehicle in front of the shop, a man quickly strode in front of the car and entered the store ahead of them. He had a very youthful face, yet his hair was almost completely white. It was well trimmed and he bore a white beard and mustache equally neatly groomed. Casually dressed in jeans and a black leather jacket, he could have easily passed for an average person on the street.

As Damian gathered up his paintings and took them inside, Cory remained stationary in his car. Damian began to pile the paintings on the counter as the man they saw earlier approached from behind. He said nothing until Damian pulled out the painting entitled, "Revelation."

"I really hate to part with this one. I really love it!" expressed Damian emphatically to the owner behind the counter.

At that point the white-haired man behind spoke up. "Oh, yes – that painting. – Do you know the story behind it?" When Damian declared he did not, the man continued. "It's taken from the book of Revelation from the Bible, you know." He eyed Damian as he spoke. "The center figure is really Satan, and his demise at the end. During the first resurrection, a resurrection to life, all the believers in Christ or God are raised and are transported to heaven. Those not with Christ or God when Christ returns are struck down by the falling rocks, and put asleep. They much await the second resurrection, a resurrection to death. The in-between time is the millennium, the one thousand years. This is when Satan roams the earth isolated with no one to tempt. Those who did good deeds are in heaven. Those who did evil are asleep. That is what this painting depicts, the in-between time. At the end of the thousand years, the second resurrection occurs in which the evil people and Satan are cast into the fire and destroyed."

Damian began to glare at this white-haired man as he spoke. Damian loved that painting and he did not like this interpretation of it at all. He liked the power that the painting evoked, not the story of the end of this powerful person in the center of the painting.

Damian's expression was well noted by the white-haired man when he at last asked Damian, "What resurrection do you plan on being in – the first or the second?" He then spun around on his heels and exited the store.

Furious of that question, Damian ran out to Cory. "Did you see where that man went?"

"What man?"

"That white-haired jerk who just came out of the shop!"

"I've been sitting here all this time watching the door waiting for you, and I tell you no man came out of the store!"

Frustrated by Cory's answer, Damian went back inside to collect what little he could get for his art work. Dissatisfied, yet with no other viable alternative, he took the $50 for all the paintings and rode off in Cory's car.

Yet Damian was not the only one having money troubles. Interest rates had skyrocketed during President Reagan's years, and many people were finding mortgage rates in double digits with credit card debts mounting as well. This was known as the "trickle-down theory" as those at the top only filtered down very little funds to the underlings. At that time George H.W. Bush was Vice President from 1980-1988. Reagan, Bush and Cheney had vaguely heard about the upcoming "meeting" scheduled for Friendly's and with Reagan in his second term, it was decided to try to promote George H.W. Bush for president. As a result there were underhanded blackmailing aimed at Damian in order to get him to comply and if so, then that would resolve his bankruptcy issues. With things not going well in the CIA at the time, it would be necessary to put pressure on someone who could help resolve the crises arising from CIA activities in the Middle East. So it was arranged that Damian would force issues at this meeting at Friendly's. Until then

Damian had no alternative, but to oblige while his money problems needed to disappear.

Although Krystal and Wilbur were careful with their money and had no real investments other than the old farmhouse they lived in, the distressing economy took their toll on their lives as well. When Wilbur announced that he was being laid off, they had to dip in whatever savings they had to make ends meet. The unemployment checks would only last a while and did not cover enough.

As a result Krystal began to get resourceful and looking around the surrounding community, she began taking on several in-home part-time computer jobs.

"They may not bring in a whole lot of money," she told Wilbur one evening, "but at least I can be home with Joshua, and not have to pay for child care." And indeed the jobs did help take care some of the bills. By fall of 1985, Wilbur was called back to his job and so the money problems in the household began to ease off.

Krystal continued to work for the two companies at home, when finally both announced that they were no longer going to use at-home services. Krystal once more had to become shrewd in her approach to employment. This time she located an out-of-state job as an assistant director for a church-operated day-care center in Charlottesville, Virginia. She spent a long time talking over the opportunity with Wilbur, stating that perhaps once she got established there, she would be able to find him work there as well. Before she made her final decision she prayed about it, asking for guidance in what she would embark on.

As she was praying a feeling of *I need you to come away for a while to show you something* pervaded her mind. Not disclosing this feeling to Wilbur, she ventured to Virginia with Joshua coming along as well. Wilbur stayed behind until she would be settled.

In April of 1986, Krystal took Joshua for a weekend meeting with the Virginia congregation to finalize plans for her new position there. Krystal had hoped that the weather would be good and they could camp out. Watching her money closely she wanted to utilize as little as possible on this trip. When she had arrived in Virginia there was still snow on the ground and any available firewood was quite damp. It had been an eight hour dive and Krystal was getting tired. Finding no suitable open camp ground, she finally pulled off the road and settled in on the front seat. Joshua was already sleeping soundly in the back seat. As she laid there with her eyes closed, just barely starting to drift off, she heard a car coming from behind. She noted from the sound that it had slowed down considerably as it crept past hers. Even though the doors were locked, she felt very uneasy about who might be peering into her car. *And what would they see*, she thought, *a helpless mother with a young child. This is not good!*

Then as if the other driver was scared off, the car sped off. Krystal sat up in the seat and noted that it was an older model Pontiac Bonneville. As soon as it had gone around the curve and out of sight, Krystal started up her blue Plymouth Horizon and continued driving down the road. She was awake now envisioning what could have happened to the two of them. Earnestly searching for a motel, she traveled several miles finding nothing. At last she found a park that led well off the road. Seeing no other vehicles around at all, she drove down the path which twisted around and let to a very secluded parking lot. Making sure no one could see her from the road, she decided to stay here for the night.

At daybreak she looked out her window only to find an older red pickup truck had also pulled off the road. Relieved that it was not the car she saw earlier, she still wondered who it might be and why they would have picked the same spot to pull off as she did.

Getting out of her car to rummage through the belongings for some cereal and utensils, she noted a white-haired man come around the front of the truck. Dressed in jeans and a black leather jacket he said nothing to Krystal, but only took note of her as well as her son. Krystal stared at him for quite some time saying nothing, but only observing that he appeared very clean-cut with a well-trimmed white beard and mustache. There was just something odd about him as she watched him. It was almost as if he had followed her there or was there to make sure she was okay. He said nothing to her, but she wondered why he was there.

When she thought, *who are you?* he appeared to read her thoughts and smirking he looked away from her. Watching him as she readied their breakfast, she perceived that he appeared to be enjoying the cold spring morning, taking in the sounds of nature surrounding both of them. Krystal wondered if he knew who she was and why she was here.

Perhaps with the CIA headquarters not too far from here, he's one of them, she contemplated. Krystal observed that he seemed to be quite content, not interested in approaching her, though.

When she had rinsed out their dishes and packed everything away, he finally spoke to her in a very gentle-sounding, sounding voice, "You might want to stop and get some hot chocolate. That will warm the two of you up."

Krystal just looked at him without responding.

He continued, "You have about an hour's drive before you have to meet your friends."

Krystal's mouth sprang open as she questioned *how did he know that?* She stared at him for a few moments longer and noted that he got inside his truck, but continued to sit there. At last she started her car and as she backed around she waved at him. He waved back. Then she drove off. He did not follow her as she kept looking in the rear-view mirror. Once away from the park, she entered the freeway watching for any restaurant that might be open.

"A cup of hot chocolate sound good to you?" she asked Joshua.

"Yeah! That would be nice and warm!"

As Krystal finally found a Wally's Waffle House Restaurant, they both enjoyed a warm soothing cup of hot chocolate complete with marshmallows. Krystal sipping on the foam then began to think about the man she had encountered. Not sure if he was CIA or not, she recalled his mannerisms. He seemed to know where she was going. *Could he have been an angel?* she queried. *Was he there to reassure me and watch over me from the previous encounter?* She had no answers, but felt confident that God had indeed provided protection in some form for her.

Upon having a successful meeting with the congregation and day care center staff, Krystal spent some time searching for suitable living quarters for both Joshua and her. Some problems began to surface almost immediately. In Charlottesville, apartments and houses were too high priced for Krystal's budget. She then looked into renting a motel room, but again in the city she could not afford such. Then Krystal began looking at living further away from the city. For several weeks they both lived in a cramped motel room. At last, Krystal could not bear the lack of room for Joshua to run around in, and so began searching for something else.

Frustrated that she was not finding anything suitable she turned to her Higher Power and prayed, *If You want us down here, then You find us someplace to live.*

As if in answer to her prayers, the following day she located a newspaper ad for renting a house trailer on private land. It was nestled on the eastern slope of the Blue Ridge Mountains just about halfway down from Wintergreen Ski Resort. The owners lived in another trailer that they had built onto. The trailer was surrounded by trees and was beautifully placed so that the adjoining mountain chain could be viewed.

When Krystal first viewed the naturalistic setting of where the trailer was she fell in love with it. Although it would mean a 40 mile drive to work, she felt the sanctuary this place provided would be a blessing. As if to place an exclamation point that this is the place her Higher Power had selected for her, she made an interesting discovery once she viewed the inside. Upon entering the living room she noted two items that she was desperately in need of, an alarm clock and a couple of mattresses which were promptly displayed on the floor in front of her.

No one could have known I needed these things, because I've been in the motel room for several weeks, and I never said anything to anyone. Yet, here are the two things I need the most right now.

Declaring to the owners' next door that she would indeed take the trailer, she quickly settled in with Joshua sleeping in a cot she rented from the church. He was quite happy and spent a lot of time playing outside while Krystal worked on materials for the day care classes. Then in the mornings they would pack their daily necessities in the car, and while Joshua slept in the back seat, Krystal drove to the day care where Joshua was able to get a nice warm breakfast and then join the others in another classroom.

In the late afternoon when Joshua and Krystal would return to the trailer, Krystal would fix a simple supper and settle down with some paperwork. For a break she would go outside and just saunter across the acreage viewing the lofty mountains. As she would watch the sun sink behind the mountaintops, she would sit and listen to the birds singing.

Sometimes she would hear a train whistle off in the distance echo through the valley. Other times when it would get darker and she would lay on the mattress before falling asleep she would hear a fox call out in the nearby woods. It was so peaceful, Krystal just wanted to stay there forever. Many times she would get up before sunrise and anticipating it arrival, she would view the vast array of stars strewn across the sky. She felt a lot of peace and serenity in her surroundings.

On several occasion while she was waiting for the glow of the morning sunrise, she contemplated the many miracles she read about in the Old Testament, about how Elisha when surrounded by the Assyrian army had prayed that the eyes of his servant would be opened so that he may see God's majestic army protecting him. When his servant did open his eyes, he viewed the mountainside covered with horses and chariots of fire all around Elisha – an invisible, yet protective mounted army, ready to intervene when necessary. Krystal thought about that army and wondered if anything like that could happen in modern times. Yet when she thought how God's hand seemed to be guiding her, she knew even though she could not see a direct army, there had to be one somewhere there.

Krystal attended church services at an Adventist church nearby the ski resort. She enjoyed the weekly sermon/ studies, each one focusing on a different human aspect of one of the Biblical prophets. She learned that they all had frailties, yet God used them in spite of that. Sometimes it was something about their nature that God seemed to bring out and build their characters in that way. She felt that it was faith that enabled them to carry out whatever duties were asked of them. When she would return back to the trailer on Sabbath afternoons, she would contemplate on how Elijah ran scared after he brought fire down from heaven on Mt. Carmel. Then God found him hiding and called him out, strengthening him to continue on in his rebuke of what was happening to the kingdom. Other times she would think about Abraham and how he lied about Sarah being his wife, calling her his sister instead, and almost causing the king to sin. Yes, they had their flaws, but God still worked with them, and she felt she could trust God more and more to lead her in a direction that He wanted her to go.

Krystal did not keep up much with the news while in Virginia, although from time to time she would read over the newspaper at the day care center. The Iranian situation was worsening with the Middle East once again heating up. President Reagan and Vice President Bush were deeply involved in trying to avert this from becoming the hot seat for World War III. The CIA was highly interacting as well. Then there was Iraq still continuing its war with Iran and Saddam Hussein, Iraq's leader, becoming more and more ruthless in his attempts to win the war. There was great concern in the news about the entire situation especially with interest in the oil fields, prices for crude oil and the stock market in general. Saddam Hussein was concerned that Kuwait would undersell oil on the market thereby cutting into profits for Iraq's oil. Krystal only read parts of what was being reported, looking more for jobs for Wilbur in the paper. Yet she still would at least read the headlines and be somewhat familiar with what was going on.

Turning her attention back to more immediate matters on the home front, she was disappointed finding nothing in Virginia that Wilbur could even apply for. Discouraged she visited Wilbur every other weekend relaying to him that the work situation for him was not very prospective appearing. When in the late summer, the day care board approached Krystal about signing a year contract with them, she relayed that she had to discuss it further.

Upon returning to the trailer one evening, she prayed to her Higher Power about what decision she should make. Awaiting an answer, she contemplated what she should do. If she stayed, economically it would be rough getting through the winter on her salary. As if in response, she heard a small still voice, *your work is done here. I have things for you to do back at home.* Sensing this as her answer, she bid farewell to all her friends and staff of the day care center and returned to Ohio.

Once home she had to look for some other employment and decided at this time to look at sales. She then began selling some products from home until something else would come along that would be better suited for her. She was also able to once more regain her at-home part-time computer job. Wilbur continues at his job with no more lay-offs occurring. Financially, the family was doing okay, able to set aside extra money in case the economic situation would deteriorate again. Having gone through lay-off once, they learned that they needed a certain amount to keep ahead even with unemployment compensation. So they rebuilt their savings to help offset any future catastrophes amid the financial concerns encompassing the world as well.

Then in November, 1986, the shocking information leaked out. The CIA had been selling arms to Iran to fight against Iraq, only the weapons and parts were being sold at inflated prices. Now the Iran-Contra Affair began to surface as Congress began delving into the mechanics of the situation. There were other questions related to how Saddam Hussein got to be so powerful and was there any connection between the CIA some time back and Saddam Hussein's rise in power. William Casey, then director of the CIA, was being called upon to testify before Congress. He suddenly became ill with a stroke. In time he would develop a brain tumor and die before he ever stood before Congress and revealed the truth behind the Iran-Contra Affair.

On the other hand, there were those in the White House administration who did not want Iran to win the war and so supported Saddam Hussein by supplying Iraq with various materials.

Krystal paid attention to what Congress was trying to do. Noting that several reports emerged questioning the tactics and methods of the CIA, she read each newspaper analysis of them wondering all the time if the CIA had any good features to it at all. She questioned whether Casey's death was an accident or was it purposely set so that the truth would be covered up once more.

As if someone had been watching her, since she had returned to Ohio the phone began ringing more often. Once more the person identified himself as "George." Krystal never saw Ernie Wilson after she made the promise to meet at Friendly's in 1987. Having left the hospital work in 1981, keeping busy with Joshua in his early years, trying to earn money with the part-time jobs, and finally her trip to Virginia, she had not thought about the promise to meet again.

Ernie, however, still not knowing who was playing the "voice" game with him, was plagued with a desire to talk to Krystal, although when she would answer the phone, he would talk about something entirely different.

Damian once again viewing Ernie's reactions, spent more time working on Brittany. He utilized the friends Elliott provided him naming the group the "Wolf Pack." Eyeing that she did well in response to the prompts he was giving her in taking money on several occasions from Melody's purse, Cory and others decided to play more of a game with her.

"If you don't take the money, I'll tell your mom that you were touching yourself in the bathroom!" he would threaten her. As a younger child, she had obliged to these voices.

When the Wolf Pack became involved in his game, they began to encourage her to do other things such as run around the house naked when Melody was gone. Keeping pictures of such, they encouraged more of the same. Then as if to play the same "give and take" amusement, they too would threaten to tell on her for her activities. Jerking Brittany around back and forth with these tactics over several years took its toll her on. Although she complied with the men's voices, upon hearing them speak in public to her, often making crude remarks, her attraction to men dwindled. She did not know they were the ones teasing her, but the content of their conversation made her feel ill at ease. Even though she would show them what they wanted in front of the cameras at home, now 15, she was developing an interest in her girlfriends, not other boys.

One day Brittany's good friend, Jasmine came to visit her at Brittany's house. Brittany was aware that she was more homey-looking than Jasmine, a brunette, but of a comparable stature. The two would often spend time together discussing their other classmates' relationships.

Kyle and Jenny, two acquaintances of Brittany and Jasmine's, had been the talk of the sophomore class for quite some time.

"They're on again, with each other, at least for now," claimed Jasmine.

"Oh, that's not what I've heard. Kyle was quite angry with her the other day, yelling at her in the hallway, and I saw Jenny crying."

"Great! Why doesn't she just dump him, then? It's a good thing we're not involved with boys, like she is with him."

"Yeah, but she seems to be quite agitated lately. I hope she makes it through this okay. She's talked about hurting herself if he leaves her."

The two girls continued exchanging hearsay and what they knew about the two the rest of the afternoon. At last they decided to go for a walk around the block. Brittany's house bore a run-down appearance compared to the other in-town houses on her street. Her father was in construction, but had gone through some hard times with the inflated economy and housing industry deterioration. Interest rates in the double digits put a halt on new homes being built. Melody, in turn, resorted to caring for invalids in their homes. With the two parents gone much of the time, Brittany was left alone a lot. So when Jasmine came to visit, Brittany always looked for an opportunity to get away from the house.

After their walk, they decided to go meet with some other friends downtown. Returning to the house, Brittany ran upstairs to grab some money. With the "voices" telling her it was okay to take from Melody's purse, Brittany had learned that her mother was not suspicious, if only a little was missing at a time.

Today as she fingered the coins in her dresser drawer, she thought about how her friends thought she was not living in dire poverty, but that the appearance of her run-down house was only a temporary thing, "until my Dad gets a better job," she would tell them. Brittany wanted to be accepted by her friends and so did what she could to be accepted. When they had more money to spend than she did, she rationalized that her stolen money was justified in making her appear okay in her friends' eyes.

At the same time these two girls were walking into town, Kyle and Jenny were at the city park attempting to reconcile their difference. When Jenny upon hearing that Kyle had no intention of staying with her anymore, she once more broke down and cried, claiming that she would kill herself if he left her.

"Go ahead!" he finally told her in disgust as he turned his back and stomped off. He only vaguely noted that there was someone else roaming through the park at this time, but did not really pay much attention to him.

Ernie Wilson often went to the city park when his shift was over, and this late afternoon was no different. He saw the two teenagers talking, but kept on shuffling his feet as he would kick up a small stone or two and sail it down the pathway. Having separated from Lily, he often contemplated if he had done the right thing or not. After several hours spent walking and talking to himself, he at last returned to home barely able to make out the front door steps in the darkness.

The following day Brittany and Jasmine had much to discuss at school. The newspaper headlines read, "Girl found hanging in a city park." The article went on to suspect that it was a murder.

When Sheriff Cory Dumas related to both Damian that this had to be a murder, because of what he overheard from the city police detectives, Damian's eyes lit up. He concluded, *this just might be the murder we're looking for. I was watching Ernie last night and he went to the park about that time.* Then grabbing his coat, he told Cory he had some arrangements to take care of and drove up to the regional field office of the FBI to see what information he could provide other agents.

NOTE: Presidential and White House administration information was gleaned from the National Archives.

CHAPTER 9

Damian sauntered into the regional office of the FBI at Burning Bridges. Approaching Agent Art Castle, he smirked as he flashed his badge at him.

"I don't know if you know that I've been working as an informant for the Bureau, but I have some information that could have far-reaching consequences," Damian stated casually, but seriously.

"What kind of information?"

Noting another agent, younger in age than Agent Castle, sitting at another desk, Damian motioned if it was okay to speak in front of him.

"He's okay. He's been assigned to us from the Cleveland office. Meet Agent Gary Scambolini."

The agent bore shoulder-length black curly hair, was somewhat shorter in stature than Agent Castle, and of slighter body build.

"Scambolini," Damian repeated out loud. "I've heard that name before."

"I come from a large family in Cleveland. Maybe you've heard of one of my uncles or someone."

Damian thought for a short while and then dismissed it, still not recalling where he had heard the Scambolini name before. "Anyway, the information needs to be shared with the Cleveland office. It concerns one of the state troopers and a possible murder charge. – There's something else," Damian continued. Then bearing a more arrogant look to his face, he went on to describe Krystal's upcoming arrangement to "cast out a demon" from Ernie Wilson.

"What has that got to do with the Cleveland office that I should contact them?"

"Well, if she really can do this, and with the situation going on in Iran and Iraq, perhaps she can be of some value there." Then wetting his lips, he asserted, I've been approached by the CIA concerning the well that is on her family's property."

Agent Castle stared at him waiting for more information to be spilled forth and yet puzzled as to the contents.

Smiling as if Damian had scored a point he went on to describe the consideration about the CIA's interest in the well. After some time, Agent Castle agreed to contact Agent Robert Snuggles, who by now had become director of the Cleveland office of the Bureau.

Phoning him immediately, Agent Castle claimed, "He's got some information that may be of importance to us, I don't know."

Agent Snuggles replied, "Let me set up a meeting between us and the CIA and we'll lay this all out." After several phone calls back and forth, a meeting was scheduled for the following day at the Cleveland office with Damian to present what he knew.

When Damian entered the Cleveland Bureau he noted Director Snuggles now had a larger desk in a mahogany paneled office. On the wall behind the desk bore a large FBI plaque flanked by portraits of J. Edgar Hoover, Richard Nixon, Gerald Ford, and Ronald Reagan. There was a conference table set up with soft leather chairs. Scanning the room he noted Elliott flanked by several other men, whom Damian was introduced as being other CIA agents. Seated on the other side of the table were several other FBI agents along with Agent Castle.

After Agent Snuggles made sure all the introductions were under way, he asked Damian to present the situation at hand.

"I wish I could do this another way," he sighed deeply and looking across the table, but not at anyone's face he continued. "It seems we have a state trooper, Ernie Wilson, who I have been seeing as a patient and whom we suspect committed murder. We're not sure, but there may be a chain of murders that he could be linked to. The problem is getting through to him. There's a mental barrier there. Apparently he had asked for a person who supposedly can cast out a demon for him. When I first heard about this I was skeptical, and when she gave a date of October 26, 1987 as the date for such an action, I was even more skeptical. The problem is she mentioned there would be one more murder, and Scoria, where Ernie lives, has just experienced another murder case. We suspect this person, Krystal Kruczyinski, whom most of you know from the family property near Cleveland, is that person that can draw this out of him."

Several people in the room nodded their heads in agreement as Elliott began to cough and reach for his water glass. Damian paused as he did so.

"Sorry," he claimed, "it's that smoker's cough I get every so often." When he downed the glass and poured another one, he sat back and stared at Damian, waiting for him to continue.

"With this being September, I think since she was correct on things so far, perhaps we need to question her about things. She arranged to meet at Friendly's in October, so we need for one to see if this is possible for her to do, and then ask her about other things.

Director Snuggles snorted, "That two-bit whore from Kent State? Ha!" He shouted in disbelief. "Why Richard Nixon's been trying to find some way to get rid of her for years."

One of the other CIA agents immediately responded. "Yes, and do you know why? The property on which the Kruczyinski family sits has the well that we need for leverage, especially now."

"That's exactly my point," agreed Damian. "Now there are several ways we can do this."

Another CIA agent added, "We need that well in our hands so that we can keep Saddam Hussein at bay. Once, he finds out we have the one last well, he won't be so bold to attack other countries."

"Yes," replied another. "We need something to protect our vested interests in the oil market. With the Iran-Iraq War continuing, we're afraid if we don't find a way to stop him, he may start to destroy oil fields elsewhere just so he doesn't get undersold."

"So," began Director Snuggles, "What's to stop us from taking the property?"

Elliott looked directly at Damian, "That's been tried before – unsuccessfully."

Damian stared back at Elliott. "That's where I've heard about Scambolini before! He took care of Chrysha's father, Frank!" he shouted out loud. Then realizing everyone else was staring at him, he apologized and motioned for the CIA agents to continue.

"Richard Nixon's been advising the presidents ever since he left office about foreign policies. Now that the Iran-Contra affair surfaced supporting Iran, both Reagan and Bush wouldn't look so good in the public eye. We were lucky Casey died of that brain tumor in May before Congress could pick him apart. We had a lot of clandestine projects going on under his direction. If the news got out to the public just how much was underhandedly done, especially supporting Saddam in Iraq – well, the Democrats would have a field day in the next election. Richard Nixon advises that we just can't afford to have that happen." The first CIA agent finished his rhetoric as he folded his hands in front of him on the table.

After a few moments, Director Snuggles responded. "This would not look good for our President at this time. We've got to do what we can to support him. So what is your plan here?" he asked as he looked over at Damian.

"Well, just suppose Krystal gets Ernie to confess to these murders and supposing she can cast out this demon, why then she would virtually be undefeatable. Send her over to Saddam to take care of him."

Director Snuggles eyed Damian as he spoke, not immediately commenting on his words. Then he posed the question, "Supposing Saddam destroys her before she gets a chance?"

Then Damian smiled. "Either way, the government gets the well. Henry Kruczyinski is getting up in years. Once he dies and with Krystal out of the way, the family won't keep that well. It will be ours!"

"Before we get too far ahead, let's take a look at this closer. Supposing she can't cast out the demon and Ernie doesn't confess to the murders, then where do we go?" inquired Agent Art Castle.

Nobody spoke for a few moments until one CIA agent replied,

"Well, we'd better give her all the support we can – something to make sure she can do it."

"Krystal did want music provided as she said these type of events can be draining." Damian looked away from everyone when he spoke. Then returning his gaze to those about him, he claimed, "I can get some seminary students from a nearby college to help out," replied Damian. "I think we need to have this even taped so that we can use it for reference."

"We'll be ready," replied one of the CIA agents.

"Yes, we'll be ready also," agreed Director Snuggles. Then leaning over to Agent Castle, he whispered, "Get some locals involved in this. We don't want to be caught in any embarrassing situations." After specifics were laid out in details as to who would have equipment placed where, the meeting was adjourned.

Early Monday morning, October 26, 1987, Krystal was awoken quite readily. She looked at the red gleaming 3:00 on her nightstand. The abruptness of her awakening and inability to roll over and go back to sleep made her wonder what exactly woke her up. Compelled to read some, she came downstairs and picked up her Bible. Turning to whatever page she opened to, she began to read several chapters. Many times before she had felt that she was being directed by her Higher Power to read certain passages, and this time was no different. At last she prayed, "Father, I feel that You want me to do something today, but I'm not sure what it might be. Give me strength to perform whatever it is that You wish. Put the words in my mouth You wish me to speak." Nothing in her memory was aroused at this particular point about her commitment she had made at the psychiatric hospital seven years earlier.

Later as the sun began to appear on the horizon, Krystal dressed warmly for her trip to Burning Bridges for a sales meeting. She was still recovering from a head cold and bronchitis and her lingering cough convinced her to dress heavily.

During the meeting, one of the other managers, Laura, invited every one afterwards to meet at Friendly's for lunch which she was buying to celebrate her successful year.

Laura turned to Krystal and said, "You're going to be there, aren't you?" Though Krystal was starting to feel the effects of disturbed sleep earlier in the morning, she obliged and said she would be a little late, but would be there.

After dropping Joshua off at the Y for swim class, she made her way to Friendly's for her meeting with her friends. The sun was brightly shinning, although the air still remained cool. As Krystal entered the restaurant, it appeared to be quite busy. She did not spend too much time noticing the other people as she made her way to the table with her sales friends, yet during the ensuing conversation she did begin to take in the faces sitting at tables across from hers as well as in front of her. As she glanced around, she did not readily recognize them. She paid them little attention at first now that her lack of adequate sleep was beginning to take a toll on her. She did note two state troopers sitting at one booth, although the one facing her concealed his face quite well. The other trooper sat across from him with his back towards Krystal. Behind them in another booth sat another figure almost completely obscured by the trooper, whom Krystal did not notice at first.

A light-hearted conversation began between several of Krystal's friends concerning trivial events of the day. Several jokes and jabs were passed back and forth amongst the friends. When Krystal made a sarcastic comment in jest revolving around her marriage, the figure behind the trooper emerged in plain view.

"Trouble in Paradise?" posed Damian.

Krystal did not look directly at him as the waitress appeared immediately at Krystal's side to take her order. Not being hungry, she instead asked just to have a glass of root beer brought. She continued to joke with her friends, knowing that the laughing would keep her awake as well. They chided her about drinking root beer.

"I always drank root beer as a child, and I still enjoy it. – It brings out the inner child in me," claimed Krystal. With that conversation then focused on childhood stories with several of the ladies relaying what happened to them. Attention was then drawn to Damian as he emerged in full view from behind the state trooper.

Krystal affirmed loudly, "Oh, I know you! You're Damian L. Madden, Ph.D., psychologist." She recalled the first time she encountered him at the psychiatric hospital and his antics at that first meeting between the two.

Claiming that he did not recall her at all, he strove to get her to relay where he would have known her from. Krystal did not think much about stating what she could remember about him, yet her lack of sleep hindered some things in her memory. At this particular time, she could only recall him being there and that he liked to entice married women. Krystal continued to make other jokes about her life to the other women and ignored Damian's comments. As she sat there, Krystal could not help but watch Damian scan Nanette's body up and down. When Nanette became aware of Damian's leers, she rolled her eyes as she looked over at Krystal.

"I'll tell you later," replied Krystal, as the joking once more continued among the women. As Krystal looked about the booth, she noticed that each booth had a small juke box to the side. Relaying that she had not seen these in the restaurant before, she began scanning through the selections.

As she did so, the one trooper who had concealed his face previously now spoke up. "They're microphones! Watch what you say!" Ernie Wilson looked directly at Krystal as he proclaimed his warning.

Krystal looked back at Ernie, not recognizing him as he had his hat pulled down low across his eyes. The rest of the women and Damian began to jest that Ernie did not know what he was talking about. Still in a jovial mood, Krystal moved closer to the juke box and began talking into it.

Then Ernie indicated to Nanette that he knew Krystal from high school. Upon hearing this Nanette repeated what he said to Krystal across the room.

Krystal stared at Ernie, yet could not recall his face, or what she could see of it at this point. Still jesting with her friends, in a vampire-like voice, she commented, "I'll have to look through my collection of human heads!"

"She's a witch!" yelled Ernie to Nanette who immediately burst out laughing.

"That's her yearbook she's talking about!" claimed Nanette. Several people now were beginning to enjoy the scenario and Krystal started to look closely about her. Across from her booth sat two middle-aged men. She recognized neither, although later on realized one was a court bailiff named Phil and the other was Danny Boy. Danny bit his lip and nervously shifted his eyes back and forth, hoping she would not remember him from seventeen years back, which at the time she did not.

Krystal's attention was distracted as Damian attempted to bring the conversation back to himself. "You look so familiar, yet I just can't recall you," he asserted.

Still only recalling Damian's attempt to ask her out then, she decided to have a little fun with him. Quoting from a love sonnet she stated, "Ah, come live with me and be my love!" Then she went on to say they could have been married.

Shocked by the assertion, he denied the absurdity. Redirecting the conversation somewhat he began, "When last seen…"

Finishing the sentence Krystal stated, "When last seen I was with child."

Damian got a horrified look on his face, recalling his request to borrow her child.

"That was my child!" claimed Ernie. As he did so Damian relaxed somewhat hoping that was enough to throw Krystal off from openly relating about the baby-borrowing incident.

Krystal, however, was still fighting lack of sleep and so those memories were not surfacing at this particular time. She could only recall his play on women and she strove to 'upset his apple cart.' The other women were still in a teasing mode and began singing.

"Damian and Krystal sitting in a tree, k-i-s-s-i-n-g. First comes love. Then comes marriage. Then comes the baby in the baby carriage."

Now wide-eyed and once more bearing a shocked facies he glared at Krystal.

She quickly cut off the song stating. "Don't listen to them. That's not the way it happened."

Yet embarrassed, he quickly retorted in an insulted manner, "I should say not! I had a vasectomy!"

"Gee, I didn't mean to get so personal!" Krystal quickly replied as her friends and many other customers continued to laugh.

Damian, however, did not laugh and only turned away from Krystal trying to regroup his thoughts and save his reputation from being exposed to others present in the room.

Ernie, though, was softly commenting, "You whore." It was so quiet at first, that Krystal did not hear it, but only noticed Ernie's partner, attempting to make him stop saying that over and over. As the partner turned to look back over his shoulder at Krystal, she remembered seeing him before on the road here and there. Suddenly a quick flash in her mind occurred as if someone instantaneously placed a picture before her and then removed it. In the picture Krystal recalled seeing either this trooper or someone very much like him standing on the porch steps of the Kruczyinski house talking to her father. Krystal did not know that this was Trooper Otto Hartsel right at this time.

Damian, however, was busy trying to entice one of the other women to 'draw Ernie out of himself.' He posed that they do something more risqué. When another of the women approached Krystal, she decided to embarrass Damian, rather than Ernie. So using an ice cream cone as a prop, Krystal strove to 'turn the tables' on Damian. He sat there nervously squirming in his seat, and as Krystal then smashed the ice cream cone into a plate, he blinked uncontrollably thinking, *I don't believe she did that!*

At this point Krystal looked past Damian to notice two figures sitting in the farther booth. They almost appeared to be opposite in dress. One wore glasses, had peppered hair and was taller than his partner. He was dressed in a casual suit and stood up to move away from the booth. The other figure had shoulder-length curly black hair, had a dark-colored casual shirt on which was unbuttoned and opened to mid-chest, exposing a full growth of black chest hair and a medallion of some sort hanging on a thick chain. As Krystal looked in his direction, he separated his shirt at his chest even more. Only noting his actions, Krystal said nothing.

When the first figure turned back to look at his partner, she heard him say, "Come on, Agent Scambolini, we need to move somewhere else." The figure with long black curly hair got up to leave as well. Krystal had no interest in this second figure. It seemed as if there was something very macho about him that he wanted to portray, a trait Krystal found more repulsive than enticing. Krystal thought to herself that he kind of looked like "Goldilocks" only with long black curly hair.

Something about the first figure though held Krystal's attention.

There was something attractive about him, and yet a familiarity about his as well. She watched as the two walked down another isle to sit at a table behind Krystal. Her sales partners noticed her actions and made joking comments about that as well.

Fearing that Krystal would take on a more supportive role for Ernie, Damian strove to focus the topics on fear. Trying to get Krystal to view Ernie as a "dark figure" and one not to associate with, Damian asked, "Would you ever marry a black man?" Hoping that she would view Ernie as an evil person, he was taken back by her comments.

"It wouldn't bother me any. – Probably would bother someone else," she commented taking his query at face value. Then she relayed, "Some of my best friends are black!" Krystal noted that those remarks did not set well with Damian and she surmised that he had no interest or use for black people in general. She observed his reactions as she made other comments about her relationships with other blacks.

She relayed, "We even had a black male teacher at that day-care center I was at in Virginia."

"Weren't the kids afraid of him?" inquired Damian fearfully hoping to convey the idea that the black skin color should have been scaring the children.

"They loved him!" shouted Krystal exuberantly. "They would hang on him and crawl on his back. And he was good with the children. He also made them mind. They thought he was the greatest thing since sliced bread!"

He was hitting a raw nerve with Krystal when he talked against black people. Many times she had heard inferences from other people debasing black people on their skin color and the association of such to Satan. Damian began to reiterate some of these blatant irrationalities. She was not aware that he was referring to Ernie as a "black" man with the question of Ernie's possible hand in committing murders. However, he did not come out directly and state that, but indicated that black people belong to Satan.

"It's not that simple," countered Krystal. "White and black for good and evil. – Skin color would be too obvious." Then paraphrasing from 1 Peter 5:8, she stated that the devil goes about like a roaring lion seeking those he can devour. He tries to hide himself, so to be so blatant with skin color in white or black would be absurd! It doesn't matter what color you are. There are bad apples in every basket. We white folk have bad apples too!"

Krystal continued, "We should have been listening to the black people. When the blacks began having drug problems in their communities, we turned a deaf ear." She recalled that J. Edgar Hoover as well as other high-ranking officials in the government ignored the problem. "Now the drugs are in whitey's neighborhood! And everyone's upset! – We only get on the bandwagon when the problem comes to our house."

"You know, there's something in our skin and we all have it. It's called melanin. It's what makes you tanned when you sit in the sun. Some of us have more of it than others." She began singing, "I've got you under my skin. I've got you deep in the heart of me." Then she went on to describe how her family was Polish and that some of her uncles had darker skin color than others. She relayed that Poland centuries ago had been invaded by Moors and other Arabian and Muslim groups, and that there probably was some mixing of the races then. "So I probably have some Arab blood in me as well."

Damian countered stating that his mother belonged to the Daughters of the American Revolution and therefore was of English descent. In order to keep the purity of the lineage, he claimed to have "blue blood."

Krystal was not aware at the time that Damian was being prompted with his assertions from others in the room, and being a "scout" with those assertations.

Krystal then reasoned that since all the races came from Adam and Eve, one of them had to be black. She stated that many of her black friends felt it was probably Eve, the mother of the nations.

"We need to get along down here. There's going to be black people in heaven as well." Noting Damian's scowl, Krystal went on stating, "If you can't get along down here, then you sure aren't going to get along up there," pointing upward. "Then you don't get to go up there. – There will be no such thing as a white heaven and a black heaven. We'll all be together, sitting at one table."

Krystal mentioned about Dr. Martin Luther King and his "I Have a Dream" speech. When she mentioned the word 'doctor' by his name, there were several people sitting at a table of four that winced at that notation. Krystal went on to exclaim 'I have been to the mountain top.' Two people at the one particular table of four, did not like hearing that at all. This table of men were between Danny's table and the state troopers table. The two men facing Krystal seemed to have a keen interest in her. Although she did not recognize them at all, she would later discover that these two people were none other than George H.W. Bush and Dick Cheney in disguise.

Krystal finally asked Damian, "How do you know God's not black?"

Trying to get things back to where he wanted he interjected comments about the movie "The Exorcist." Krystal relayed that she was only vaguely familiar with the movie, had not seen it, and went off on a tangent related to her growing up as a Catholic. From there she expressed her conflicts in her beliefs at the time and her questioning of the Catholic doctrine she was raised by.

As she talked about her younger years, Ernie, in his own way, tried to get Krystal to remember things from her childhood and so began asking if she remembered "talking to God in the woods." With several topics begin thrown at Krystal at once, it was hard to spend any time delving into one topic before begin interrupted with another. As such, Ernie then mentioned that Krystal was supposed to marry him.

Damian interjected, "But he HAD to get married," hoping to dispel any lingering attraction between the two. With his comment, though, several people began to talk how they had married under "similar" circumstances, and even Krystal relayed that she had been pregnant when she got married.

One of the sales managers sitting at Krystal's table, Pauline, posed, "If you were pregnant when you got married, then how come Joshua is only 6 years old?"

Realizing that she had now opened herself up to controversy, Krystal strove to explain that she had an abortion, but it had been a mistake.

"And they still let you come to the Catholic Church?" Pauline inquired.

"No, I left before they had a chance to throw me out," related Krystal. When Pauline asked if Krystal went to church anywhere,

Krystal related her search for God and truth in her life, amid some humorous comments.

Once again Ernie tried to redirect the conversation back to her childhood.

Yet Krystal commented, "Now wait! – I'm still working on 'talking with God in the woods! I've done things like that many times," though at this particular moment she could not zero in on any specific incident that would have involved Ernie. When she did mention that she and Chrysha "built a church for dogs" she did not think about him watching the two at that time. Immediately Krystal described many other antics that the two girls had been involved in.

In vain Ernie tried once more to get Krystal to remember him from her younger years, and so commented that he used to watch Krystal go to church and confession. Again Krystal talked about various church doctrines.

With the conversation circumvented with a combination of religious attitudes, Krystal tried not to be preachy in any way, but endeavored to insert humor into the topics and make those around her feel a little more at ease. This had always worked when she lead out in the 12-step self-help groups she had run, and so felt that this would be a good way to relax everyone. She had hoped that they would see that yes, she had made a mistake, but that was not the end of the world for her or anyone else.

Finally, she commented, "You know what's going to happen – some Baptist preacher is going to come along and get really upset with me for this!" As she said so a figure moved from the far right side of the restaurant, circled behind Krystal and then sat down in the booth across from her.

"I'm Bruce Frost and I'm the minister at the Hill Street Baptist Church. I want to ask you a question. – Are you saved?" At this the crowd groaned as they had enjoyed the more light-hearted approach to the topics at hand.

Krystal, however, felt that a verbal attack was eminent, yet she stood firm assured that she could defend herself. She replied, "The only thing I need to be saved is from myself!"

"What about Satan?"

"Well, if you believe in that sort of thing," Krystal responded in a coy manner, a technique she often utilized in her life in order to uncover just exactly what the other person was getting at. Krystal herself was well aware that there was an evil force at work in the world.

"Are you saying that there's no Satan?" His words were harsh-sounding. Krystal felt that this was definitely going to be a battle – one she really did not want to get involved in.

"I believe there is something evil, but I don't really know what to call it." Krystal had encountered a lot of antagonism in her search for truth, and knew than many Christians did not even consider that even Satan existed.

Pouncing on her answer, he immediately chided loudly, "Well, God spoke to me this morning and told me you needed to be saved!" Then in a very stern and exacting manner he exclaimed as he pointed his finger directly at her, "You committed a sin by having an abortion! Now just what do you think sin is?" he demanded standing up from his seat.

Undaunted by his condemning attitude, Krystal chose not to raise her voice at him, although inside was festering a desire to set things straight. She responded calmly, "Actually sin is a broken relationship. It's a result of abridged feelings between God and another person, and sin results from this abridgment." Then she commented, "You believe 'once saved, always saved,' don't you?" When he replied to the affirmative she went on, "Well, what about having to be 'born again?'"

Resorting to his stern reproach and loud voice, he shouted, "That doesn't matter! You committed a sin and you can NEVER be forgiven! Now what do you have to say to that?" He sat back down with a smug look on his face as if he had scored a lot of points.

Krystal noted his antics. She felt she was being attacked much the same way Captain Kirk was when he was on trial in the beginning of the Star Trek IV movie. The Klingon ambassador was demanding justice for the death of his son by Captain Kirk. Krystal felt likewise being accused in the same manner. Comparing herself to be in a similar situation for having committed various sins, including her obvious abortion and her language, she commented that she also had been "charged with nine violations of Star Fleet regulations." So continuing to take script from that movie, she answered, "Klingon justice is a unique point of view!"

"I am not a Klingon!" he indignantly replied. Then jumping up to his feet again, he shouted as he scolded her, "That's not funny! Just what is it you think we're here for! We have a job to do and you're messing it up!"

Krystal reeling from the attack responded that she was here with her friends, not specifically recalling the promise made seven years ago. Endeavoring to get her to remember that promise, Ernie openly began to agree with the minister. When Krystal began hearing his attack as well, even though it was a mere assertion with a "yes" response to the minister's accusations, she now considered Ernie to be taking the same view point as her attacker.

"Oh, two against one, eh?" concluded Krystal. "I'm gonna go home and get my momma and she's gonna come back and give you a good whomping!" As Krystal described some of the fear tactics her mother used when all the children were young, she noted Ernie recoiled from his claims. Those reactions of his were too obvious for Krystal to ignore. Krystal sensed that perhaps in his younger years he may have been abused. Somewhere in the back of her mind came the recollection about a patient at the hospital. She recalled that he had been physically abused by his mother. Although she did not immediately make the connection at that time, Krystal watched Ernie physically retract in his seat, appearing almost afraid that she really would do as she had said.

"You say you've watched me in my younger years always going to confession – maybe it's about time you went to confession!" Krystal felt that everyone had made mistakes and to be so boldly attacked in public by two men only infuriated her inside, especially when one was a minister. She reasoned that she felt like the adulteress brought before Christ whom the people wanted to stone to death.

"Do you really think all these people are going to help and save you?" the minister sarcastically claimed.

Feeling a surge of need to defend herself once more, Krystal spoke, "That's the same thing the Pharisees accused Christ of – hanging around with the riffraff! Of course, Christ's answer to them was that it was not the well who need a physician, but the sick. Actually, no, I don't expect anyone to come to my aid. Most of these people came here for a lunch. There's no need to involve them. No, this is just between you and me!"

Continuing with his relentless accusations, the minister began implying that women were the cause of the problems in a man's world. He particularly claimed that it was Eve who caused all the problems, and that if it had not been for her, there would not be a sin problem in the world. This was too much for Krystal to bear.

"Oh, yes!" she exclaimed. "Eve ate the apple! She wandered away and it's all her fault! Did you ever wonder why she wandered away?" Krystal tried to suggest that perhaps if Adam was as stern as this minister was, Eve had every reason to wander away. When the minister did not respond immediately, Krystal seized the opportunity and claimed that woman was made from man's side to be a partner, a "help mate." She was not made from the head to rule over him, not from the feet to be held under him, but from his side to be next to him and to be a partner."

After a few moments, the minister, once again launched his criticisms of her. "You can never be forgiven. I suppose you think YOU HAVE been forgiven."

Undismayed that he would continue his assault, Krystal asserted boldly, "I not only think I've been forgiven, I KNOW I've been forgiven. If what you say is true, then let me ask you this. Why does it say in Isaiah that although your sins be red as scarlet, they'll be washed whiter than snow?"

Bellowing out, he claimed, "That's for saints!"

"For the saints!" Krystal repeated. "Then in other words, the saints must sin."

"What do you mean?" he inquired in a quieter tone as he was taken back by her immediate reply and U-turn in his claim.

"Well," Krystal explained, "it talks about sins being washed whiter than snow, and if this is for the saints, then the saints must sin."

He paused for a moment and then stated that it did not matter. Then he went on to once again claim that Krystal had committed the unforgivable sin, and will never be forgiven.

"The only sin that's unforgivable is when you totally reject God and don't want anything to do with Him. No sin is beyond forgiveness, except that of total and complete rejection of the truth – the sin against the Holy Spirit!" When he said nothing, she claimed, "Yes, I committed murder, but Christ also forgave a murderer when he was hanging on the cross. Am I any less of a person that He cannot forgive me? – I think not! When I worked at the hospital, and someone brought a baby for me to hold, a voice came from the back of my mind, and claimed that I murdered something as beautiful as this!" Krystal's voice began to crack as she recalled the incident.

"But you laugh at all of this now!" he shouted. Regaining her composure, she asserted,

"Oh, yes! Don't come out of this whole thing laughing. You want to keep a person in a living hell, and as I crawl out of the pit, a pit I dug for myself, you'd be at the top with a cattle prod shoving me back in! Burn baby burn!"

The minister had sat back by now and just stared at her.

Krystal took note of his response and then posed the question, "What is the Good News? That you're damned to hell? – I think not! The Good News is forgiveness – we have an Advocate, someone who was tempted in all things, who stands at our side, as we come boldly before the throne of God." Citing 1 John 2:1, she paused as he still did not respond and she asked him, "What gives you the right to judge me?"

"I have every right. I am to rebuke my brother."

"Yes, that's in Galatians chapter 6 verse 1. Finish the sentence." She paused and then stated, "You know it must be nice to just pick out a phrase here or there out of the Bible and claim it to be true jut to suit your needs. You need to read the whole section, not just a part. So finish the sentence."

At this the minister was stumped, claiming that he did not know the rest of the sentence.

"Are you sure you've read this Book?" she queried. "Yes, it does say to rebuke your brother, but then it goes on to say 'with gentleness and kindness.' You know, when I worked at the hospital, one thing always intrigued me and that was the number of people who came in with such guilty feelings. What are you doing to your people to make them feel this way? – There's a warning for you in Ezekiel. Woe to the shepherd of the flock, that he knows where he is leading his sheep!"

Undaunted the minister tried to challenge her some more by stating about Ernie, "This man claims you can cast out a demon!"

Krystal looked over at Ernie and asked, "Is this true?" She really wanted to know if Ernie really felt that she could do such a feat. Ernie responded by shaking his head affirmatively.

"I've never cast out a demon before," she honestly replied. With that the minister pounced on her claim and denounced that she would even be capable of such.

Krystal immediately responded, "But that doesn't mean I couldn't do it!"

Then the minister claimed that Ernie should go back to his wife and make amends and his life would be better. When Krystal looked at Ernie as the minister spoke, she noted him to be shaking his head negatively. Krystal stated that maybe he did not want to go back to his wife, that maybe there were more problems there that were not known to the minister.

Thinking that Ernie was still on his side, the minister continued stating, "This man speaks in tongues! He has every right to call you a whore!"

"Speaks in tongues?" Krystal queried unconvinced. "Who interprets for him?"

When the minister did not answer her Krystal stated that there must be someone to interpret what he is saying, otherwise it is just babbling and it does not mean anything. Then Krystal went on to describe that when the apostles were given the gift at Pentecost of the Holy Spirit descending on them and giving them the gift of tongues, that it meant they were able to speak in different languages. "When that occurred other people heard the message spoken in their own language and understood the message of Christ."

Once more the minister challenged Krystal's abilities to perform any restorative aid. Convinced that the minister was seeking almost a duel with regards to his healing against hers, Krystal asked, "Shall we see which one of us can draw fire from heaven?"

"What do you mean?" he asked in the same subdued tone as before.

Once more Krystal reiterated, "Are you sure you've read this Book? – Mount Carmel revisited. Elijah drew fire from heaven to prove his God was the true God."

"God shall not be mocked!" he replied indignantly.

"Oh, I assure you. God shall not be mocked. In fact, He'll be revealed!"

"Then let's see your God!" he asserted.

"He'll be here when the time is right. It's not the right time just now." She claimed, feeling no sense of urgency at the immediate time. She felt that in essence she would be "testing God" in this particular context. Yet she knew she could draw on Christ's power when the time was right. When the minister once more began to accuse her and attacking the God she believed in, she challenged him.

"Talking with God is like have a fireside chat. He's really a great Dad, because He sits and listens to me, and I can talk freely to Him about what's bothering me. That's the kind of God I worship." Saying nothing in response to her statements, she further added, "If your God is a condemning God and that's what you worship, I pity you! Do you really think that after condemning me to hell that I'd be interested in joining your group?"

The minister indicated that he did not want her in his group. Krystal sensing that he was going to say something to that effect, she decided she had had enough of his antics. In response she undauntedly stated, "I think the whole problem here is that you haven't read this book at all! I think you'd better go home and really read it!" Then pointing in Ernie's direction she stated, "Get out and take your friend with you!"

Ernie immediately shook his head negatively, softly claiming, "I want to stay here with you!"

"Why not leave? You've been calling me a whore all this time?"

"You're not a whore!" Ernie apologetically stated. This time he spoke up more loudly stating that he indeed did not want to leave.

"Hmmm" claimed Krystal, "There seems to be a difference of opinion here. It looks like there's a change of heart. He doesn't seem to want to go with you." Then once more she demanded of the minister, "Now you take you bill of goods and you peddle them somewhere else. They'll be no buyers here today! Get out!" With that he got up to leave and the rest of the restaurant clientele began to applaud loudly.

Krystal took a long drink of her root beer hoping that something in it would rejuvenate her departing mental strength. Damian noted that she did appear somewhat worn, and thought to himself how he could use this to an advantage.

"You know your Bible well," remarked Damian.

"I have read the Book," Krystal replied.

From what seemed to be behind her and to her right, came a soft voice that stated, "He's waiting for the movie!" Krystal did not know who said that, but that whoever it was referring to Damian. Then she pondered over Ernie's claim that the juke boxes were microphones. *Perhaps he's right,* she mused. *Maybe they're two-way radios.*

"You're the one we're looking for," Damian claimed.

"Who's looking for me?" Krystal questioned feeling edgy.

"Do you remember any patient at the hospital coming into your office to visit with you? Do you remember what you said would happen before this day?"

Krystal sat perplexed for some time. When someone in the crowd mentioned something about a murder taking place, then Krystal recalled just that part of the conversation at the hospital. Again, a voice from behind her and to her right asked, "Did he do it?" Krystal then recalled not only her statement about one more murder taking place, but also the news about the teenage girl they found hanging in the park.

Astonished she exclaimed, "But I never said he did it! I was only relaying the events in the course of time." She sat quiet for a few minutes as she contemplated, *this is a set up! – They're trying to pin a murder on an innocent man!* Noting that Damian seemed to be gloating as those around her waited for her response, she fixed her gaze upon Damian's reactions. *There's something not right here, but I don't know what it is.* At once she saw what appeared to be a heavy iron shackle encompassing Ernie's neck with a long heavy chain leading back to Damian. Krystal interpreted this as Damian somehow controlling Ernie.

After analyzing this Krystal then claimed out loud, "He didn't do it!"

Damian, however, refuted her statement, describing how the teenager was found at the park.

"Actually it was a suicide, made to look like a murder. I think you'd better look closer at the crime scene. She slashed her arms and then hung herself." Krystal was familiar with similar attempts made by various patients when she worked at the Hospital. As she watched Damian she noted he was talking to some sort of handheld microphone. He paused as if listening to someone and then responded. Noticing Krystal looking in his direction he quickly placed it back in his coat pocket. Krystal said nothing, but wondered who he could have been conversing with.

No one said anything for quite some time. Krystal, again drawing on her collection of folk songs, began to sing on Eric's behalf. Taking the verses from "Hangman," another Peter, Paul and Mary selection, she tried to express how Ernie might feel in this situation, dejected. The last verse related that unlike the others, a person comes forth to bring hope and pay his fee so he doesn't hang.

Damian was infuriated that Krystal did not claim Ernie to be the murderer and made him look foolish by involving other officers in this investigation. He began appealing to Krystal in a different approach trying to get her to reveal more about herself. Somewhere along the line he was hoping to find something she would trip over, exposing her as some sort of fraud.

"You have to go as a sacrifice!" Damian demanded in a very angry tone.

"What sacrifice? What are you talking about?" At this point the effects of lack of sleep, coupled with the draining attack by the minister had begun to take their toll on her, and Krystal began to cry. "I didn't ask for this!" she pleaded.

"Didn't your family tell you?" he tried to innocently ask. Then more sarcastically, he stated, "Aw, that's too bad!" Then more demanding he asserted, "You don't have any choice in the matter. You have to be the sacrifice!"

Krystal, confused, now stated that she had no idea of what he was talking about.

"Big Brother is watching!" he exclaimed hoping to produce more fear that the FBI and/or CIA was after her.

With tears streaming down her face, Krystal prayed, *God help me!*

Looking up as she did so, a figure appeared before her. *I'm here for you,* He stated. The ghost-like figure she recognized as Christ, but in modern attire. The tears stopped as she grasped the full implication of what she was witnessing.

Wiping her face off and composing her feelings as well as her thoughts, she claimed, "You're right! – Big Brother is watching! – The Real Big Brother!" As she stated this, she pointed with her thumb up above to indicate that the real God was watching this scenario. "And this is His little sister, Little Liza Jane!" she claimed as she pointed to herself. Hint, hint, hint. – You don't hear too much about Elijah returning before the end."

Then the Christ-like figure said softly to Krystal, *and He's getting sick and tired of His little sister being jerked around by a bunch of bozos!*

"Boy, You got that right!" she exclaimed conclusively.

"But," Damian asserted, "Elijah was a man!"

"One little mistake," replied Krystal.

Then Damian went on to ask Krystal about a doll that she had when very young. She did recall the second doll, the one her father had no picture of. She began to describe it with the straps on the feet and that she used to dance with it. Then she remembered the yellow and red doll she posed with, although not the circumstances.

Not knowing what Krystal had seen, Damian went on to demand that Krystal go as a sacrifice for this country. "This is the first time God has used a woman and she'd better do it right!"

"The Gospel according to whom?" inquired Krystal reasoning that whatever god Damian was talking about was certainly not the God Krystal believed in.

"The government is concerned about the crisis that has developed over between Iran and Iraq. And we are looking for someone to resolve the crisis. You're who we're looking for." It was felt by the powers to be that if Krystal could cast out a demon, then she could do the same for Saddam and thereby alleviate the troubles that several agencies had caused. Krystal was unaware how devious the agencies were with one working against Saddam and supporting Iran, and the other working with Saddam against Iran.

Krystal, however, felt that she had already seen some underhandedness displayed by Damian with Ernie, and wondered who the "we" included that Damian referred to.

Since Damian had referred to her family not telling her about such, Krystal thought back about the family activities as she was growing up. She thought perhaps it was related to the family sending packages overseas to Communist Poland. From those sitting right behind Krystal, they softly stated that they knew all that. Krystal then surmised there had to be FBI agents in the restaurant.

She continued "We sent packages so our family would not starve. We could not get them out from behind the Iron Curtain."

Looking at Damian and his ambivalent attitude and lack of interest in her description, she cried, "Perhaps YOU ought to take the silver spoon out of your mouth and see what it's like to go hungry for a whole day and sleep outside with no blanket!"

She further explained, "When the packages would arrive, they would thank God that someone across in America had enough thought to care for them. The packages were sent with a letter that was in code and described where they would find the money, using verses from songs."

She momentarily paused and then asked, "What are you rooting around in my FBI file for anyway? Actually I could care less what the FBI has on me!" Krystal thought briefly and then stated, "I know what you're looking for!" Reasoning that it probably had something to do with the well on the Kruczyinski property she exclaimed, "I'm telling you right now, if you try to use that well by force or ill-gotten gain, it's going to go dry on you!"

Again from behind Krystal someone stated softly, "There is no well!"

Unsure who the speaker was, Krystal stated, "Now I know that and you know that, but he don't know that!" as she pointed in Damian's direction. Then in a softer voice, she claimed, "I was going to find one and stuff him down it!"

Then Damian mentioned that there was a "think tank" whose decision was that she go as a sacrifice.

"Is that anything like a fish tank? They get pretty skuzzy on the bottom when you don't clean them out!"

"You have no choice in the matter!" he exclaimed conclusively.

Raising her voice a little louder she exclaimed, "Who died and left you boss?" Chuckling sounds were made behind her with the comment, "That sounds just like her dad." Since it appeared that they knew the family, Krystal concluded they had to be FBI.

"I have a Ph.D., you know," Damian asserted.

Krystal responded, "Ph.D. only stand for Piled Higher and Deeper!" as she strove once more to expose a lot of his self-assured attitude.

"Where did you go to school?"

"Kent State."

"I was at Ohio State. I went to Woodstock," boasted Damian.

Blatantly she responded, "Kent State, May 4th 1970 – a day I'll never forget!"

"I am Phi Beta Kappa," he asserted.

"More like Phi Beta Kappa piece of crap!" she snapped. "I belonged to the Lunch Bag Five!"

Shifting his eyes nervously from side to side, he inquired rather subdued, "Was that some sort of singing group?"

"No," she claimed, "we had no need for fraternities or sororities, so we formed our own – four guys and me! We used to study together."

Once more insulted by her attitude he shouted, "You were supposed to die at Kent State!"

"You missed! Next time, I'll paint the bull's eye bigger!" she responded as she drew an imaginary target on her chest.

"Where were you when the shootings took place?" he asked irritated.

"I heard a voice – the voice within that said don't go up there! Right after the shootings took place I was locked in a building."

"You were supposed to die at Kent State," he bellowed. "Don't you know that from the song, 'American Pie' is about you and the fact that you were to die then?" At this point Krystal turned to the juke boxes at each table. Finding "American Pie" by Don McLean she began to play it with a quarter.

"You don't need to do that," Damian stated referring to quarter. Krystal looked around thinking, *so they are microphones and probably FBI at that.*

"This is the part I like best," and she began to sing along with the one verse, "And the three men I admire most, the Father, Son and Holy Ghost – They caught the last train for the coast, the day the music died."

Damian insisted that the song was about her. Krystal knew better and so changed the conversation about the rumor about Richard Nixon wanting a female shot.

"That was supposed to be you!" he roared.

Krystal had wanted to lay this matter to rest and rather than evoke a lot of emotion she stated that it was a rumor among many at that time. Then she mentioned, "I would hate to think that four people died because of me." She went on to describe some of the after-shocks from the shootings, encountering job discrimination simply because they had attended Kent State University at that time.

Seeing that he could not evoke any other fear from her, Damian chose another avenue to once again try and reach his goal.

"Your number has come up. You have to go as a sacrifice!" Once again, he seemed to be prompted by someone else, and Krystal wondered where or who was doing this prompting. She paid little attention to the table/booth that held four men. Yet every so often the two facing her would whisper back and forth to each other. Krystal observed this, yet said nothing.

Krystal then became more direct in her approach and accused the CIA of plunking people's numbers into a computer.

"You'd better watch just exactly who you're plunking into your computer," Krystal warned. " Maybe you need to hang a mirror next to that computer, and put YOUR number in the computer!" she reasoned. "No more – the buck stops here!"

"You don't have any choice in the matter!" he shouted once more. "Your number HAS come up!"

"Yeah? Well your number's come up too. It's zero! You don't count!" she emphatically stated. With that several people began to snicker. Damian looked about realizing that he was being made fun of and appeared irritated.

"Are you Democrat or Republican?" Hoping to bank on the idea that she probably was a Democrat and that the majority of the Ashland community was Republican. However, he was one more side-railed as he heard Krystal's reply.

"Neither!" she shouted having an inkling that he wanted to somehow brand her this or that. "My mother always told me that one party start the wars, and the other party finishes them. I vote accordingly. – Do I want to start a war or finish one?"

"But you didn't do as you were told," he began loudly scolding her. "You were supposed to vote for Nixon!"

Recalling the incident about the man telling Darlene that "they had to vote for Nixon," Krystal retold the event.

"I did vote for Nixon. By pulling the lever for McGovern, I voted for Nixon to get the hell out of the White House.

At that point Laura, sitting across the Krystal, stated, "You lied."

"That's not a lie. It's a half-truth. The man said vote for Nixon. He didn't say what I should vote for him. I found an X on the ballot and I thought I was supposed to make him ex-President! – I didn't know. It was my first time voting."

Then she described her tactics for voting in elections. "You don't like A, but you sure as hell don't like B. So you vote for A to keep out B. It's defensive voting!" When several people began to laugh with her logic she concluded, "I even voted for Donald Duck one time. – He was a write-in candidate. I liked his personality and I thought he would make a good President."

Damian did not like Krystal diverting the matter into jokes and seeing that she was getting a lot of comradery support from her peers he strove to inject more seriousness into the conversation.

Reiterating his initial claim with force, Damian stated, "You have to go as a sacrifice! You don't have any choice in the matter!"

"This doesn't sound like FBI. It sounds more like CIA – Chicken Identifiers of America!" Then going off on a tangent Krystal inquired, "Can anyone tell me what the CIA really does? All I ever hear about them doing is 'bugging' someone to death!"

Once more Damian asserted emphatically that Krystal was to die as a sacrifice for this country.

All of a sudden in front of her appeared a ghost-like figure walked from Damian's booth, He pointed over his shoulder in Damian's direction and stated, *he's nuts!*

Krystal responded by saying, "More like bats in the belfry!" With that statement another ghost-like figure dressed in robe and crown came from the right side of the restaurant and stood behind Damian.

With the sparkled crown on His head, He moved his hands while bats appeared circling around Damian's head.

Krystal began to laugh at the picture before her and trusted that the ghost-like figure was either Christ Himself or perhaps Elijah. Fortified by this scene, she began to sing many selections from the rock opera, "Jesus Christ, Superstar." There were multiple verses that spelled out how she felt about what was taking place in the restaurant. Yet as she was singing, she could only imagine that there would be many a brood of vipers stirring both within Damian as well as sitting in many of the booths.

Damian was getting increasingly frustrated and once again pulled out a mini-microphone and began talking to someone. She also noted that the two men who were seated in front of the troopers had their hands cupped in front of their mouths. *Perhaps they are conversing with him,* Krystal surmised.

At last Damian stated, "Then you'll go do this and be a sacrifice?" Krystal blinked her eyes as if awakening from a dreamy state, and declared, "I wasn't even talking to you!" As she sat there she noted Damian had a pad of paper and was writing down several things. She watched him for several minutes wondering what exactly he was writing.

"You don't have any choice in the matter. You have to go as a sacrifice!" He demanded.

Changing the topic, Krystal talked about her German background and learning German in high school. She mentioned that Germany had a lot more to offer than Nazis. She also mentioned that the Berlin Wall would collapse in the future. A lot of people balked at that thought, as they felt a united Germany would result in another rise of a Hitler type figure.

Krystal began to recite several German proverbs that she had learned while in high school. When she recited, "a bird in the hand is worth two in the bush," her head was automatically towards the table with the four men, and particularly towards the two who were looking in her direction. It was as though Someone knew who was hiding in disguise, even though Krystal would not discover until years later that it was George H.W. Bush and Dick Cheney.

When she was finished, the minister appeared from behind her and once again took his place in the booth across the aisle from her.

"I want to ask you a question," he said more subdued than during his previous encounter. "Are you a prophet?"

Turning away from looking at him she claimed, "Oh, there's a long list of criteria for prophets!" Then she surmised, *you're not even sure I know Christ. If I were anything else, you wouldn't believe that either.* He waited for a more direct response.

"I don't claim to be anything. Just a sinner that's been forgiven."

"How do you know you've been forgiven?" he asked as his voice began to get louder.

He persisted in obtaining a more concrete answer, and so she finally responded, "I have been washed by the blood of the Lamb." Then she sang "Amazing Grace." Yet he just glared at her and reiterated that she will be plunged into Hell.

"I don't think so," she stated in response. "The Bible says that prostitutes and murderers will make it into heaven before the self-righteous will. – You know, the people we think will be in heaven, won't necessarily be there, and the ones we think absolutely not, just may be. It's going to be very interesting to see just who is in heaven. – When the roll is called up yonder, I'll be there!"

Her confidence irritated him even more. He stated that there would be no way she could be in the Rapture.

"Oh," she stated, "You believe in the Secret Rapture, don't you? – Well, from what I read, that rapture is not so secret. – It says in First Thessalonians, chapter 4, verse 16 *For the Lord Himself will descend from heaven with a shout, with the voice of the archangel, and with the trumpet of God; and the dead in Christ shall rise first.* – That doesn't sound very secret or quiet to me. That's pretty noisy with shouting and a trumpet sounding!" She continued the verse, *"Then we who are alive and remain shall be caught up together with them in the clouds to meet the Lord in the air."* She added, "You see there is no secret rapture. When Christ returns those who are dead rise to life. Those who are alive in Christ are transported to meet him in the clouds. That's not a secret to be hidden. The whole world knows about it."

"What about the millennium?" he asked. At that Damian shifted nervously in his seat. He recalled the painting he loved so much, and then recalled what the man in the pawn shop told him about the meaning of it. He glared at Krystal as she now spoke.

"Well, the millennium occurs between the resurrections. When Christ returns, those who are with Christ, be them dead or alive, are brought to eternal life in the first resurrection. Those who did not believe in Christ when He returns have the rocks and hills fall upon them. So they are dead then. During that 1000 years, the millennium, those in heaven will be going over the books, understanding why so-and-so was not in heaven and how so-and-so did get there. It's actually a time where we discover is God a just God. In the meantime, Satan is chained to the earth, with no one to tempt. At the end of the 1000 years, there is the second resurrection in which those who did not believe in Christ are brought to life for one last battle – the battle of Armageddon. The city of God descends from heaven. Along with Satan those who are raised in this second resurrection try to storm the city of God to take it, but are destroyed by fire from God. That is when they get thrown into the lake of fire, not to burn forever and forever, but to be complete and final. That is when evil dies in the world. – Then Jesus forms a new earth where we reign forever."

At the mention of Satan being destroyed, Damian once more tried to divert the conversation elsewhere. Interrupting the discussion, he began focusing on other interpretations of demon possession.

"Have you ever been exposed to those who deal with begin able to handle snakes?"

"You mean snake charmers?" she inquired. She smirked then and brushed off his statement with "that's based on fear. They believe that if you can handle snakes, you can handle Satan."

Then swallowing hard, Damian stated, "I've been to such an even in Louisiana." As she spoke his eyes widened in a manner suggesting that it had been something to fear. "It was pretty scary!" He was hoping by now with being attacked that she would not comply with Ernie's wish.

The minister, however, did not like being distracted from his questioning of Krystal and so once again began to attack her, claiming that she was on the side of Satan. She turned to look at him, but out of the corner of her eye she now noticed Ernie beginning to shake and writhe in his seat uncontrollably. Although diverted by her attackers, a picture came into her mind that reminded her of the scene from the "Jesus" movie, in which a young man began to shake in a very similar manner. In the movie then Christ moved towards the man and cast the demon out. Luke 4:35 indicates what Christ said.

Damian leaned forward with an almost penetrating glare at Krystal. With so much taking place at the same time, Krystal began hearing the bellowing of the minister's condemnation begin taking a hissing sound to his words. She felt a little faint. She retreated for a minute and then gathering what strength she could she pointed back at the minister emphatically stating, "Leave me alone." Feeling some strength returning, she repeated it more loudly this time. "Leave me alone." The hissing continued until she boldly shouted as she pointed directly at him. "Come out of that body!"

Ernie began wildly jumping in his seat. Now turning her entire body, as if it was almost frozen in its pose, Krystal shouted loudly to him, "In the name of Jesus Christ, come out of that body!" Something was holding the demon back. Krystal told Ernie to speak the name of Jesus. He tried, but was unable to.

"Say it, or it doesn't work!" Krystal claimed. Damian withdrew and hid behind Ernie's silhouette, hoping Krystal would not find him. Krystal realizing that there was a strong force here, implored Ernie's partner, Otto Hartsel, to hold Ernie's hands across the table and speak the name with him. Together the two of them were able to get Ernie to say the name of Jesus.

At once Ernie's body began to go limp. Then Krystal turned towards the direction of the minister and following a dark figure shouted, "Trouble him no more!"

At once the building shook and doors to the entrance banged open and shut. Everyone except Krystal was cowering in the restaurant.

"Must be having a sale today – two for the price of one!" she exclaimed.

Krystal looked about and seeing everyone was sinking somewhat in their seats, she asked if everyone was okay. She did note the two older men she mentioned earlier seated facing her, had sunk quite low in their seats.

Turning to Ernie she asked, "When was the last time you had something to eat? A couple of days?" Ernie nodded.

Calling out to the waitress she said, "Make sure that he gets something to eat." The waitress responded immediately taking Ernie's order. Slowly the lunch crowd began to relax and resume their previous more upright positions.

"There were 10 lepers…" she began to say.

"Thank you," Ernie called out with much more strength in his voice.

"You know the story well."

Then Krystal went on to tell the story of "The Touch of the Master's Hand." An old battered violin is brought up for auction before an eager crowd wishing for something more valuable. The auctioneer thought about it, and decided to go ahead and see what price he could get. "A dollar, two dollars, and who'll make it three?" But wait, from the back of the crowd comes a gray-haired man and picking up the bow, he wiped off the dust and tightened up the strings. Then he began to play a melody that was so sweet it made the angels sing. The music ended and the auctioneer with a voice that was quiet and low asked "What would you give me for the violin and he held it up with the bow?" Came one, "A thousand dollars." "And who'll make it two and then who'll make it three?" And the people cried out, "What made the change? We don't quite understand." Quick came the reply, "It was the touch of the Master's Hand." – And so many a man with life out of tune is battered and scarred with sin. And he's auctioned cheap to a thankless crowd, much like the old violin. But then the Master comes and the foolish crowd can never understand the worth of the soul or the change that is brought by the touch of the Master's Hand." (Anonymous version)

Damian now emerged from behind Ernie, and began writing vigorously on his pad of paper.

"Now," she bellowed, "You say someone wants me dead. Where are they? Well, bring them on. We'll settle this thing here and now." Her eagerness to terminate this line of thinking was replaced with a calm resolute, an Oriental mode and purpose. Using wise instructions given from the teacher in the movie, "The Karate Kid" Krystal recited the lines, "Daniel-son, Mr. Miagi say karate here (pointing to head) and here (pointing to heart), never here (pointing to hands at the waist as a show of force). Mr. Miagi also say, he who catch fly with chopsticks, can do anything – We catch fly with chopstick."

Damian now moved more into the open, but continued to write, which Krystal noted.

"You're awfully eager to get your signature on my death warrant!" she proclaimed as she zeroed in on Damian.

At once, he put his pen down and shifting his eyes from side to side, said nothing, but would not look at her directly. Then easing back in the booth, he inquired, "What would it take...?"

Stopping him in his sentence, she claimed loudly, "You can't buy me! I'm not for sale." Then raising her voice and standing up she proclaimed, "I don't belong to you, the FBI or the CIA or anybody else! I have been bought with a price, a very high price," referring to Christ's crucifixion. I belong to Him and Him alone!" she stated as she pointed upwards. "I take my orders from Headquarters. When He says move, I move. When He says stop, I stop! I'm not some trinket that you can dangle in front of somebody else's face to get whatever it is you think you want! DO YOU GET THE PICTURE?"

"Quite clearly," muttered Damian.

"Then remember it!" She sat down. After waiting for her heart to stop the loud pounding in her chest, she looked up towards the Christ figure before her. Sarcastically she asked, "Was that loud enough?"

Then looking about the people seated in the various booths, she decided to inject a little humor to get them to ease up a bit.

"These people are going to think I go to church with the Mafia. Believe in Jesus Christ, or your mother's out on the street." With that several people began to laugh.

Damian now knew that he was not going to easily get her to do what he wanted, yet he felt a surge of energy inside him. He then asked what happens to the evil spirit when it is cast out.

Smiling Damian paraphrased from Matthew 12:44 that the demon goes out seeking rest and does not find it. "It returns to the house from which it came and finds it unoccupied..." Damian knew what he could do to continue the games he had already played on Ernie.

However, in this passage, which should be read in entirety, from verses 43 through 45, it says that the demon does return to the house and when it comes it finds it unoccupied…Damian had not banked on the idea that the Christ-like figure had put a "guardian" in as soon as the demon went out. Furthermore, the demon was instructed to 'trouble him no more,' and therefore the demon could not come back. So this house of Ernie's was now occupied. Now the demon has to do what is stated in verse 45, and find more wicked spirits than itself and occupy another house. In this case Damian's house was "open for business." So the demons took up residence there. Yet seated in the restaurant there was more than one "open for business."

Krystal looked over at Damian as he was proclaiming the above, and she noted his face began to beam very darkly.

"Ah, yes!" she said insightfully, "the angel of light." She knew that Satan will try to portray himself as an angel of light in the end times. "So we meet again," she exclaimed. She recalled that the Native American Indians referred to the evil spirit they encountered as the "being without a face." Concurrently as Krystal looked at Damian's face, it darkened.

Pursing a more intellectual note to the conversation Damian began to spout off about the Middle East crisis and the need to divert world war from erupting, to what he referred as "Armageddon."

"You really are a prophet!" he exclaimed, as he smiled hoping to entice her with his train of thought. "Prophets have to write a book." Then once more pursuing his desire to get rid of Krystal, he claimed that she could draw fire from heaven as Elijah did and destroy Saddam Hussein. As he spoke Krystal could almost see the dollar signs forming in his eyes. He went on to talk about the mounting sale of arms to Saddam Hussein that had taken place already.

At this point Krystal very bluntly expressed her opinion of that entire scenario.

"This is like three little boys playing together, but somehow that never seems to work. Two of the boys will play and the third one gets left out. – Now the U.S. has arms and the Soviet Union has arms and with the Cold War, we have been playing back and forth, and we keep telling Saddam, 'you just hang on to those in your living room. You can't use them, but just look at them.' - You know what happens then? He's going to get mad because he can't play in your game, and he'll start picking on one or both of you to play."

Damian reiterated his claim, "You have to go as a sacrifice."

Krystal continued with a German accent, "Now ve had created a Frankenstein monster." Then going back to talking normally, she said, "And you want this littlest kid on the block, this dumb Polack, to go over there and say, 'Hey, you can't do that!' – I'm not the one that started selling him these arms in the first place!" she pointed out.

When he insisted that she could draw fire from heaven, she shook her head no. Krystal knew that the only time fire comes from heaven was first at Mt. Carmel with Elijah and then at the end of the world when all evil is destroyed.

So she bluntly taunted him, "Why don't you come with me, and I'll show you how it's done!" As she said this Damian sunk down in his seat a bit and shook his head no. Then pantomiming with her fingers, she pointed to a spot on the table and said, "Here, you stand over here!" Then looking up to her Christ-like figure from where the fire would come up above, she indicated that she would have Damian struck by fire from heaven, instead.

"Why not come along?" she asked. "Isn't that what you want all the fame and glory of all this?"

Then moving on to interrogate some of his background she asked, "How did you get out of going to Vietnam? You'd have been about the right age." He stared at her as she continued. "A little money under the table to a few senators and you're scot-free?" Now he began to glare at Krystal and he did not like the mind probing.

"Oh, don't looks so surprised, my dear! What's the L stand for in your name, loveable?" she asked sarcastically.

Then turning to her Christ-like figure she asked "Who is he?"

The figure responded, "FBI."

"He is…"

"Not now."

"He was…What's he now?"

"CIA." As the Christ-like figure responded he casually looked at the fingernails of His hand, suggesting that she should not get too alarmed by the fact that the CIA was as well amongst those in the restaurant.

"Both? – Can they do that? Don't they have rules? You can only be one, but not both?" Then thinking about coming from one to the other organization, she remarked, "His mama don't dance, and his daddy surely don't rock and roll!" referring to FBI and CIA respectively.

"Who are you talking to?" Damian questioned perplexed.

"That's Irving," she said in a Jewish accent. "He's Jewish – use to work with wood a lot!"

At that point from far across the restaurant came the chorus of several college students well versed in the Bible. They laughed as they stated, "He's a carpenter!" Hoping to help Damian understand.

Damian continued to spout off to appear intellectually educated and insisted that Krystal is a prophet and that she has to write a book. "All prophets write books." Krystal knew that he was wanting something published so he could denounce it in some way, much like he tried to denounce the 12-step programs belief in a Higher Power was preposterous, and that he himself is god.

Krystal instructed Damian that not all Biblical prophets wrote books.

When she talked about Daniel, who did write a book, she enthusiastically described how the angel of the Lord shut the lion's mouth so that Daniel was not harmed when he was thrown into the lion's pit.

"That's a myth!" he declared.

"That's no myth!" she retorted. "That's the truth! Angels encamp around those who fear the Lord and protect him."

He balked at that trying to declare that he once more felt he was god and a king as well. He also stated that the government was "like a god."

Krystal then stated "the government!" in horror. "You've got a postage stamp size god. My God is a very big God!"

Krystal began telling the story of King Nebuchadnezzar in Daniel, Chapter 2. "King Neb, for short." She described the story of the dream that the king had concerning a statue. The king found Daniel who interpreted the dream for him. Daniel also went on to describe exactly what the king was looking at in his dream. It was a statue of a man with a gold head, silver breast and arms, belly and thighs of bronze, legs of iron with feet of iron mixed with clay. Daniel explained what it all meant. King Neb thought about it and decided to make a statue of himself all in gold and wanted all to worship it. However, there were three youths who did not and were thrown in the fiery furnace. Yet God protected them and they emerged unscathed. King Neb then realized he is not God and had to learn the lesson the hard way.

"But like so many of us, we get accustomed to having it good," declared Krystal. "In time King Neb had the same thing happen to him. King Neb's kingdom was prosperous and he began to take credit for the prosperity. Krystal stated that King Neb was therefore reduced to wandering with the animals until time had passed and he acknowledged the power of the Mighty God.

Damian appeared bored with this conversation. He brought up the topic of the Koran and four prophets of doom.

"Well, I have not read the Koran yet, but I do know that there is mention of a seventh heaven and that there are a lot of overlaps with what is presented in the Bible. The Muslims believe in God, Allah, as well as a day of judgment and resurrection."

Trying to get away from any type of religion that expressed the fact that there is a resurrection, Damian expressed that he believed in Zen Buddhism because that religion had no need for any resurrection. It only entailed sitting and mediating.

Krystal was somewhat acquainted with Far Eastern religions from a philosophy class at Kent State. As soon as Damian mentioned Buddha, Krystal recalled a picture of one statue of a fat man with a large belly in a seated position. She went on to explain that the reason that statue was made that way was a reminder that expressed the philosophy, "Don't be lazy." She then went on to explain that Buddha was not a prophet, but a philosopher, along with several other Far Eastern religious leaders, and that these religions center on correct and positive thinking and not prophecy. She also pointed out that the central theme of these philosophies actually arose from a woman, not a man. These religions were brought in an attempt to bring social reform to the respective societies.

"What about the Hindus?" inquired Damian hoping to catch her off guard. Krystal mentioned Vishnu, part of the gods that included creator, preserver and destroyer.

In a last ditch effort, Damian thought he would throw Krystal off balance by stating that the Native Americans, including South American Indians had no formal religion.

This time Krystal really paid him his due. "They believe in the Great Spirit, the giver of life. When they would be hunting and kill an animal they would thank their Creator for providing food for them and for the animal laying down his life for their needs. So they have a very strong belief in God. They see Him in everything, all aspects of nature."

"But what about a resurrection?"

"They have the Ghost Dance. – 'Bury My Heart at Wounded Knee' when the natives were massacred, they believe the spirits did a ghost dance looking forward to a time when they would once again live in peace on the earth. That's a resurrection. They also believed that God was a woman."

With Krystal mentioning that a woman was behind the religion and not a man, Damian became offended.

Damian, after circling the conversation again returned to her going as a sacrifice and that it was inevitable in order to avert Armageddon.

"Is that what this country believes, that the Middle East is Armageddon?" she inquired as she looked about the faces in the room. "No, no, no, no, no. Turn the ship around! We're spiritual Israel. If this is taken as literal Israel, where does that leave the rest of us? Then there is no room for us in what is prophesized in the book of Revelation."

But Damian was not impressed and tried to come up with political arguments to convince her.

In an Indian accent she replied, "Many people will go floating down the Ganges with no wind in their sails." She felt many would be deceived into thinking their philosophies and political agendas would be right with regards to not only viewing Armageddon in Damian's description, but in their personal desires as well.

Damian wanted to know about spies and if there were any in the Bible. Krystal proclaimed that spies did go into Jericho before it was overtaken and sought out Rahab, a prostitute who owned an inn. She not only helped the spies, but she told them that she believed in their God. As a result she let them leave by the red cord out the window. When Jericho was overtaken not by Joshua's army, but by the hand of

God and a shout, Rahab's household was rescued by hanging out the red cord from the window.

As he continued in his trivial pursuit of his goal, he tried to explain the concept of the four winds, but called them the four corners of the earth, as in Revelation 7:1.

Krystal was becoming a little tired from Damian's supposed knowledge of government philosophy. Seeing that she bore a scowl on her face, he said, "You have to understand this."

Resting her head in her right hand, she urged him to continue as she stated sarcastically, "Believe me, I'm trying." He smiled as he tried once again to reiterate that war in the Middle East as was eminent, would be the end of the world and thus, the reason for her to stop it by being a sacrifice.

At the end of his speech, he claimed, "Hence the four corners of the earth!"

Allowing her right hand to fall against the table, she looked up in the direction of her Christ-like figure and said, "That's what the problem is here – they got the four corners of the earth – they still think the earth is flat! If you go with them, you'll never make it because you'll fall off the edge of the earth."

Then becoming even more sarcastic, she said, "You didn't see the pictures they sent from space, did you? This is something man has wondered about for centuries. They finally sent up the astronauts and all their questions were answered – it's really round!"

At this point her Christ-like figure might have as well handed Krystal a slice and dice machine, because she continued to throw sarcastic remarks back to him.

Damian then went on to describe that Krystal did not fit in anywhere in the scheme of events, other than to be disposed of and claimed that heaven would be emptied out and there would be no more angels.

Krystal never heard of such a notion, as she knew God as Creator had the ability to make more angels. "Besides," she pointed out, "In the book of Revelation, John describes thousands upon ten thousands" as a display of innumerable angels.

Damian claimed that Heaven would be emptied out of all the angels, and that they are just sitting up there until the end. Krystal went on to describe as in the book of Isaiah about Heaven and having gardens and building houses. She stated that with Revelation those in heaven will have a house in the city and a house in the country. Then she proclaimed jokingly, "a chicken in every pot and two cars in every garage."

With that the four men at the table all shouted out "Harry Truman's saying" Krystal noted their response and again wondered who these men were.

Finally, turning to Damian, she inquired, "Just suppose in your wild imagination that I am the person you claim me to be. You bump me off and you've just doomed the rest of mankind. – Lest I smite the land with a curse! That warning is in the Bible for a reason!"

However, Damian did not want to hear this and started to bellow out, "If you don't do what you're told you're never going to be able to hold a job in the United States again!"

This in turn just irritated Krystal and she replied, "You come get me! I'll be waiting for you. I have a double barrel shotgun up at the house and I know how to use it. – I'm gonna blow your head off!"

Trying to appeal to a softer side of Krystal, with coddling mannerisms, he stated, "You wouldn't do that."

"I wouldn't be too sure about that!" she exclaimed. "We're going to have a new Rorschach test. Your brains splattered all over my porch steps. And when your head rolls down my porch steps, I won't bat an eye, because it will be in self-defense. Of course, it will be a small test. You don't give Us much material to work with."

Otto Hartsel was enjoying the salad shredding efforts and remarked about Damian, "You don't have any brains at all!"

Finally she said to Damian, "You don't exercise your knees very much, do you. Well, that can be arranged. I pity you, and I'm serious when I say that because the lesson you have to learn is one of the hardest." Then paraphrasing from the Scriptures, she reiterated, 'It is much easier for a camel to go through the eye of a needle than for a rich man to enter heaven.' - I would really like to see you in the new kingdom, but from what I've seen so far I don't think you have what it takes to walk through the fire. I see you going into the fire, but I do not see you coming out. – No name, no memory of you. You will completely cease to have existed. – Think about it!"

"But then where will you go?" he inquired.

"As far away from you as possible," she replied.

No! responded her Christ-like figure standing directly in front of her. *I want you to go see him.*

"Great!" she stated sarcastically, "Why don't we just march into the lion's den!" She sat there with a perplexed look on her face trying to understand what that was going to prove.

Just go see him, came the reply. As she sat there contemplating what was at stake, she felt His reassuring presence and that in time she would understand.

Her Christ-like figure finally said, *I'm going to make you forget this whole event ever happened. Then when the time is right I will bring back the memories to you.*

She sat there still thinking about everything when Damian claimed that she had a story to tell and that she indeed needed to write a book about it.

Once again, her Christ-like figure gave her advice regarding these matters.

Thinking about 'we catch fly with chopstick,' she stated to Him, "We're going to need some fly paper!"

Your book will do the trick! came the swift reply of the Christ-like figure. Krystal pondered this and wondered if He was referring to Damian, Saddam Hussein or both. Then He continued to advise her some more. A picture came to her mind. This one had Damian manning a bunch of controls, laughing all along that he was in charge. However, the Real Master of the controls appears behind him and Damian becomes horrified. "Beautiful picture!" exclaimed Krystal and she gave her Christ-like figure the OK sign.

Looking back over at Damian, she stated, "This is going to be easy."

This is going to be rough on you! Claimed the Christ-like figure as He proceeded to present brief images she would have to endure.

Finally she remarked about going fishing down at the fishing hole and stated, "We're gonna pull a whopper up on this one." Then referring to Irving she stated, "We're going to have to put flashing neon lights on all the confessionals saying 'Open 24 hours.' You tell your friends, Damian, they should not only pack a lunch when they go to confession, but they better bring breakfast and supper as well. They're going to be there awhile." At that point Laura who had been sitting across from Krystal nodded her head affirmatively.

Once more her Christ-like figure advised her again, *they're going to try to kill you. – They'll try to poison you.*

"Do I make it? she inquired unsure of what was being proposed.

Trust Me! came the reply.

She considered, *if I can't trust Christ Himself, who can I trust? After all, He had risen from the dead and was now right in front of her. What's not to trust!*

Would you be willing to undergo a spiritual crucifixion? the Christ-like figure asked.

"What's that?" Again very rapid progression of scenes was displayed before Krystal's eyes. "They'll crucify me too! They don't care that I'm a woman. They'll nail me to the cross!"

Then the Master Planner proposed some exchanges to be made. *In order for this whole thing to work out, I'm going to have to take your father.* Even Krystal knew Henry was aging and would die someday soon, he had been a source of strength for her. As she mulled this proposition over the Master Planner then said, *Trust Me on this one! I need him up here with Me.* Krystal only understood that perhaps he would be put on the council of 24 elders referred to in the book of Revelation.

Damian, unsure who Krystal was talking to, inquired, "Then you'll do it?"

This time she responded, "What's the matter? All the black people saying no? – Well, they're not going and neither are we. – You've been doing this to the black people for a long, long time! – Irving says No More! – The buck stops here!" She told him to take back a message to whoever sent him. "You tell those shit for brains in Washington that they'd better be careful who they're picking out for sacrifices!"

Then in a calmer tone she relayed, "You know, down in Africa when they come across a white man like you they put him way in the air with his legs attached to two long poles. And one group of people pick up the pole and run in one direction. The other group of people pick up their pole and run the other direction. – Make a wish!"

Damian sat there trying to envision what she was describing and all of a sudden he became very wide-eyed realizing that he had become a wishbone to be split in two. He responded by saying that if she did not do what he wanted, "The gods will be angry with you!"

"What gods?" she asked trying to narrow down exactly who was behind this scenario.

"The government," he replied casually.

"The government! They can't even balance a checkbook!" she replied thinking *and you think they're god?*

Aware that the Christ-like figure would bring back memories for her at a later date she grabbed Laura's glass of ice water as well as her own and began adding just ice cubes. In a German accent she stated, "We must return to the laboratory und dann ve add ze secret formula and ve make kaboomba. Big Kaboomba!" Just ice would portray justice!

She tried to explain to those who were listening about probation time and the investigative judgment, and using the same train of thought she spoke to the Christ-like figure, "So, while they're investigating me, We'll be investigating them. – That's rotten! – I like it!"

Turning to Damian she stated, "You have been weighted in the balances and found wanting!" Once again she referred to the Biblical reference of the handwriting on the wall in the book of Daniel. "You're bankrupt!" unaware that just two years earlier he had actually filed for bankruptcy in U.S. District Court.

"My assets are good!" he replied, knowing that Bush and Cheney would pay him well for his efforts.

"Not that type of bank account. Next floor up, third door down on the right. You can't miss it! A three-man accounting firm. They just sent down an auditor's report. You're bankrupt! – It seems you haven't been making regular deposits to your account and They're thinking of foreclosing on you!"

Then the voice that was behind her and to her right said, "We're going to drain his bank account." Krystal was hoping that whoever this was would do the right thing in this matter. Although she was speaking of spiritual assets, she considered that there could definitely be monetary assets to be drained as well. She figured whoever had said this was going to definitely put Damian out of operations, particularly with respect to making money off deceptions he was baking up. Yet, it was not his deceptions, but those higher up in the government.

Then Krystal looked up and she saw a crowned Christ seated on a throne with a sickle in His hand. She knew this image represented judgment as well as reaping and harvesting and giving just rewards, separating the sheep from the goats.

Excitedly, she began to dance around the room with excitement. She looked back at Damian and said, "Lucky Eddie! – Gonna play the numbers!" making reference to his comment about her number coming up. "You're gonna lose – big time! And you will be ashes under my feet!" She thought about the judgment throne scenario she had just envisioned. Then she paraphrased the warning given in Revelation Chapter 3, "I wish that you were hot or cold, but you are neither – I will spit you out of my mouth! You say, you are rich and have need of nothing, but you are wretched and blind and naked… Christ admonishes you to buy from Me gold refined by fire, that you may be rich and buy white garments to cover your nakedness and eye salve so that you may open your eyes and see the truth." Yet Bush and Cheney were only concerned on making money from oil and nothing more.

Then in a black dialect she stated, "Five little monkeys jumping on the bed. One fell off and broke his head. The momma called the Doctor. The Doctor said, 'No more monkeys jumping on the bed!" She was referring to end times, the judgment and that with Damian's expression of his views and plans, it was as if he broke his head.

Upon hearing the number, five, Damian tried to assert that there are five world leaders in place and that there was no room for a woman. Picking out from Scriptures that the Queen of the South was black, he tried to assert that Krystal portrayed the same features. He went on to try to instill the notion that a black man and a black woman would rule the underworld.

Krystal tried to dispel this notion by reiterating, "if God created us in His image, then black and white are both of that image. When Christ said in My Father's house are many mansions, He was not only referring to other religions, but to peoples as well, no matter what color."

At any rate with Damian reiterating the number five, he claimed that the Pentagon was a signal for aliens from outer space to land. Upon hearing about the Pentagon, Krystal began to chide with him. Then he stated the Pentagon was to represent that there would only be five world leaders.

"Oh, yeah!" claimed Krystal trying to appear that she had insight into this. Once more deriding his ideas she went on, "I see what you mean. If you keep adding points to your pentagon figure, eventually you end up with a circle. We'd all have equal rights and then we'd have a democracy. What a terrible thing to happen, especially in the land of the free and home of the brave! What was I thinking of? Where was my head?" Others sitting there agreed with her logic.

He returned to the idea that she had to do something about Saddam Hussein. Krystal did a play on words with the name Hussein stating, "Who's sane and who's insane? Well, we're going to find that out, too! By the time this is over with you're going to wish you'd have never opened Pandora's box. And before this is all over, this dumb Polack is going to show you a few things!"

Then she told the crowd that if the country is going to go to war, they should pray before going as that was what the Old Testament prescribed for success in battle. Then Krystal began to sing "God Bless America."

Damian did not like it and when she was finished he stated, "You're not Kate Smith!"

"I wasn't trying to be Kate Smith." As an ambassador for Christ, Krystal once more wanted people to pay attention to what the words of the song said. 'God...stand beside her and GUIDE her.' Then she explained to Damian, "I was asking for a blessing to be poured out on the United States." She thought, *I'm trying to give guidance and counsel here!* Yet she wasn't sure her words were taken seriously.

Asking what could people do, Damian only wanted to know what Krystal would say, so that he could divert it from happening. She counseled them to begin with reading the Psalms of David which speak of the heart and then read the four Gospels to learn about Jesus and how He treated other people.

Searching through the juke box music once more, she found an appropriate song. She played "Bridge Over Troubled Waters" by Simon and Garfunkel. When the music came to the last verse "Sail on, Silver girl. Your time has come to shine, all their dreams are on their way," Damian glared back at her solidifying his plan of action, *Absolutely not! I will not let this happen!*

Then Krystal looked at her watch and seeing it was time to pick up her son, Joshua, at the Y, she turned to Damian and exclaimed, "Physician – heal thyself!" Turning her back on him, she walked out.

DISCLAIMER: In the original book, there was much more of the conversation that took place. For those interested in more detailed description, please contact <u>maxineoday@gmail.com</u>.

CHAPTER
10

Damian sat in his booth for some time before leaving the restaurant. He then received a phone call.

"You'd better get over to the hospital here in town and quick!"

When he arrived at the emergency entrance, Damian was whisked away by two other CIA agents to a room on another floor. Elliott was laying on the bed. Greenish drainage was seeping out from under an eye patch which was covering over his bulging right eye.

As Damian looked at him all he could think, *Krystal did this!*

"He's had a stroke! He can't talk sensibly and he can't see clearly out of the left eye!"

"When exactly did this happen?"

"We were viewing the restaurant scene from a distance and as Krystal began talking and singing, Elliott started groveling on the floor. Then other things began to happen. We really don't want to talk about it right now. We don't think he's going to recover from this and be back to his old self. He'll be a cripple until he dies, at least that's what the doctors are saying right now."

Damian left the hospital and made his way to the local FBI field office, branch of the Cleveland office. Director Snuggles along with several other agents were going over their losses when Damian walked in.

"What are we going to do about this?" cried one agent. "She brought so much out in the open. We didn't want that!" The agents gathered around the table hashing back and forth what would be their next move.

Damian finally spoke, "Well, it's rather obvious. She's not going to do what we want! She was pretty clear on that! Yet, we really need to train her to do what we want. If she is a prophet, then we can show her the right direction she should go. Either that, or dispose of her."

"And how do you propose we should do that?" inquired one agent.

"Well, perhaps if we write some of what happened, change it around."

"I'm not sure I'd want to do that! There were a lot of people in that restaurant. They might put up a fight about it," declared another agent.

"Maybe not. That's pretty strong Republican town. Let's use that aspect to our advantage," touted Damian. "After all, her father is a Democrat and voted for Kennedy."

"But she said she was neither," replied one agent.

"Well, we know she didn't vote for Nixon, so let's bank on that. We'll get local law enforcement involved. When they see she did not oblige either Nixon or Hoover, they they'll have to be against her. That way, we can put a hold on her, keep her where we want, and quiet!" concluded Director Snuggles.

"Regardless, I'd like a copy of this for my own use," stated Damian. "After all, she was speaking most of them time directly to me."

"I guess that would be okay," claimed Director Snuggles. "What's it going to hurt?"

Another agent stated, "Yeah, but if word gets out about the Kent State shootings that she talked about and all the rest – well, you know what can happen? They'll come after us!"

"Maybe, we'll just kind of lay low for a while. Keep quiet, say nothing. Then people will forget about it, and things won't get out of hand," contemplated Director Snuggles.

"You know, if we just change the story around to make it more in line with what we want, we could make a lot of movies – lots of money to be had!" baited Damian.

Director Snuggles' eyes began to glaze over, "Yeah, we could, couldn't we." He contemplated for a moment, then asked one agent to replay the portion about the well. As they listened to it, Director Snuggles thought, *there has to be some truth to that well. Why would she say if it's taken by force or ill-gotten gain it will go dry? It sounds like there is something there to be had. It belongs to the United States and we have to protect it.*

"I have to get back up to Cleveland. I have some talking to do with the higher-ups," claimed Director Snuggles. "Make me a copy of that recording. I'll get in touch with the rest of the CIA agents who were there, and we can get our project on its way."

"So many of us in the CIA have been masking things when they happen like this. We really don't want the public to know what's going on. Perhaps the two organizations can work together, but in different ways to accomplish our goal." taunted Damian.

With copy in hand Damian departed to his psychology office to begin his writing. Calling Sheriff Cory Dumas, he told him to make sure there's surveillance on Krystal's house now. "We want to watch everything that happens there." He pondered to himself, *I hope I can stop her from doing anything. I'll turn her into that black woman that I want!*

Now the county surrounding Scoria, where Krystal lived, was in the sheriff's territory, so they claimed they had jurisdiction and squatter's rights to be there. Sheriff Cory Dumas along with other sheriffs and city detectives, who were of the same disposition, continued the surveillance. So once again Keith Munson and Greg Fleuzy were involved. Believing like Damian they felt women were only good for one thing, and were beneath men in intelligence, they decided to mock Krystal as much as they could. These particular people had no interest in God or any religion and so sought to discredit Krystal in any way. They noted Krystal's reactions when she returned home after the restaurant scene.

She was mentally exhausted walking in through the door with Joshua.

"How was your lunch?" asked Wilbur.

"It was okay," she stated. Then she contemplated *how could I tell any of this to him? He doesn't believe in God, at least, not like I do. If I told him*

I was able to cast out a demon, he would think I'm nuts! She said nothing and laid down to take a nap as Wilbur played some games with Joshua.

"This will work out just fine," stated Sheriff Dumas to his friends the next day. "Why her husband is pretty dense. He doesn't know anything about what happened. She didn't tell him anything."

The problem behind this whole scene was that George H.W. Bush was looking at his election campaign for 1988 with Reagan becoming a past president, and he was not interested at all in what Krystal had to say in Friendly's. So with Dick Cheney, Robert Gates and other from the CIA, they strove to engage other local law enforcement to do whatever they could to destroy Krystal's household.

"Then we'll keep it that way," surmised this group of saboteurs. "And we'll work on driving him away from her as well. She'll be so alone and isolated. If we keep going, she'll have no friends, no one to talk to. She'll either concede to our wishes and go as a sacrifice or kill herself."

Turning back to Sheriff Dumas, Damian stated, "Let's just keep a watch on what she does. Then we'll go from there as to what we will do next."

The following day Krystal took Joshua into town to go grocery shopping. As the State Highway Patrol was conducting roadside vehicle inspections, her car was pulled over. Trooper Ernie Wilson carried out the inspection and then leaned over to speak with Krystal.

"I was listening to everything you said yesterday. You know a lot. There's a lot of that I didn't know. But you like him, don't you?" he inquired about Damian.

But Ernie failed to realized Krystal tried to refute everything Damian said and was not interested in him at all.

Then he asked, "What are you going to do?" referring to sacrifice notion.

"I'm not sure right now. I'll have to see," she replied as the previous day's memories were already fading.

Then Ernie asked, "Did you really not remember me at first in there?"

"No, I didn't remember right away, but then I recalled a lot later on."

"Then you do remember me!"

"Yes, now, but it took a while for the memories to come back." Then they parted and Krystal drove into town to finish her errands.

Meanwhile, Damian had been in contact with friends of Elliott who had transported him to an obscure private location in Virginia, where he could spend the rest of his days confined to a cryogenic nursing home. These CIA agents wanted to know if Damian was making any progress in his attempts to get Krystal to do what he wanted.

"No, actually, I'm just observing, seeing where I can put forth some pressure in the household. Wilbur knows nothing about what happened and the sheriff's department is cooperating in keeping it that way." Damian stated on the phone.

"Well, I'll be coming out in the next several weeks," began one CIA agent. "I'll be bringing some high-tech equipment – something to add to the household to provide incentive, if you get my drift."

"Oh, yes, that would do just fine." When Damian hung up the phone he thought, *That Wilbur is such a poor schmuck. I'll have fun targeting him. After all, he does have a temper problem.* Damian smiled thinking about destroying the remainder of the household as well.

For the next several weeks, Krystal managed to see Ernie along the road several times. So she would stop and they would spend some time in conversation. By now, however, Krystal could only remember events from her childhood that related to Ernie. Her memories from the Friendly's conversation had faded. Ernie then went on to explain that he and his wife were divorced and maybe Krystal should divorce Wilbur and then the two of them could be together.

Krystal thought for a moment. There really had been no reason so far to divorce Wilbur and she was somewhat mystified about the prospects of marrying a childhood sweetheart. She told Ernie she would see what she could do. As she departed from Ernie, she thought, *Wilbur would never go through with a divorce, no matter what the reasoning.* Later that evening she proposed the idea to Wilbur, mentioned that she had come in contact with someone she knew before. Wilbur, however, was insistent that the two of them should stay together no matter what and so would not hear of it.

When Krystal encountered Ernie several weeks later, she told him that it was of no use. Ernie became somewhat jilted and then accused

Krystal of being too fat anyway. Krystal considered herself chunky, but not excessively overweight, and so balked at his accusation. Then Ernie whispered in her ear that he could get her some drugs so she would be thinner.

"Look," she began, "if you want to do drugs, that's your business, but don't try to peddle any on me!"

He then began to taunt her a little bit. Krystal finally stated to him, "Stop it, Ernie! The more you threaten me, the stronger I'm going to become." As she spoke she felt the words were coming from somewhere deep inside her and she could not explain why she said it exactly the way she did. Krystal drove off irritated, set in her mind with the same attitude she had throwing the drug dealer out of her house back at Kent State. Her resolve was made up. She wanted nothing to do with any kind of drugs, no matter what they might do for her.

"Hmm," said Damian as he as well as Sheriff Dumas and others from law enforcement viewed the surveillance tape from Krystal's car. "We'll have to do something to stop that! – We can't have the two of them hooking up together! This really would sabotage our goal." Then turning to his CIA friends, Damian asked for more micro-chip cameras and microphones to be placed not only in Krystal's car and house, but in Wilbur's car, too. "I'll have to go more to work on Ernie as well."

So for several months, Krystal returned to her bland lifestyle of attending church, her home duties and her retail sales business. She was unaware of any "bugging" taking place at that time, until one day driving home a radio commentary mentioned Ernie and how ignorant Krystal was. She decided not to listen to this rabble, sounding like Damian. She played the tape with the hymn "Shall We Gather At The River," As the music came to the verse, "feeling doubt around me, there is no place I can hide…" she noted that a sharp scratchy sound occurred. When she played the tape the next time, the flaw in the music was very evident. Krystal did not like this and considered it was Damian taunting her.

However, all was not lost. Krystal decided, *okay, you want to mess up my music, let's just see what happens.* Then whenever the radio commentary and/or music would sound odd to her, not like the original piece, she would insert a tape of some sort of music and crank the volume up loud.

I might as well blast his ear drums out of his head. And so this began a long, long series of "radio wars." She did manage to get headaches from this tactic, but she felt she had to do something.

One night she had a dream that she found very disturbing. It was what she called a "special dream, one sent from a Source, because it was prefaced by a Christ-like figure standing off to the side. He indicated the events could happen and would jeopardize the message she was seeking to proclaim. In this dream Krystal is "tricked" into her sexual vulnerability, and her feelings not only get once again ripped to shreds, but she literally becomes a "toy" for others' sexual pleasures. Krystal woke up startled and felt hot and sweaty from the ramifications of what she saw. For three days she pondered over the significance of this dream and how it related to her situation.

Finally she prayed, *whatever You need to take away from me, do so, that this may not occur.* Krystal recalled her life's events, and how she had wandered away from God. Yet she became a little wiser and a little stronger in her efforts not to backslide.

The radio wars continued to escalate. Even in the home Krystal noted things were more strained. Wilbur seemed more irritated, upset that several pieces of equipment in the household had broken down. He seemed on edge walking around the house with clenched fists. Then he would start swearing when working on something that would break. He could not figure out what could be wrong with the knobs or internal wiring, becoming more frustrated and swearing vehemently.

Sheriff Dumas played back some of the household surveillance tapes. "Look at this one. Here he is the big oaf trying to get the lathe to run and it just quits. – Now he's swearing at it. Boy, what a schmuck!"

"Yeah, and look what happens when we start playing that high-pitch squeal. The dogs are going nuts with all the barking!"

"If he doesn't have a heart attack or blow up, I'll be surprised. Let's see what else we can do to have his car malfunction."

Krystal started wondering about all the equipment breaking down. When she started to think about how much they were spending to replace broken down VCRs, and other items, she became quite suspicious.

She mentioned something to Wilbur questioning the possibility of the house being bugged. Yet his nerves were so on edge and was so tired that he snapped at her, "You don't know what you're talking about. Why would anyone do that? There's no reason to. It's just things are cheaply made. Nothing but damn junk!"

When she tried to explain what little she could remember of Damian wanting her to be sacrificed and the entire scene of Friendly's, he exclaimed how absurd that was. Finding no way to resolve the matter, Krystal finally stopped in to see her old friends, Melody Gable and Brittany. As they sat on the porch talking over how things were going for each, Melody mentioned that she and her husband, John, were finding more work in Virginia and wanted to move, but Brittany wanted to stay in high school in Scoria. Krystal relayed some things regarding the home situation and suggested a separation. Melody then suggested becoming Brittany's guarding and living in Melody's house.

Krystal returned home and read through the newspaper. An article caught her attention. Entitled, "Child Raised by Wolves found in Wilderness," it had a picture of a very young blonde-haired, 5-year-old girl, who had been found out west, perhaps Wyoming that had been raised by a pack of wolves. To the average reader it sounded plausible, but the question was, was it real, or was it something else. The child in the picture did appear quite cute, somewhat shy-appearing, and had big blue eyes similar to a very young Brittany. Krystal looked at it for quite some time, not recognizing the child, but then decided the article had to be true. When Krystal turned on her TV and radio, the essence of the article was portrayed. As it was reverberated throughout the media, Krystal began to wonder if her home was bugged.

One weekend Wilbur took Joshua out of state on vacation. It was then Krystal moved to Brittany's house. While they were gone, she was able to avoid a heated confrontation with Wilbur. Melody had legal papers drawn up on guardianship by lawyer, Shep Gridlock. Melody specifically wanted Brittany disciplined with her almost 17. Krystal was not sure she would be able to do anything to Brittany anyway, so she agreed.

Prior to moving out, Krystal had contacted several counseling centers with regards to her separation. All centers were booked with appointments for several months, except one. When she called, they told her she would be seeing Dr. Damian Madden. She wanted someone else, but there was no one else available. So Krystal decided he would have to do.

After Krystal had moved in with Brittany she began her counseling sessions. As she entered the room for her first appointment, Damian replied, "So you've finally come to see me." Krystal stared at him vaguely recalling the request to go see him.

His unsatisfying session focused mainly on Damian himself and his line of thinking. She went for weekly sessions for several months. From time to time he would underhandedly introduce ideas about her having to go as a sacrifice.

She would return to Brittany's house and contemplate her next move. The meager living arrangements required wood heat. Delivery of cut wood never arrived. So Krystal went to her house where Wilbur was and gathered what wood she could find.

One night Krystal was unable to stay warm and sleep comfortably. She laid there shivering and she prayed. All of a sudden she felt a warming sensation as she felt arms of an angelic being enveloped her. This Christ-like being maintained this position until Krystal was comfortable and able to fall asleep.

When Krystal first moved in with Brittany, she thought their relationship would be a good one. But as time progressed, the relationship deteriorated and Krystal could not understand why. She basically kept to herself with her work duties and home schooling Joshua. And Brittany pretty much did what she wanted. With John and Melody both finally working in Virginia, at last they were able to install a gas furnace back at Brittany's house.

One weekend after Brittany had spent time on the phone talking to her mother, Melody then called Krystal and began berating her for treating Brittany so harshly. Krystal denied having done anything of the sort, but it was to no avail. Melody did not seem to be buying Krystal's story.

Brittany and her female friends would sometimes volunteer to take Joshua for ice cream. At first Krystal eagerly allowed them to do so thinking it was all a nice gesture. In time, however, Krystal began paying more attention to Brittany's attitude, and she became more leery of Brittany's motives.

"Where did you go?" asked Krystal to one of Brittany's friends.

"Oh, we just went out and about. Lots of people like looking at Joshua."

Krystal became nervous as she mentally pictured ill-tempered and evil motive men who seemed to be ogling Joshua for some ulterior motive. She sensed from this picture that these men, whoever they may be, meant to do him harm.

She then asked that the girls not take Joshua out any more. As the girls departed to go elsewhere and Joshua went to sleep, Krystal laid awake contemplating those mental pictures. A sequence of images began to fill her mind. Joshua had been taken away from her and was screaming for help, and Krystal could not reach him.

Krystal jerked with her heart racing. She decided to start making arrangements of getting out of this supposed "guardianship" for Brittany.

John Gable had now earned enough money to buy Brittany a used car. It was not anything to brag about. It was dull gray in color with the paint gloss mostly worn off and part of the front grill was missing, but it ran. Brittany named the car, "Ernie." Krystal thought that odd and so began asking unobtrusive questions about Ernie. As she did so, Krystal began to notice Brittany respond to something and get quiet and shy appearing. She wondered what was really going on inside her head. In time Krystal would discover the "give and take game" that had been and was still being played with Brittany from the outside 'wolf pack.' It was then she recalled the articles about the child raised by wolves, and she now understood it was a ruse.

If Brittany would have spoken up at that time, she would have relayed what those 'voices' were telling her. This "wolf pack" had played the game well with her and now once again one of its members stated to Brittany. 'Get me what I want! You have to do as you're told, or else, your mother will know everything you did!' Then those in this pack would use images of torture in various manners to get her to oblige.

The next day the school contacted Krystal. As her guardian they wanted her to know that Brittany's grades were falling. Krystal asked to see the grades when she went to the school. She had mostly C's, but she was on the brink of failing other classes.

Krystal began paying more attention to Brittany, noticing that she and her friends were dressing up to go out with more spiked hair, leather outfits, etc. She also noted that Brittany would come home usually acting like she had a cold and would want Krystal to have her call off sick from school the next day. Although Krystal was not sure, she surmised Brittany and her friends were getting into drugs.

At one point Krystal approached Brittany and tried to have a talk about how things were going for her, and trying to get a reaction from her. Krystal proposed that Brittany come with her to see Damian for counseling. As soon as Krystal mentioned Damian's name, Brittany looked away and would not have any straight eye contact with her.

I don't know what's going on here, but somehow he's connected to her as well, Krystal concluded. This only distanced Brittany further from Krystal along with the rift between Melody and Krystal.

When Krystal tried to tell Melody of what she suspected, Melody claimed, "No Way! Brittany is a good girl! She would never do anything like that!"

One afternoon a teacher/coach came from the high school and dropped off a bouquet of red roses for Brittany. Although Brittany was not home, Krystal took them and put them on the kitchen table. As she did so, she wondered what Brittany would have done to earn these. The note attached with the bouquet thanked Brittany for a 'job well done.' Since Krystal knew it had nothing to do with grades, she wondered what portion of Brittany's soul she sold out for something else. The roses remained on the table for several days. Yet Krystal noted Brittany had no boyfriends, only her close friend, Jasmine.

Just by chance, Wilbur presented Krystal with a bouquet of yellow roses obtained from a friend of his. He had decided to pass them on to Krystal. She displayed them on the kitchen table next to the other roses.

When Brittany walked in and saw them she stated, "What are these? Where did they come from?"

Being rather coy, Krystal said, "Well, you got red roses for whatever, and I got yellow ones," hoping to get her to say more.

"What did you do to get yours?"

Krystal shrugged her shoulders nonchalantly, "Maybe the same way you got yours."

The next day when Krystal came down for breakfast, the red roses were gone, never to be displayed again.

One evening when Brittany was out with friends, another friend finally called the house because Brittany was in the emergency room from a car accident. Upon arriving at the emergency room, Brittany was reluctant to tell her anything.

Later the State Highway Patrol contacted Krystal with the full report. As it turned out Brittany had been to a party and had either some alcohol and/or drugs. She misjudged a curve in the road and totaled her car. When confronted Brittany remarked that the radio had been playing "Bad Moon Rising," by Credence Clearwater Revival, when the accident occurred. Brittany was on crutches for a sprained ankle and Krystal ended up taking her back and forth to school.

One morning, as Krystal was ready to drop off Brittany, none of the cars seemed to be advancing.

"Why are we just sitting here? What are we waiting for?" posed Krystal.

"We have to wait for the king!" replied Brittany. "What king?"

"Benny Soper. – He's the drug lord and he thinks he's king! That's why everyone has to wait. His escort blocks the drive so that every day there is a parade for his entrance to school."

Krystal paid attention to the car that he came in. The next day Krystal dropped off Brittany just a little earlier than usual. As soon as Brittany exited the car, Krystal saw the drug lord's car coming, and she pulled out in front of him, not waiting for any parade, and drove around all the other cars in a display to show that she would not pay tribute to such absurdity. Then she returned to Brittany's house.

John Gable got rid of Brittany's car and wanted her to come back to Virginia with him. Brittany played up to her mother's feelings and convinced Melody that it would still be okay for her to be here and that Krystal was being too harsh with Brittany. John was skeptical, but decided to go along with the plan.

Krystal had been advised for a partial hysterectomy. With Krystal going to be in the hospital for a few days, she decided to teach Brittany how to drive stick shift on her car so she could get herself back and forth to school. In the meantime Krystal planned to have Joshua stay with Wilbur for those few days. As she made the arrangements with Wilbur, she exclaimed she felt there was something going on in that house, but did not know what. One evening Wilbur brought Pepper, a large black cross between a Labrador Retriever and an Irish Wolfhound as a security measure to Brittany's house.

When Krystal went to her counseling session with Damian, she mentioned that she would have to have surgery.

"Well, divorce is like surgery!" he insisted.

Krystal continued to explain, but Damian kept thinking she was talking abstractly. Finally, when she said she could not come back the next week as she would be in the hospital, he remarked, "You really are going to have surgery, aren't you?"

Krystal looked at him and wondered where his brain had been all that time and said, "Yes, and if I get pregnant after that, it will be like the Immaculate Conception!"

The surgery performed by a Hindu wife and husband, graciously allowed Krystal's pastor phone call praying that the surgery went well. Krystal felt reassured and so when she left the hospital after her short stay, she resumed living with Brittany. Yet she was determined to dissolve the guardianship.

Krystal's successful surgery did not set well with George H.W. Bush, Dick Cheney and the CIA. They were still trying to concoct another method of getting Krystal to go as a sacrifice. A notion that a marriage between Saddam Hussein and Krystal would unite Muslim and Christian world was proposed. There would be world peace then, at least on the surface. Now that Krystal could no longer have children, this proposal was rejected.

Saddam Hussein's cabinet in the meantime had been infiltrated with CIA operatives. They were telling him that Babylon would be rebuilt with him as king. Saddam bought into this idea for a time until he realized he was being made a fool of by part of his cabinet. He then uncovered who was CIA and ordered them executed. Krystal read about this incident and began to contemplate the CIA's motives.

The following week Krystal had her counseling session in the evening with Damian. Listening to Damian babble, she felt a strong presence in the room. Damian began to mock Krystal accusing her of being fraudulent and not keeping her end of the bargain in dealing with the Middle East crisis by going as a sacrifice.

Finally, taunting her, he asked, "Do you really think you can draw fire from heaven?"

Sternly she replied, "If I felt it was absolutely necessary – yes!" As she spoke her eyes began to glow. Damian was taken back as he gasped. Krystal continued to glare at him with her beaming eyes thinking *how can I slit this guy's throat – I have no intention of drawing fire from heaven, except to get rid of you!*

Over Christmas Brittany stayed with her family in Virginia. Upon returning, she began spending an exceedingly great amount of time with Jasmine. Krystal noticed that they seemed to be quite hyper. As they shared the same refrigerator, Krystal went to retrieve some of her dinner. The casserole seemed to have more a gritty texture. For the next several days, Krystal did not sleep well after eating dinner.

One night she felt quite ill and not thinking that she was in town and should call the local police, she thought she would call the sheriff's department for help. She told them, "I think someone's trying to poison me!" When she told them where she was at, the conversation seemed to be interrupted, and there was a lot of disturbance in the background. At that point the call was disconnected, and they never got back with her.

During the next afternoon Krystal herself felt very hyper. Jasmine and Brittany took a particular interest in watching her. Brittany insisted that they were going to have a party that night. They spent the afternoon getting ready with much conversation trying to elicit from Krystal anything about Ernie. Krystal was starting to feel pretty spacey and so the conversation took an odd turn. It centered on Ernie hanging from a tree in the park, and the body would need to be taken down. Both Jasmine and Brittany kept smirking and eyeing one another.

At some point, the two girls left for a while. Krystal sat there contemplating what was going on, feeling her head reeling in circles, unable to pinpoint exactly why. She decided this would be the time for her to make a break from this house. She gathered up some things on the dining room table.

Brittany and Jasmine returned and as they came through the house, they noted the items on the dining room table. "Going somewhere?" they remarked.

Brittany was taken a little off guard and acted surprised, but seemed intensely interested in Krystal's actions. As both Brittany and Jasmine sat in chairs opposite Krystal on the couch, Krystal noted that they were staring at her, watching every reaction she made. Finally, Krystal took the party hat from her head and proclaimed, "The party's over." As she did so, a voice came to her from inside and said, *Get out! And get out now!* She knew neither of the girls heard the voice, but watched her as they maintained keeping Joshua in the living room.

Krystal began to gather her items from the table and indicated that she wanted Joshua to go with her, but both Jasmine and Brittany blocked Joshua's escape saying that he could stay. Deciding on a more drastic approach, Krystal concocted a story about suspicious activity in the house, and that she wanted to bring her dog back to protect her. Yet, the girls continued to block Joshua's escape.

Finally, Krystal told them that Pepper is a big dog and she would need Joshua's help getting him in the car. She reassured Brittany and Jasmine that they would return later. When she finally was able to trick them with her story, they let Joshua go.

Both girls sarcastically remarked, "Drive carefully!"

It was a fairly heavy foggy night and Krystal wondered about that as well, As soon as Krystal and Joshua were safely in the car, Krystal remarked to him, "We're never coming back here!" And Krystal did not care what would happen to Brittany as there had already been too many lies told to Melody about what was going on.

They arrived safely back at their own home. As they watched television, Krystal became increasingly weak and ill feeling. She mentioned to Wilbur that something might be wrong, and that she may need to go to the emergency room. Wilbur said that 'nothing was wrong' and continued to watch TV. After a time, Krystal though did not feel calm. So she went out and drove around in her car, finally ending up on Interstate 71. Playing her tapes, she decide to pull off the road, ahead of a patrol car. She listened to the words of Steve Camp's "Revive us, O Lord," gaining spiritual strength and feeling better she returned home.

The next day, Saturday, Krystal's family went to Brittany's house to remove all belongings. Brittany was not there, but there was a note left on the kitchen table stating, "Krystal is sick! She needs to go to the psychiatric hospital!" Wilbur read the note and commented that he thought it was right, but he did not know or comprehend what had transpired or what the community was involved in. Krystal was unable to convince Wilbur otherwise.

Since Krystal was still considered Brittany's guardian, she called the sheriff's department to report that Brittany may be missing. Krystal had made mental plans to see Shep Gridlock and have the guardianship revoked. Although the sheriff's department listened somewhat to what she said, there was never any formal report made out and no officer came to the house to investigate the situation.

They instead remarked, "Just stay in one place!" and that they would search for Brittany. As Krystal was talking on the phone she was half watching the TV which was on in the other room. She noticed that the scenes changed completely to a different story whenever Wilbur would walk into the room. Not paying much attention to what was on the tube, but rather more engrossed in other thoughts, he took no notice of that. When Krystal tried to point this out to him, he was slow to respond and did not see what she was talking about. Krystal wondered *who is watching this house, that they are controlling the TV pictures so well?*

Sunday night Krystal decided to check on Brittany's house as she had heard nothing from the sheriff's department. She noticed that all the lights were on and upstairs she found the windows open letting all the heat out. Krystal shut the window, turned off most of the lights and shut the door. It appeared to Krystal that this had been staged as if someone knew she would return. She decided to leave the house a different route and driving her car through the backyard, she intersected an alley and continued through town. As she did so, Krystal noticed that there was no longer regular music on her radio, but that there was singing portraying a black séance with instructions leading her to the city park. Krystal noticed as she turned the corners of the various streets, the cars behind her did the same. At one point she stopped the car, as the séance music continued. Noting that the other appeared to be waiting for her and for what she was not sure, she decided to leave. She made several turns to see if this trailing pattern continued, even back-tracking along the way, while the cars behind her followed suit. Krystal drove through the park and then the surrounding streets.

Approaching a sheriff's house with the outside lights on, she noted Damian's car parked in front. As she passed the house, her rear view mirror showed Damian getting into his car and drove in the opposite direction. Krystal sped up and exited out of town as fast as she could.

As she drove out of town the séance portrayal on the radio changed into more a directive tone, indicating that she should turn back and return to the park. Krystal did not, sensing that there was too much danger involved and instead returned home to Wilbur. As she neared her house, she noted that the radio music once again returned to normal and no longer played any séance music.

Krystal was now quite distressed over the last several days' events and coupled with not sleeping well, Wilbur remarked that there was indeed something wrong with her. He thought about the note left by Brittany on the kitchen for admission. Although Krystal, too, sensed something was wrong, she was quite reluctant to go. *I'm not crazy! These things are happening here and at Brittany's house, and I can't convince anybody about what's going on!*

Krystal was admitted that night and given medication to sleep.

The next day, Wilbur went to see Damian and began questioning what was going on. Damian, however, liked the Give-and-Take-Guilt-Trip-Game he had played so many times, not only with Ernie, but with Brittany and others, and now he could play the same with Wilbur. Basically it revolved around the premise of 'you give, and I take.'

"She should not have gone there!" Damian cried. "She is a queen and should not be treated so poorly!" Wilbur sat there not understanding anything. As Damian continued to play the game on Wilbur, he at last told him, "That was the right thing to do!" Confused, Wilbur left not knowing what to think.

As Krystal was placed on a locked unit, Joshua was unable to visit her. Yet the staff found a solution to that problem. When Wilbur and Joshua came to visit, they stayed on the elevator and Krystal was able to hug and reassure Joshua. That way there were no children on the ward.

Joshua looked very distraught and Krystal wondered what more harassment could be taking place at the house. As she embraced Joshua she told him that she would be home soon. She could sense that Wilbur once more was up tight as she noted his rigid stature and clenched fists at his side. Kissing Joshua she told him things would be better once she came home and to be patient.

Wilbur had decided to pull Joshua out of the home school program and enroll him directly in the Christian school. Even though Wilbur was not in any way accepting of Krystal's religious beliefs, he at least saw the need to continue Joshua's education in this direction. This proved to be very fruitful and worthwhile, and this reduced a lot of stress in the household for both Wilbur and Joshua.

The next morning Dr. Klone came to see Krystal in the hospital. As they talked she felt her thoughts were rather foggy and jumbled, but she did convey to him that she had been seeing Damian for counseling at the counseling center. Dr. Klone listened and then made the comment, "Stay away from him!"

Yet Krystal thought, *how do I do that if someone is pursuing me? There is no way to get away from him!*

In Dr. Klone's assessment of Krystal, he wrote that she had had a hysterectomy and that a week to 10 days after that 'things went sour.' Dr. Klone also included statements that she had made which comprised of becoming suspicious. He wrote, 'She stated that she thought someone was poisoning her or drugging her. She also had a fear that somebody was trying to kill her, according to her husband.'

During the hospital stay, she had a battery of tests done. Even though she felt rather 'spacey' as she did the tests, when she took the intelligence test, she noted that the evaluator appeared to be rather surprised when she answered the questions. Later on she received a copy of the assessment: 'Her IQ test indicated her to have a verbal IQ of 143, in the range of very superior intelligence. She indicated no behavior of anyone who was an alcoholic, and there was not dysfunction of any kind of brain activity on any of these tests. Her depression indicated that she was in the normal range of dealing with the usual ups and downs of daily living. Her projective personality assessment indicated that she was under a lot of environmental pressure. She had a high energy level, and may have a need to get increased power of strength.'

Krystal returned home after a two-week stay in the hospital. Her medications seemed to give her the sensation of being "spacey," but she continued to take them. Then one day she noticed that her tongue appeared red and raw. Wilbur noticed it too and wondered about it. They contacted Dr. Klone who changed the prescription.

Then Krystal was contacted by Melody Gable. They all met in

town in which Melody began to berate Krystal, accusing her of scaring Brittany and abandoning her.

Krystal sat there wondering, *who was scaring who?*

Melody finally told Krystal that she was taking Brittany back to Virginia and absolving Krystal of all guardianship responsibilities. Krystal did not care for the accusations, and feeling the dulling effects of the medications, said very little in response. She was glad to be out from under the guardianship responsibilities. John, on the other hand, was not so quick to point the finger at Krystal. He felt that perhaps there was more to this and that Brittany needed to be back with them in Virginia where they could better control her. The families parted although the friendship between them had now dissolved.

After returning home, even though she knew Joshua was better off in the school setting, she felt something had been abruptly taken from her. Being falsely accused by Melody did not help. Krystal contemplated her situation and became more despondent. Although she could not put her finger on what was transpiring, as she watched TV one evening, she noted that sounds in the house seemed to be elevated. Any equipment used had sharp grinding sounds to them. The burners on the stove grew hot exceedingly fast when turned on and food would easily burn if not watched. Wilbur appeared more distraught and frustrated on trying to understand what was going on, not comprehending what Krystal had tried to tell him about the house being bugged.

Although they enjoyed watching the Dr. Who series, Krystal began paying less attention to the story and more attention to her environment. She noted that there would be sharp, piercing sounds at times, emphasizing various phrases of the characters' script. This occurred especially when the scene displayed would focus on someone being destroyed or used for ill purposes. She began to wonder just how strong a hold Damian had on the household or if all the bugging was done by others and why was there no one on the outside seeing what was going on. After watching several episodes and various programs, she was convinced that that was what was occurring. She once more tried to relay this to Wilbur who was not able to be persuaded. At last she retreated upstairs and remained in bed for hours during the day.

Wilbur, noticing that Krystal seemed distant, talked to Dr. Klone wanting to get some ideas about how to motivate Krystal. He finally came upstairs to her with a bowl of cut up fruit for her to eat. Then he relayed how he felt when he went to visit Damian and how confused he was when he left the counseling center.

"I don't know if I did the right thing by putting you in the hospital," he confessed.

Krystal listened to him and then said it was probably necessary to go somewhere, at least to get a break, but whether the hospital was right or not was uncertain.

Her tongue continued to look worse and raw, and finally after several days, Wilbur took her back to the hospital. As they sat talking things over with Dr. Klone, Krystal was demonstrably irritated. She felt that she was not being addressed directly, like she was not even in the room and that her opinions did not count.

Finally, she said, "Yes, I need some R and R. I need sensory deprivation!" When she tried to explain that the house might be bugged, Wilbur claimed that she did not know what she was talking about. Dr. Klone observed Krystal go from being quiet to irritated. Without knowing the reason, he once more admitted her. This return visit would put a strain on the their household expenses.

This time a psychological report appeared from the last admission that included this assessment: 'Krystal and her husband separated approximately four months ago. She stated that the main reason for her leaving him was that they couldn't seem to talk about things and that their sex life was down. Krystal had been working two jobs for over a year, and she was pressured by her husband about the need for more money. When Krystal moved out of the house from her husband, she moved into a friend's house where she was to look after their 17-year-old daughter because the parents had moved out of town. Krystal became her legal guardian so that she could finish school in the area. Approximately a week and a half later after her hysterectomy, Krystal had a sudden onset of paranoid delusions. She began thinking that food in the house was being poisoned and she questioned whether the girl was drugging her food. Krystal felt so unsafe in the house that she returned to her husband's house.'

During this hospitalization, Krystal's medications were changed and her tongue regained its normal color. As she sat in the lounge reading the newspaper, she noted some electrical workers doing repairs on the overhead intercom. She noted that one worker kept intensely looking at her. She took note of his actions, but did not recognize him. She continued to read the article, but was aware this worker kept watching her. Finally she retreated to her room.

Dr. Klone came to visit the next day and after a discussion, Krystal finally asked if she could have some paper and a pencil to write with. When he was gone she wrote out her own treatment plan including her own goals. This list included a general medical view of her health, including eating right, exercising, drinking plenty of fluids, and also encompassed working on activities that included making new friends, being involved in Joshua's school programs and other group functions. In short, it was an all-around plan for better health, including physical, mental and spiritual aspects.

When she showed what she had written out to Dr. Klone, he only commented that it was nice, even though she included in her assessment that she felt her problems were herself. Yet she felt he was not listening to her. Perhaps because of insurance payments for psychiatric hospitalizations, he felt that he needed to cover up a loss monetarily. He then place her on lithium to 'deal with her mood swings.' The insurance companies would not accept 'nervous breakdown' as an appropriate diagnosis, so something else had to be utilized for payment of her hospital stays. As a result manic depression was placed in the diagnosis, even though Dr. Klone clearly felt she was not a manic depressive.

It was Martin Luther King Day and Sherita, Krystal's black friend from church, decided to come and visit Krystal at the hospital. When she walked in, the receptionist said that visiting hours had not begun yet.

"But what about on holidays? Aren't visitors allowed in on holidays at any time?"

"Well, yes, that's true, but..."

"Well, this is my holiday," stated Sherita bluntly, and she was then allowed to visit with Krystal in the afternoon. Together the two of them chatted. Finally, Sherita concluded that there was nothing wrong with Krystal and returned to the church family to let them know.

By now George H. W. Bush was president and the situation in

the Middle East was getting increasingly tense. Krystal continued to read the newspaper and then retreated to her room one evening. As she lay there contemplating the facts, and the articles she had read, she began feeling a spinning sensation. All of a sudden she envisioned herself spinning in a huge whirlwind, and her feet were no longer on the ground. The whole scene was brownish in color. She was being spun so fast that she could barely hang on. Finally, the whirlwind stopped its intensity and began to slow down. As she slowly circled around descending to the ground she noticed a casket draped with the American flag.

She asked, "Who's in the casket?"

A Christ-like being off to the side in this vision answered, "That's Thomas Jefferson." She then asked more questions which were answered by this being. Finally she landed on the ground which was a ranch where there were several cowboys dressed in that attire, and she recognize one of these cowboys as Bush himself. Then the vision was over.

As Krystal prepared to leave the hospital from this admission, she asked Dr. Klone, "Do you still have the book I gave you long ago with poems in it?"

"Yes, I do," he replied.

"Well, I'm coming out with another book. This time, it will tell the real story!" She remarked as she set out to begin recounting her experiences, so someone somewhere would understand her. In early March 1989 she once again returned home.

As she managed the household finances, she began looking over the bills. The previous month's electric bill, which normally had run about $50, was up to $90. Krystal suspected this may have been because of the bugging taking place. So she watched the next few months' bills and noted that they had now returned back to approximately $50 a month.

NOTE: The information concerning the psychiatric hospitalization records and notes from various assessments are true and copied directly. They were obtained to verify these facts presented here.

CHAPTER
11

This time when Krystal was discharge from the hospital, she used her medication effects to her advantage. If Damian and others were trying to enrage her and react in anger, this wouldn't happen. She basically sat back and observed all that occurred in her household. Often when Krystal was alone pornographic images would appear on her TV screen, and then disappear when anyone else entered the room. She surmised that if they were sheriffs doing this, as the county was their territory, they acted like little boys who never made it out of high school. She wondered if they had a personal vendetta about her being female and not obliging to their wishes. She decided to once again seek counseling.

Although Dr. Klone advised seeing someone else at the counseling center, she did try another psychologist/ psychiatrist. However, he was very cold, showing almost no emotions and would not listen to anything she had to say. Deciding that she needed information on what occurred while hospitalized, she sought out Damian purposely.

Damian was surprised to see her return. As Krystal sat listening to him babble about himself, she took mental note of everything he did and said. At one point he insisted that she start a journal to write down her thoughts. However, she pondered, *if he has my house bugged, he will be able to see everything I write. He really wants to know what I'm thinking, so I won't keep a journal for him.*

She continued to see him for several sessions in which he related one time in a jovial manner, "We need to get you some sexual toys to play with!" His eyes beamed as he spoke and he almost appeared to blush.

Krystal concluded, *so they've invaded the bedroom as well. – Hmm, I may have to curtail some of my openness then.* Though she felt mentally violated by such, she began to build a wall around her heart. The medications helped with this in keeping her emotions subdued.

Still beaming sensually at Krystal, Damian went on to describe knowing several friends of his in Columbus owners of pornographic shops that he visited several times. Krystal made no comment, but vowed to return to get other information from him.

When she arrived at her next session, Damian wanted to know why Krystal was not having any affairs. Claiming that he was now divorced from his wife, he stated he was looking for a partner.

He continued to talk about himself claiming that with all the AIDS epidemic, "wouldn't it be safer to have sex with someone you know?"

Krystal let him babble on, thinking, *if I give him enough rope, he's going to hang himself with it.*

"Well, you know, you need someone to teach you how to have fun with sex!" he claimed eyeing Krystal. She stared at him wondering what kept the stupidity from oozing out of his ears and said, "Who gets to be the lucky fellow?"

"Why you're looking at him!" Scowling, Krystal just glared at him saying nothing.

When Damian realized that she was not buying his story, he claimed in a jilted manner, "It was just a thought!"

Krystal realized that she could get him on this point, that he could have his license revoked for soliciting a patient for sexual favors. But she was not yet ready to make a full-fledged complaint against him.

She decided to change the subject and asked about her tests performed in the hospital, especially the IQ test. He indicated that he had received a copy of such.

"So what was the result?" knowing that it was high.

Not looking in her direction, Damian mentioned that it was just average, and tried to dismiss the question. Then he sarcastically described another couple who he was counseling. He laughed describing them shooting each other to resolve their differences. Again, Krystal showed no response.

Damian then switched the topic back to discussing his sexual fantasies. When Krystal began asking about his background, he indicated he was leaving the counseling center and would no longer see her. Since Krystal had no idea where he was headed, she reserved her complaint against him for a later date.

About this time Scoria's law enforcement agencies were ridding the community of many drug dealers, including Benny Soper. As the police investigated his transactions, they stumbled across a connection with Damian. Several detectives searched further to discover that Damian was fueling the Republican Party with misinformation not only about Krystal, but about the health care/insurance provider payments. Healthcare became a hot topic politically and debated in Congress along with doctor malpractice suits. Damian's revenge was partly aimed at George H.W. Bush who saw no real need now to help him out financially. Prior to 1985 when Damian filed for bankruptcy after trying to double-bill Medicare, Bush helped him out then. It was only after Damian had to resort to compliance with Bush's wishes. Now that Bush would not rescue him financially, Damian had to resort to other tactics.

Krystal returned home from the counseling session, now knowing that the cameras and microphones were still active in the house, and that there were now others watching the scenes. At times she felt at ease. Other times it made her skin crawl. She wondered if there were any good people watching the house, along with the bad and the ugly.

Although the medications did deaden her feelings, she noted she was not able to cry as easily or express much in the way of emotion. This began to affect the marital relationship and sexual activities, and she did not want to put on a show for someone to view and criticize her.

As she tried to exercise in her home's privacy, she began hearing cat calls and whistles, not loud, but just enough to be heard. She surmised it could not be Damian doing all this. She realized they were working in shifts.

Krystal then contemplated, *what if they are trying to discredit me? What avenue would they take? – What better way than to invade someone's home, take nude pictures in the bathroom and bedroom, paste them with either different faces or in different situations and sell them as pornography! If they chose to do this, that will be their demise. I can't stop that they come here.*

On her next trip into town, she spoke with various police officers, and she mentioned the bugging in her home. Each time she was cut off in mid-sentence or totally ignored. She finally conceded *well, this is a Republican town. Perhaps that is the crutch they hope will hold them up and keep them safe. But in the end, the Judgment, how will they stand when they deny me justice here?*

She became preoccupied with world events, hoping to forget the disturbing issues in her home. She did note, however, that since speaking with the police, the bugging attacks considerably lessened in her home. After George H.W. Bush became president. Salman Rushdie published the book, Satanic Verses of Islam. It seemed to incite the Muslim world with gross conclusions that Satan was harbored by Muslims reading the Koran. Then there was Exxon Valdez oil spill which endangered the fragile Alaskan environment, destroying its wildlife.

Just what kind of president is this? Where are his priorities? she queried. *Was the entire situation in the Middle East solely for oil and nothing more?*

Then Krystal discovered a double murder/suicide event took place in Scoria, whereby the husband and wife shot each other. This made her contemplate if Damian was involved in some way. Again she approached law enforcement, but they brushed her off saying she did not know what she was talking about.

She decided to go to the library and began an archival search. She did find a photo album of the Highway Patrol. As she paged through it, she discovered a picture of Ernie Wilson, when he first joined the patrol. Then she searched through the local newspaper on any articles that might aid her.

The search continued for months. In the late 1960s, she found an article regarding a discontented FBI agent named Damian Lear. It described coming from the Philadelphia office to Louisiana with another agent. As Krystal continued to read, a picture began to form in her mind, and she visualized two agents observing a snake charming event. The event managed to evoke demons out of one person and then possessing others. The scene shifted to where the two agents struggled and one ended up dead. Damian Lear then fled the scene and Louisians as well.

Krystal searched for more articles, but this was the only one. At the end of the article it did state that Damian Lear would be pursuing a career in psychology. Krystal contemplated, *is this possibly the same person, the same one who is now a psychologist here?* although she only knew him as Damian L. Madden.

Meanwhile in politics things were not looking so good for George H.W. Bush and reelection. Although he touted the fact that he headed the CIA, he was only director from 1976 to 1977. Also, Krystal read that Bush first claimed to be an Episcopalian, then a Methodist, and later on aligned himself with the Baptists. *How odd,* thought Krystal, *that you seem to bend whatever direction the wind blows.*

Then she thought about her own religious journey, how she started out as a Catholic, visited various Protestant churches and ended up then an Adventist. Perhaps he was on a journey, too.

When the Iraq-Iran war ended in 1988, Saddam Hussein began to exhibit greater ruthless power. It appeared war was inevitable. Oliver North began blowing the whistle about the Iran-Contra Affair and Congress was starting the slow process of hearings to uncover the truth. Damian once more used his influence politically, and so a long series of "buying and selling" between various agencies began. It was an exchange program of misinformation whereby one set of lies was sold for another. Damian claimed that Krystal was very shy in order to keep her quiet while the household was continually disrupted.

When Krystal attended church, Damian would follow sitting in the parking lot listening to the sermon and then rewrite it, claiming this was now New Age thinking. The CIA of course, gobbled up the lies and produced mass misinformation as well.

When Krystal had first attended an Adventist church, Lydia began verbally bullying her. Krystal ignored her for the most part, and learned that Lydia voiced the idea that she was like Ellen White and wanted to write for the church. Some other members ignored Lydia as well.

When Lydia's bullying continued, Krystal finally wrote her a nasty note. Krystal then got accused of hurting Lydia's feelings. Church service began to drain on Krystal as she thought *what about my feelings?* That's when Krystal decided to attend a different church and where she met Sherita, the church she was now attending.

As more tension surmounted about what to do about Saddam Hussein, Damian as well as others involved with the CIA and FBI, decided to try to physically take Krystal as a sacrifice. One was an FBI agent Krystal named as Woolly Bully, who later became head of the Burning Bridges field office of the FBI. Following her on Sabbath, Woolly Bully and others arrived at her church. Once Krystal was inside they decided to band together as a show of force. Yet they were surprised when Sherita met them at the door. They were not expecting a black woman to confront them.

"You can't take her!" affirmed Sherita. "She's here seeking sanctuary!"

When they showed their guns, Sherita only replied, "You'll have to go through me first!"

Not wishing to have to deal with a race issue, the agents turned away. Sherita approached Krystal assuredly explaining, "We tried to tell them, didn't we!" Then she laughed and walked away appearing to understand the role she took in defending Krystal.

When the church service began, one of the elders stood up to speak and made the statement, "I don't know if that is how I would have handled the situation, but then maybe I don't know the whole story." As he spoke he looked directly at Krystal and Krystal became aware that at least some of the congregation had become aware of what transpired in the restaurant in 1987. Krystal thought, *this is true. You don't know the whole story, but in time you will.*

Then Pastor Andy got up to speak. As he laid hold of the microphone, Krystal motioned silently to the pastor that the microphone was bugged. When he perceived what she was indicating, he finally said, "I think there's a lot more to this than we know!"

Krystal rolled her eyes around as if to say, *yeah, a lot bigger!* She indicated with hand signals in an "OK" sign, that he was correct. She prayed that her congregation would take to heart to trust God and bear out the storm that would come upon them.

Yet the war in Krystal's household still continued. Although taking on more subtle methods, Wilbur's car was still bugged and Damian used that avenue to his advantage. Convincing Wilbur of space creatures and aliens, he promoted his book, <u>Communion</u>. It was at that point that Wilbur brought the book home and urged Krystal to read it. Right at this point, Krystal did not recall that Damian had claimed this was his story, but to oblige Wilbur she agreed. Krystal only half-read it, but when she came to the part where the character supposed had been abducted and a female ant alien with greater intelligence than he approached him, Krystal became suspicious. She read on that this abducted person supposedly could not have sex with her because he was not attracted to her. Krystal finished the book, but considered that this was Damian's rendition of how he viewed Krystal.

"I think the book's stupid!" she claimed as she finished it handed it back to Wilbur. *If I try to explain what is behind this, they will bug his car more and convince him that I am crazy again. So I will just keep quiet for now.*

The attacks in the household continued. She waited several months continuing with her medications to dull her emotions and when this pursuit calmed down, she would go off the medications, knowing that she really did not need them in the first place.

On occasion Krystal and Joshua would visit her mom and dad in her home town. Her brother, Matt, was home for a visit at the end of May 1989. As they sat around the dining room table, Matt began chiding Henry because he said he was going to die soon.

"You're not going to die!" claimed Matt almost mockingly.

Henry looked up at Krystal and Krystal recalled the promise made in the restaurant whereby her Chist-like figure said He needed Henry 'up here.' As Henry continued to stare at Krystal, Matt turned to look away from the two. At this point Krystal shook her head affirmatively at Henry. Then the conversation was quickly changed to another subject. After a lengthy visit, Krystal and Joshua returned home.

By now the insurance company had only paid a portion of the hospital bill, and it became necessary to look for better paying work. In June she began working at a hospital in a nearby city with Joshua spending the summer in a nearby day camp.

In early July, Krystal was notified that Henry had had an accident and had broken his leg. Upon attending his side at a Cleveland hospital, Krystal discovered that Henry had become despondent over various things. Martha claimed that he had been talking about moving back into the old neighborhood somewhere in Cleveland. Martha had no intention of doing so and knew that Henry wanted to stay where he was, but these statements seemed so out of character for him. As a result Henry tried to string a rope from a tree overhanging a cliff in the backyard. However, he slipped and fell and ended up breaking his leg instead.

Krystal sat with him several days later in the hospital with Henry having been placed in a leg cast. Martha was anticipating bringing him home soon. As Krystal sat there she wished that there could be a way for her to communicate the conversation from Friendly's in 1987. All of a sudden Henry began repeating phrases from that restaurant conversation. Krystal realized her Higher Power had immediately answered her prayer. She then asked Henry if he remembered certain events when she was growing up.

Henry responded out loud by saying, "Yes, I do," as he looked directly at Krystal. It was an interesting three-way conversation, but it worked. This three-way conversation continued with Krystal praying that Henry would understand what role he was going to play once he died. Although Krystal was unsure exactly what that role would be, she trusted in her prayer.

Krystal came to visit Henry one more time at the end of July. He had been sleeping and when he saw her, he eagerly grasped her hand saying, "I'm so happy you're here!" He hung onto her hand for a long time and Krystal realized that this would be the last time she would see her father alive. At last she bent down and kissed him on the cheek as she mentally said goodbye. Several days later Henry passed away.

After the funeral, Krystal returned to work. Several weeks later as she was sitting at her desk, Krystal felt an intense sense of loneliness. It completely overtook her and so drawing a picture of a broken heart and leaving it at her computer terminal, she left work. Her coworkers were concerned and notified Wilbur, and Krystal was once again admitted to the hospital. Although Wilbur explained that Krystal had been very close to Henry and that his death probably had a major effect on her, the hospital was in a dilemma whether to admit her or not. At last, a relatively unknown physician took her case, claiming that her previous hospital records had diagnosed her as bipolar and that this is what she was exhibiting. Nobody bothered to read through the records and check out the real story behind the first admissions. And nobody bothered to check what was happening in the Scoria community.

In time, Krystal discovered that this physician was a fraud. First of all, he gave Krystal incorrect combinations of medications, and over the next week Krystal began having muscle contractions drawing up her arms and legs. This made it awkward for Krystal to do physical activity and even her gait was thrown off. When she tried to write out checks to pay bills, it was almost impossible to write a legible signature. Krystal did some checking into what medications she had been placed on and confronted this physician. She then told him she wanted someone else for a physician.

By now her medical records were embedded with the diagnosis of bipolar, and there was no stopping this misguided railroad that she was on. The same physician then tried to bill her for appointments that Krystal never made. Krystal began notifying the insurance company of billing for services not rendered. When the insurance company investigated, they refused to pay this physician. Over the next year, this physician demanded payment from Krystal. She did not consent and finally wrote a nasty letter to him indicating that she knew he was a fraud and had notified the insurance. The letters and threats then quit and Krystal was left alone, not having to pay any more. In fact, the hospital paid all other related bills, so there was nothing more Krystal needed to do.

In September 1989 Krystal decided to move to the bigger city to be closer to her work, once more hoping to find decent work for the family and moving out of the house by Scoria. She found an apartment only 15 minutes from work, very simple and suitable for her budget. Discovering that Damian was living in the same area, she sought to contact him just to see what he was up to. When he answered the phone at his home, he replied he had been watching children play.

Krystal listened to him talk once more, thinking, *he doesn't even like children! Just what exactly is he watching?* As the conversation ended she then remembered him mentioning he was going to have a child, right before their sessions ended. Krystal thought it was odd since he claimed he had a vasectomy, and thought he might be talking about her childhood friend, Chrysha. In time she would discover that he never had a vasectomy and indeed did have a child.

Sitting in her apartment one night, the memories of everything that occurred in Friendly's in 1987 began to come back in full force. Krystal felt it was almost like watching a movie. She immediately grabbed a notebook and began writing everything down. It was at this time that she recalled every encounter she had with Ernie Wilson from her childhood on when she first met him. The pictures were very vivid. She remembered her Christ-like figure's promise in Friendly's *I'm going to make you forget this ever happened, and when the time is right I'll bring back the memories to you.* In the next several days, she began recalling the complete restaurant conversation. For several weeks Krystal kept her notebook with her at her side to write down things that jogged her memory.

Yet financially, she could no longer stay in this city. Wilbur could find no work there and so Krystal once more forced to return home to Scoria. She put in an application at a subsidiary of a former agricultural research firm, FarmAgriMark.

Once more she would return to her home and have to face all the bugging that continued there. However, before she did so in November 1989 the Berlin Wall collapsed and the Communist empire began to erode throughout Europe. Krystal recalled that she did state in Friendly's the Berlin Wall was going to fall.

Krystal began working at this company in January 1990, and the work was more in line with her degree in biology. But there were problems here. There were those who had heard something about Krystal's conversation in Friendly's about black people and didn't like it. Other were simply scared of her.

Yet Damian began to think about what Krystal said in Friendly's, and wondered if perhaps there was something he was missing in his own personal life. Damian then began reviewing the tapes from 1987 and thought maybe Krystal had more to offer him spiritually than from Bush, Cheney or others in the government.

Krystal was left little time for herself, after working and providing for Wilbur and Joshua, but she did manage to start writing her book. She remember the promise the Christ-like figure had said that her *story would do the trick*. Using fictitious names she kept the details of the story as they remained true. It began as a very beautiful story, one in which she introduced each chapter with appropriate song verses.

As she put in information gathered from her own family history as well as local history, she never thought that someone would try to circumvent her story and make it appear as something else. When Krystal got to the chapter where she began describing what took place in Friendly's in 1987, her computer would break down, and eventually being replaced with a new one. Fortunately, she had always saved copies of her work on a disk, so all was not lost.

"I don't like this!" claimed Damian as he viewed the surveillance tape once more provided to him now by others involved. Then thinking to himself Damian muttered, *Krystal! If I allow you to continue you will reveal everything about me! I can't have that!*

Krystal also got called for jury duty. As she had to report to the court house in Scoria, she went and met Phil, the court bailiff, who was present in Friendly's. He began telling her about jury duty, when he abruptly changed the subject to the imminent upcoming war with Iraq. Recalling that Krystal had told those listening to 'pray before going into battle,' Phil whispered loudly to Krystal, "Let's just hope this works!"

"Oh, it will work all right!" Krystal immediately replied. As she did so her eyes began to glow. Phil gasped and was taken back. Scared he looked about the room to see if anyone else was there that would help him. Krystal gently placed her hand on top of his to reassure him.

"Don't be alarmed by this," claimed Krystal referring to her shinning eyes. "I have friends in higher places, and we keep in touch!" She pointed upwards to indicate heavenly places.

Then Phil began to smile as he comprehended what Krystal was saying. "They're going to be surprised, won't they!" he claimed. Krystal figured he was referring to the CIA and others of like thinking. For some time he sat there basking in sunshine or more appropriately, 'Son shine.' Finally, Krystal departed from the building, not knowing that her glowing episode had been caught on security cameras in the building.

Although Krystal reported for jury duty on two cases, neither case went through with actions and were dismissed before any jury heard the cases.

Now as Krystal watched the news she saw that the Middle East situation with Iraq and Kuwait began heating up. Saddam was invading Kuwait to try to gain control of the oil market. As Krystal watched the news, memories of what she had discussed in the restaurant in 1987 came to mind. Yet, as she watched other programs, there seemed to be an intention portraying the idea that she should go over there. There was even an effort by President George H.W. Bush to "go and deal" with Saddam as portrayed by what was on her TV screen. Acting on a hunch, she decided to do something as she felt Damian was behind this. She called her pastor relaying some of her anxious feelings. He gave her good advice to consult Proverbs 3:5-6. She felt if the phone was bugged, then Damian would hear the conversation and then make some attempt to sway her in the direction he wanted her to go. Her hunch proved fruitful as she soon saw displays of sit-coms, and the like, that appeared to portray her going as a sacrifice. Krystal sat back and did nothing to oblige. Instead, she continued to work on her book.

Krystal frequently would visit Martha back home making sure that she was doing okay since Henry's passing. There was much family discussion about selling some of the property because of the taxes to be paid. At last it was decided to sell off most of the surrounding property, except the house and where the spring was, the one that the government had been interested in known as "the well." Then upon returning to her home in the country, she added another chapter to her story.

One day she had the tape player on as she was listening to recordings of music she wished to place in her book, when they became distorted in sound. Figuring that Damian or someone else was once more trying to ruin her tapes, she got up and turned the radio to one station, the TV to another, and various other radios throughout the house to entirely different stations.

"There!" she said. "Now you can all listen and talk to each other, trying to tell me what to do! I'm going to work on my book!" With that she closed the door to her room, leaving all the other equipment on. *Maybe now I can concentrate!* she exclaimed, hoping whoever was in the house would get the message.

At church now and for several years to come, the bugging continued. At times the sound system would be affected. Other times the heating system would give out with the members as well as repairmen scratching their heads, trying to figure out exactly what was wrong and why things would not work like they should. Yet Krystal prayed that the church would hold on. As Krystal looked back on the 1960s and how the black churches were fired upon with tear gas and burned, many times the parishioners were locked inside. Yet they continued to preach the truth praying earnestly at all times. And they survived. Krystal wondered, though, how well the white church would fare if faced with similar circumstances. She would soon discover that the white church would easily succumb to pressure and not be bold enough to take a stand for justice, even though they preached being able to stand up in times of trouble.

One night Krystal was awoken from sleep by Joshua talking. It appeared he was having a conversation with someone. When he said yes to whoever, Krystal became concerned. She asked him as she whispered to tell her what was going on. Then he started crying because he 'could not perform the task asked of him.' Krystal suspected that this was more of the Give-and-Take-Game of Damian's. So Krystal woke up Joshua from sleep so that he would think it was only a bad dream and not think about it anymore. Then Krystal whispered loud enough for any microphones in the house to pick up.

"Get out of my house! I know it's you, Damian!" Then Krystal seriously threatened to come after him. Krystal was determined that Damian was not going to destroy Joshua this way. After all, Krystal was becoming convinced that Brittany was being used by Damian or someone and had already showed signs of damage done. No way would she allow Joshua to be tormented in the same direction. However, at that time Krystal had not had enough time to consider the possibility that Brittany might be so brain-washed by Damian or others that she would play the same game on another child.

On January 18, 1991, Operation Desert Storm began the Persian

Gulf War. Krystal watched as chaplain after chaplain prayed for the troops' success, much like what Krystal had indicated in the restaurant conversation. The war was a military success in terms of turning Saddam Hussein out of Kuwait and ended with a cease fire proclaimed on February 28, 1991. However, Saddam was still in power and Kuwait had suffered much in terms of the spoils of war.

Several weeks later on the way to church, Joshua relayed to Krystal that he had a strange dream the previous night. As an answer to Krystal's prayer, Joshua had dreamt that he had a helmet placed on his head. It was too big, and he could not see out of it. Krystal explained to Joshua that in the battle with Goliath, young David tried on the armor, but it was too big, so he did not use it. The helmet was protection, and even though it was too big for Joshua's head and Joshua could not see out of it, the protection was there. In this battle Joshua was the one to receive help, a battle he knew little about. Joshua had been spared at Brittany's house. Brittany, unfortunately, became the 'sacrifice' which Damian and others continued to use to their advantage.

Still continuing her book, Krystal at last resorted to writing to the Cleveland Office of the FBI to indicate that she knew who Damian Madden really was, a wayward FBI agent. She specifically wrote her letter to the resident agent. This in turn was forwarded to Director Robert Snuggles. In a few days he responded stating that the FBI had no one in their service as Damian L. Madden, and that she did not know what she was talking about.

Krystal was irritated, but continued with her book. One evening when she returned home, she noted that Pepper, her dog, was very lethargic and did not get up to greet her as he usually did. He remained motionless on the couch as though drugged. Krystal looked around the house. Nothing was missing. Then exclaimed, "There would only be one thing in this house someone would want, and that's my story!"

Immediately Krystal checked the computer. The story was still there, but in one of the chapters someone had added a few sentences. She had been writing about the FBI and the notion that she was to be a sacrifice. Someone else wrote how ruthless the FBI was and how they would 'bump off people' they did not like. Then the added paragraph further stated, "However, what they did not realize or believe is the fact that at the appointed time these things are revealed to a prophet." Taken back, Krystal still knew there were evil men surrounding her house.

Determined to get more information, she returned to another of Damian's offices and made an appointment to see him. *This time,* she reasoned, *I'll get enough on him that they'll have to take his license to practice away from him.*

In the meantime in April, she wrote to the local field office of the FBI again trying to find out more about this notion of going as a sacrifice. That letter was never answered by that office. Instead that letter was forwarded once more to the Cleveland office and to Director Robert Snuggles. Yet this time no reply came.

She then asked Damian about the tape concerning the 1987 encounter.

He answered her that "I have no idea what you're talking about!" Then he questioned if she was mentally okay.

When Krystal finally felt she had enough information to take Damian's license away, she wrote a letter to the State Review Board of Psychology, which had the ability to approve or deny one's license to practice psychology in the state of Ohio.

Then in broad daylight she snuck over to Damian's office and decorated his sign. She then began to paint strips across his name on the sign to indicate that he should be in jail, behind bars. She knew anyone driving by his sign would wonder about it, and since there was a local FBI office nearby they would see it as well.

And why the decorations? Krystal was excited. She had seen the U.S. been victorious in the war, even though Saddam remained. Her book writing was going pretty good, even though she knew Damian was watching over her shoulder. She knew who Damian really was, and she was going to get his license to practice taken away from him. Her troubles would be over, so she thought.

Yet she received nothing from President Bush in the form of thanks for what advice she had given those who were listening in 1987, perhaps he didn't want to acknowledge that both he and Cheney were actually there and heard it firsthand. But Bush and Dick Cheney were only interested in oil in the Middle East, and so none of what she stated at that time in Friendly's had any impact on them. If the FBI and CIA had taped the conversation, which they had, surely they would have shared what was on that tape. Instead, Krystal had the 'rug pulled out from under her,' and other organizations decided to keep things quiet. Keeping the tape for themselves, and utilizing for their own means, they got no official approval or signed release from Krystal to do such with that tape. So Krystal got absolutely nothing for her admonitions. What she got was a series of distorted stories in the form of various movies produced which degraded the message she provided for those listening.

Wilbur, however, noticed her excitement on this particular day, although did not know why. Thinking she was becoming 'sick' again, he took her back to the psychiatric hospital. This time she talked to a young doctor, son of Dr. Klone. He may not have been acquainted with her story or situation at all. When she relayed what had been happening, he did not believe her story and so she was admitted once more. Again, without consulting any outside sources for information he, too, classified Krystal as bipolar illness and stated his report, "Presently the patient is experiencing delusions of grandeur that she is writing a book, as well as paranoid delusions that the FBI are somehow involved in her book-writing and are trying to sabotage her life."

Krystal was not happy about her situation. It appeared once more than no one was listening to her. As she remained on the ward during this hospital stay, a small still voice reminded her that this was going to be rough! Krystal now understood what this was entailing, but still did not like it. Yet she still had hope. When her birthday came around, Joshua had hand-picked a beautiful heartfelt card. It expressed how much he loved his mother and all that she did and that he wished for all the happiness on her birthday. Krystal cherished the card and thanked him profusely.

After her birthday was over, Krystal questioned one of the nurses on the ward. Since she had been placed on lithium, she inquired what her diagnosis was. Nurse Brown stated, "They wrote down bipolar disorder, manic depressive, but that's not what you are!"

"How would one act it they were?" inquired Krystal. At that point Nurse Brown pointed out a patient for Krystal to observe for the next several days. In the mornings this patient would be talking a mile a minute. Then by the end of the day, her speech would be dramatically slowed. By the next day the cycle would begin again.

After several days, Krystal approached Nurse Brown again. "I see what you mean. – I see the bipolar aspect, but why do I have this as a diagnosis? I don't act like that!"

"No, you don't," she replied. Then much softer she relayed, "This is for your own protection!"

Krystal thought a minute, rationalizing, *true, no one's really going to try to hurt me if they think I'm crazy, but the problem is, I'm not crazy!* Puzzled, she came to no concrete conclusions and went home several days later. It would only occur to Krystal later on that the diagnosis was necessary so that insurance would pay for the hospital stay.

When Krystal returned from the hospital in mid-July, she was contacted immediately by "Rex" who said he was from the State of Ohio Psychology Review Board and that he wished to meet with her, but not at her house. So she arranged to talk with him at a small diner. He claimed that he had received her letter and that the board had received a lot of complaints about Damian and were looking into the matter. When he opened his briefcase, he bore the letter that she had sent to the review board. She also noted that that was the only thing in his briefcase.

As Krystal talked with "Rex" she felt that there was something vaguely familiar about him that she should know him. She became suspicious of him.

"Are you sure you don't want something to drink?" she politely and casually asked him. When he shook his head, no, she said, "Then do you want to tell me who you really are?"

At that point Rex turned around to see who else might be in the diner giving him away. He tried to reassure her that he indeed was from the review board and would look into the matter and then he departed.

Weeks passed and Krystal heard nothing. Krystal knew that the support for the President was very strong in the community, especially since it was a Republican town. Yet what she did not know at that time was somehow George H.W. Bush thought the interaction between Krystal and Damian was a joke and something funny to observe. He wanted no repercussions coming in his direction and so ordered that

Damian as well as others be given a Presidential seal of clemency and protection, so as not to interfere or stop the entertaining. Once more several weeks later, Krystal saw across her TV screen President George H.W. Bush inferring about the 1987 restaurant encounter and in relationship to Damian, he stated, "I think we'll just let her take care of him!" Then laughing he exited off the presidential stage.

Krystal became irritated, *You don't know what I've been putting up with, or you don't care – you just think this is one big joke!* Then she wondered also if Bush was referring to Saddam Hussein and that Krystal should take care of him.

She felt abandoned and dumped by the side of the road. *How many other people is Damian or these other misconstrued law enforcement people going to hurt, before something gets done to stop them?* she questioned. Finding no immediate relief she went about her normal routine, returning to church activities, and immersing herself with her work duties. Yet all the time she was burying a hurt that no one would be able to take away.

CHAPTER
12

Now off the medication, it was easier for Krystal to cry. Those watching her felt she was more vulnerable and once again displayed offending pictures on her TV. Rather than react, Krystal would become involved in other activities.

This game, however, began to be played at Martha's house as well. While visiting her mom, Krystal noted a TV ad about Eden Rock wine. She noted that the person looked like Goldilocks, Gary Scambolini, the FBI agent with long black curly hair. He was surrounded by other Silicians who were celebrating and blowing out the candles on a cake. Then he motioned with his fingers of a gun going off and pointed them at the camera.

I guess Goldilocks wants me to fear him portraying he's part of the Mafia, Krystal concluded. *Well, I wasn't planning on taking on the Mafia! – Now what's next?* she questioned.

Returning home, she noted no more TV ads like that, nor were there any more on Martha's TV when Krystal visited again.

As she continued writing her book, once again the printer malfunctioned and she was unable to print a copy. Yet she did have a copy on disk. The printer was finally replaced, but not without frustrating both her and Wilbur.

After making more library trips for research, Krystal purchased a copy of the Koran (Quran) and began to read it. Although somewhat familiar with Islam, she now became aware how much overlapped with the Bible. She discovered not only did the Quran follow along with Abraham, but extended to include Daniel, Elijah and other prophets. She realized the Quran did recognize Jesus.

She was already acquainted with the seven heavens. Now she understood in depth the significance. There is a battle between good and evil, much like what the Bible describes. Those who conquer the battle, no matter how small, continue upwards, while those who lose the battle, continue downwards. In the end, all the evil ones are below and the good ones are above.

The Quran acknowledges the resurrection with a Day of Reckoning and rewarding of the deeds performed. The believers of Islam were very familiar with the presence of angels, both good and evil, as well as the messages and deeds the good angels could bring or perform.

Krystal was amazed at how much the Quran paralleled the resurrection in the Bible. *If they believe in the resurrection, then perhaps what is written in Revelation is there as well,* she thought. She then spent much time in the church library. In one of Ellen White's manuscripts she read: "Satan will use every opportunity to seduce men from their allegiance to God. He and the angels who fell with him will appear on the earth as men, seeking to deceive. God's angels also appear as men, and will use every means in their power to defeat the purposes of the enemy… Evil angels in the form of men will talk with those who know the truth. They will misinterpret and misconstrue the statements of the messengers of God… We are engaged in a warfare (Ephesians Chapter 6) against the hosts of darkness."

Krystal thought, *that's exactly what the Quran is describing! The battle in the levels is the same battle described in the Scriptures.*

As she watched the news that evening, she saw several soldiers had been captured fighting in the Gulf War. Krystal feared they would be tortured and prayed for their safety.

Sometime during the night, she woke up from a very odd sensation.

Those watching her noted that suddenly she began to 'glow' and not just her eyes as before, but her whole body. The 'glowing' sensation was so strong, she felt it was lighting up the entire room. Wilbur, however, was sound asleep and not awakened by this. Then she felt she was dreaming as she was transported to where the soldiers were and where Saddam was. Then the dream and 'glowing' sensation ceased.

"Did you see that?" asked one of the sheriffs.

"Yeah, but what was that? There's something going on in this house that's kind of creepy," replied another.

In the morning, Krystal wondered if it was just a dream or something else. When she prayed about it, her answer came almost immediate. *If those watching want to see bedroom activities, then We'll give them something to watch!*

After a few days had passed Krystal found a news report that the soldiers had been released. They claimed while being held in captivity they had seen angels comforting them. Apparently those holding the soldiers relayed the sight as well to Saddam, who immediately released the captives with no further explanation.

Yet once again, the government agencies sought to downplay any of this. They released bits and pieces of this glowing sensation into science fiction movies who portrayed it as paranormal activity without any religious ties whatsoever.

To add insult to injury, those observers approached Pastor Andy claiming that Krystal had a 'sickness.' Pastor Andy later confronted Krystal. Although he did not come out directly and say it, he beat around the bush enough that Krystal knew what he was referring to. He claimed there was no way she could be a prophet if she indulged in bedroom activities that only included herself, namely masturbation.

Krystal thought, *you don't understand what's going on in my house! Or even why I would do such!'* Furthermore, Krystal never claimed to be a prophet nor did she want the church to acknowledge her in any way.

Feeling rather subdued after this episode, she noted an Adventist magazine addressing the topic of teen masturbation. Although there was mention of a self-centered lifestyle leading to an interest in pornography, Krystal was very aware of her reasoning for what she was doing. Krystal was very much aware there was no reference to such activity in the Bible.

Krystal had no interest in pornography. She was, however, concerned for the victims, particularly young children.

Trying to rebuild her self-esteem as the watchers were tearing at her on the outside, she pretty much kept to herself. Even the congregation was unaware what she was enduring on the home front.

In a few weeks, however, Damian boldly approached Pastor Andy stating that he had come to a realization and wanted to get to know more about the church. When Pastor Andy reiterated this to the congregation, he looked to Krystal for answers. Although Pastor Andy never said outright it was Damian, from all the description given, Krystal had no doubts. As Pastor Andy looked at Krystal, she only shook her head no. Then Pastor Andy stated that perhaps there were wolves in sheep's clothing lurking about. Krystal shook her head affirmatively, and no more was mentioned. Pastor Andy then began to lean a little more on Krystal for consult and support and the report concerning her 'sickness' was cast aside as nonrelevant. In turn, Sherita provided much in the way of advice for both Krystal and Pastor Andy.

Then during the winter months of 1991, Krystal's house again came under attack. There were noises just loud enough to disrupt Krystal's sleep cycle, but not loud enough to wake up Wilbur. Occurring for several nights, Krystal lacked proper sleep. Then while working at FarmAgriMark, several employees began harassing Krystal. Although she did not mention her religion or church, they taunted her concerning any religious beliefs. The two main instigators were Leonard Blare, a former patient of Damian's and Tyler Grove.

In late 1991, the movie <u>Silence of the Lambs</u> was released. Krystal was seeing enough low grade movies being released with distorted portrayals of her message, and she chose not go to the theaters to see them. This movie, however, bothered her because in the advertising across her TV, Goldilocks appeared promoting the movie as a true story. In this particular ad, Agent Art Castle, who was retired from Burning Bridges FBI field office, was displayed as being ignorant and gullible with Agent Scambolini's portrayal. What bothered Krystal the most was that Agent Castle was probably not even aware Goldilocks had done this.

Irritated with the household attacks, and still not knowing who was doing it, she decided to throw a monkey wrench in the system. Gathering up some dog excrement wrapped in a sock, she placed some in an empty box from an air pistol. As she claimed, *an air pistol for an airhead,* placed the dog excrement in it and closed it. Writing 'use as directed' on the top, she placed the note with 'eat shit' on the inside. She then took a dry cleaning plastic bag and wrote that Damian Lear Madden was an ex-FBI agent. In the evening she took her decorations making her way to Damian Madden's psychology office in Burning Bridges and posted them on the front doorway. By morning, everyone who worked there would see it.

The next day during her lunch break at FarmAgriMark, she walked out to the parking lot. She noted a gray Trans Am drive up and down the street. Damian was driving and turned around to approach Krystal. When she heard Damian's car slow down, she turned around and started walking towards him. Damian appeared scared and with wide-open eyes stomped on the gas pedal and drove off, while a satisfied Krystal returned to work.

The next morning on her way to work she heard strange messages on her radio, something to the effect of people coming after her because she did not do as she was told. Irritated she finally said, "Then you come get me!" She went inside not knowing what would happen, but anticipating there would be trouble.

Later on during the day, two shipping clerks came back to where Krystal was and told her everything was okay. Turning to Krystal's boss, they relayed that several men came with guns to the shipping department, demanding Krystal be turned over to them. These two shipping clerks stood firm in the assertion that they were not turning over Krystal to them. These men, whom it is speculated were CIA agents, persisted, but it was to no avail. Upon getting no cooperation, they left.

Krystal's boss, a strong woman, made one comment upon returning to where Krystal was. "Guess we'll all be having to pack a six-shooter just to come to work!"

Although relieved that others had stood up for her, Krystal felt drained and throughout the rest of the day, she did not function well. The following days she did not sleep or eat well.

Once more things started to go wrong in house. Wilbur was working on the computer and it appeared to malfunction again. Joshua, who had earned money on his own by delivering newspapers, had bought himself a Nintendo game system. He was also playing in the same room on a different system, and the games began messing up frustrating Joshua. There seemed to be nothing he could do to play the game without getting exasperated. Between Wilbur swearing at the computer, and Joshua crying out of being flustered, Krystal was getting a very strong headache. She tried to calm Wilbur down, but he would not hear of it. When at last she sat down at his computer, working on a hunch, the computer then easily performed the operations Wilbur had been trying to do. She surmised that someone was once again viewing this "frustration episode" as entertainment.

This episode jarred her nerves extensively and coupled with louder than usual sounds in her house, including the volume from the TV and radio, she became more aggravated than ever. *Doesn't anyone see what's happening here?*

She cried herself to sleep that night questioning, *who would do something like this, to frustrate a child to tears and aggravate someone else to a heart attack? This can't all be Damian. What if that Goldilocks character is involved? There has to be more people involved – a lot more – more than I can deal with!*

The next morning Krystal could feel her blood pressure was elevated. She sensed things were not right at work. Leonard Blare kept coming into her work area, idly milling around as if watching for something. Krystal did not care for him or his attitude and basically tried to ignore him. She wondered just how many people on the outside were involved in harassing her house.

Leonard tried unsuccessfully to have Krystal "tell him what was bothering her and maybe he could help." When Krystal heard this, she almost became sick to her stomach. Then later on he returned with a faxed drawing of a woman's head similar to Krystal with her brains blown out. Leonard laid the picture down directly in front of Krystal and waited to see what she would do. She chose to ignore it, but inside she felt nauseous.

Once again Wilbur took her to the psychiatric hospital for lack of proper sleep. This time the young Dr. Klone wrote: "This patient claims she is experiencing auditory hallucinations, feeling that the FBI was after her... Escalation of her irritability. She has not been sleeping for four days, not eating, losing unknown amount of weight. Her husband states that she is not eating and continues to obsess constantly about her psychotic system with special messages from the TV...and being monitored by the FBI." Now young Dr. Klone questioned whether there were schizophrenic features appearing, but he did note in the diagnosis, 1) bipolar manic, 2) elevated blood pressure, and 3) sinus tachycardia.

She sat in her room upset and feeling irritated. Finally, she decided to lay down and try to relax. As she did so, a still small voice came to her demanding, *Get up! – We've got to do this!* Krystal tried to resist, but this invisible being literally pushed her up out of bed and began shoving her down the hospital hallway. No matter how she tried to resist, the being kept telling her, *We've got to do this!* She then met a long-hair hippie character looking at her. Krystal did not know how he got on the unit as it was locked with limited access.

Subconsciously Krystal held out her hand at which point the hippie character handed her a large white pill. He laughed as she downed it stating, "Sweet Dreams!" Then he left.

Krystal apparently went into an episode of thrashing about for several hours. When she finally settled down, a nurse was standing beside her bed, holding Krystal's hand and reassuring her that everything was okay. Although no one from the nursing staff mentioned anything to Krystal about the episode, Krystal knew that this had been under the direction of her Higher Power. He once again had proven himself to be true. She recalled Him telling her "They're going to try to kill you. They're going to poison you!" Yet even at that time He had promised to trust Him and she would be okay, which she was.

When she returned home arrangements had been made for marital counseling. As she returned to church, there had been subtle attacks as well. The heating system and furnace kept breaking down, and Krystal realized that this was happening too often to be just chance.

There were also two church members dying only weeks apart. Both appeared to have been natural causes, but both were prominent elders. However, Krystal was suspicious that these deaths were disguised to appear as natural, when in fact they were not. Krystal was keenly aware that the CIA many times would use overdoses of potassium, causing cardiac arrest, but being untraceable. Krystal knew that there were cold-hearted people in government agencies that would stop at nothing to create havoc, and she wondered how much Goldilocks was involved.

On one such trip to church, she was passed by a yellow Volkswagen bug, with a vanity license plate that read "Chicken." His booming stereo could be heard several cars back from him where Krystal could see his long black curly hair. She figured it had to be Goldilocks, Agent Gary Scambolini. It appeared he was taunting her as if to say, *Nah, nah – you can't touch me! – I'm an FBI agent and you can't shoot me!*

Krystal he drove past her church, but did not stop to which she breathed a sigh of relief.

In fall of 1992 a short newspaper article got Krystal's attention. Although it didn't mention Damian's name, it described him complete and claimed he needed someone to "save his skin." Sometime later around September 1992 a very short article appeared in the newspaper, describing Damian's attitude and claiming that someone needed to "save his skin." Then it went on to say that he died. A few days later, several mysterious articles appeared once again describing Damian and claiming that his methods of attack had been uncovered, though not naming him. Krystal wondered, *is Damian really dead or have cryogenics taken over. Is this just a joke? And if he really is dead, then someone else will move in and take his place.*

At this time both she and Wilbur were attending marital counseling with Tom Denzel. Several sessions were spent on talking solely with Wilbur and his interests. Krystal let it go for a while figuring that he was trying to develop a rapport with him. Yet when it turned into several weeks to months, Krystal finally protested wondering when they were ever going to actually work on anything in the marriage.

As the sessions continued Tom and Wilbur began talking about how there is gold in computers, and that if someone could salvage it, there could be some money there. Wilbur was thrilled with the thought. Krystal sat there and only stared at the counselor. Suspecting that Wilbur was being lead unknowingly into a venture that had no possibilities, she proceeded to observe what Wilbur would do next.

Once more it appeared his car was bugged with talk shows describing getting gold out of computers. Krystal suspected that there were devious individuals behind all of this. If they were CIA, she would never find them. She only knew of several sheriffs possibly being involved, some other detectives, and of course Damian as well as Goldilocks, who also could hide. The problem with trying to bring about charges was that she had no concrete proof.

What if some of these people were like chameleons – begin good when others were around who might give them away, and being bad when those around them were just as bad as they were? – Then who would know that they would be acting this way? Once more she prayed for direction on what to do. She suspected that this counselor, Tom Denzel, was someone set up by the CIA to downplay anything that Krystal tried to do that was positive.

Stumbling into the kitchen at one point she almost reached for a bottle of her medications when Wilbur stopped her.

"Let's take a look at what you're taking. – Hey, these look a little different!" he claimed.

Krystal noted that the pills were indeed different. There were triangular in shape, light brown in color and had an indented circle in the center. Nothing she had ever seen before. Even though Wilbur had no interest in Krystal's beliefs, she felt he had been used by the Spirit of God, to divert Krystal from taking planted drugs. Krystal rationalized that someone else obviously had entered the house and replaced her prescription. Once more Krystal had to be aware of her surroundings and not to be drugged and out of sorts. Yet Wilbur said no more about it. He seemed to be distracted again with other thoughts.

In time, Wilbur brought the store's old computer system home, completely disassembling it, hoping to glean all the gold from it. With the computer parts mounting in the garage and Wilbur refusing to throw any parts away, Krystal finally protested at the next counseling session having pulled Tom Denzel aside. She told him in no uncertain terms that he was doing nothing, but making her husband look like a fool. With that the counseling sessions were halted. Wilbur finally quit working on the computer systems, having salvaged absolutely no gold whatsoever. All that was left was a heap of computer parts sitting idly in the garage worth absolutely nothing.

By now Krystal had heard nothing more from the State Board of Psychology Review, and so she figured that "Rex" had been a set-up to divert her attention. *I guess the FBI or CIA or whomever wanted to keep this whole thing quiet, so they tried to fool me into thinking this would stop, but it's only getting worse!* She sat down at her computer, looking over her story and began to cry uncontrollably. When she started to tear up her story, Wilbur immediately came into the room.

Restraining her hands he said, "You don't want to tear up this book!" Krystal did not know if he understood what the story was about, yet something compelled him to stop her from destroying her work.

"But nobody will ever believe me!" she replied. For the next several weeks she did not work on her story and pondered if she indeed was sane at all.

As if in response to her thoughts, someone did reply. One night while lying awake, she thought she heard someone enter the back door. The dog as well was asleep upstairs and was not alerted. She listened, but heard nothing. Then when she was about to fall back asleep, she thought she heard the back door close softly. When she heard one of her cats cry out momentarily, she thought perhaps this person accidentally stepped on one of them on their way out.

In the morning she checked all around and found nothing missing. Then when she checked her computer, she found a file that she had not put there.

The file appeared in the same format that she had been writing the drafts for her story, but this one had more information in it. Written in rather choppy half-sentences, it unveiled data that Krystal was longing to hear. It talked about the situation with Damian, how he was using cameras and microphones, and that Damian, 'doesn't believe in the power of Jesus Christ, but wants to steal away a prophet from another church. Willing to make me look bad to church, so they disband me – didn't work. Put story together how they led me to the city park and were to lead Ernie there as well, to commit murder (mine), didn't work, then they could kill off the prophet and the Adventist church; if Ernie killed me, then he would be blamed for it.' The note went on to describe some other ideas of Damian's in terms of theology and what Damian believes about being god himself and indicated that we were pawns in his chess game.

When Krystal read this, she realized this was the person who entered her house the previous night. Sighing with great relief, now Krystal had some solid evidence that she was not crazy, and that Damian was indeed doing a lot of these things. This note also confirmed her suspicions about what had transpired at the city park several years prior. Whoever this someone was that risked letting her know this, was working on the same track as she was and she let it go at that. There was no way to prove who wrote it, so she had nothing conclusive to take to a lawyer.

Perhaps there were some good people in on this surveillance, but the bad ones were organized enough to be on their best behavior while the good ones were around. In time, this proved to be true, as the bad ones let other local people in on this surveillance game. Krystal suspected Sheriff Cory Dumas had a lot to do with it, as she had encountered him on several occasions, indicating that he knew nothing about such, yet laughing all the while. Similar comments also came from Leonard Blare, at her work as well as other people at work. They were of like mind making derogatory remarks about women in general and that they could not possibly be as smart as men, about black people calling their unmentionable names and denying religious thinking having no interest whatsoever in a Savior to turn around their lives and their habits.

This attitude even included her neighbor, Randy Hellman, who began eyeing Krystal's property as something to covet. Although Krystal had been putting up a fence to divide the property and to keep her dog contained, Randy did not like it and began throwing beer bottles on her side and other various pieces of trash. Krystal could not specifically prove it was him doing it as she never saw him, but she always found the strewn items along the property line by his house.

It was about this time in the political arena that President George H.W. Bush., began to promote Operation Lock-up to give law enforcement more power to take criminals off the street. Yet this operation did nothing for the Krystal household. Equipment from time to time would break down. Lights would go out for unknown reasons. Krystal suspected Damian's death was a spoof on her and was really still alive and well. And Damian was not brought up before the Psychology Review Board, but instead was allowed to continue practicing his form of psychology and fool others into his demented way of thinking. As a reward for law enforcement to keep their silence, they were awarded hundreds of thousands of dollars under Bush under the guise of Operation Lock-up for their good work. So the blackmailing continued within law enforcement and Krystal suffered for it.

On another visit to see how Martha was doing, Krystal again was watching TV. This time a news flash came across showing several people on the golf course including former President Reagan who turned towards the camera calling Damian an "asshole". Then this ad viewed several other individuals who likewise did the same thing including President George H.W. Bush. Krystal had already been familiar with Goldilocks' attempts at these ads, but because he was not in any of them, she wondered if they possibly were from the Cleveland office of the FBI. She would find out later that her assumption was true and Director Robert Snuggles was behind these ads. She returned to her own home later that afternoon.

Once more Krystal's home situation was not improving. There were attempts at making noises at night just enough to arouse Krystal, disturbing her sleep cycle. Again, Wilbur looked tired and dragged out as well and both were once more getting on edge. Krystal decided one day to do the laundry in an attempt to put some distance between her and Wilbur. However, Wilbur followed her. Krystal turned around to look at him and noted a very tense and frustrated look in his eyes and she did not like it. An argument ensued, and although Wilbur never had struck Krystal previously, he began to take his belt off as if he would use it. Krystal could visualize a very vivid picture of him beating her with it. Scared, Krystal ran outside. Wilbur retreated back upstairs. When Krystal came back inside she put the laundry in the dryer and returned upstairs as well.

At the top of the stairs, Wilbur was waiting for her. Although he had put the belt down, he demanded that she take her medications and stood, appearing to tower over her in a posture of power. Had Krystal not complied, she felt he would have forced the medications down her throat.

Retreating upstairs she prayed as to what to do. The marriage seemed to be going no place except downhill. It was apparent to Krystal that she was unable to convince Wilbur, as he viewed her as going crazy. If she insisted on him listening to her, he would always take her to the hospital. They could not keep doing this as the unpaid amounts left over from what the insurance companies were not paying were beginning to mount up. As Krystal poured out her heart to her Creator, a still small voice answered her, *do what you must.* Krystal then made plans to initiate the divorce.

In the meantime Krystal began writing more letters not only to the FBI, but other sources of media, in order for her voice to be heard on how the CIA and others were harassing her life. Krystal never knew how far the letters got, but it gave her satisfaction of finding some way to fight back.

Now that the surrounding property by the Kruczyinski house had been sold, several homes were starting to be built there. One interested Krystal as it was planted exactly on what would have been her lot had the property been kept in the family's name. When Krystal asked Martha who bought the property there, Martha described a very nice, bald-headed man who introduced himself as a future neighbor and claimed he sold life insurance on the side. As soon as Martha said this, Krystal became suspicious. Henry had also sold life insurance before he retired.

Weeks passed and Krystal could observe the partly finished basement from the school property. As she noted a lot of standing water in the basement, she *chided all you got was a swamp!* Krystal walked around the area which led down a ravine. She used to find arrowheads there and she recalled great memories of the family enjoying the wooded area.

Upon walking along what had been the Nike Road, she neared the partly finished basement. She noted a bald-headed man in a gray car pulling into the driveway with license plate, LY777. Krystal noted that this was her father's license plate as it had been easy for him to remember. This man in the car only glared at Krystal.

With President George H.W. Bush losing the election in November 1992, he right away pardoned all those involved in the Iran-Contra affair, thereby ending any more inquires by Congress. Krystal feared that this would only allow the participants to go about and do as they pleased. Robert Gates, head of the CIA, declined to continue as director and was replaced under President Clinton by James Woolsey. Krystal wondered w*here would Robert Gates go, and what kinds of things would he do.* However, Krystal could not speculate any more on this as she neared her divorce date.

In the mean time she worked on her book, recalling more of the 1987 Friendly's conversation and transferring her notes to disks. No sooner had she done so, her computer first froze and then crashed. Her only resolve was to replace it with another computer. At least she had not lost her story material.

The petition for dissolution allowed Wilbur to have unlimited visitation rights with providing child support. Krystal would have Joshua otherwise in her care, and would take care of the unpaid bills.

No sooner had the petition been filed when a barrage of mailings and flyers arrived at the household from the Coalition for Father's Rights. Krystal noted that they were mailed in surrounding towns near Scoria. She recalled that Damian had once lived in that area. Both Krystal and Wilbur agreed the flyers were disgusting and in bad taste, and since both had agreed on visitation rights, they promptly threw all the flyers away. Krystal had noted that some of the flyers posted an older man wearing glasses with a somewhat familiar face.

However, Damian had not produced the flyers. He was involved with a divorce settlement and custody battle for his own child. Krystal later found out the flyers were from Leonard Blare and other sheriffs, but at the time she thought they might be from Damian.

As soon as her divorce was made public, Krystal's neighbor, Randy Hellman, insisted on buying some property from her. Although Krystal had been busy with trying to make preparations for the divorce, she finally obliged in selling him a half acre hoping that she could use some of the money for the bills.

In March 1993 the dissolution was finalized. The judge was Shep Gridlock, who previously was the guardianship lawyer for Brittany. Krystal had not seen Brittany since she moved back to Virginia, and was unaware that Brittany had returned to Scoria.

Even though Krystal sold the half acre to Randy, the money went towards her mortgage. She decided she would have to take on another job. Knowing that the house was bugged and with Wilbur out, she began to openly carry on conversations with those who were listening, not knowing if they were friend or foe. She reasoned, *perhaps if we have some Bible readings and other insightful ventures, they'll understand what I was trying to tell them in 1987. Maybe then they'll be ready because Christ is returning soon, and there will be no turning back then.*

At one point she expressed her disgust over whoever for bugging not only her computer, but Joshua's games as well.

She immediately heard a reply from the television speaker, although it was not on, "That was us!" was the reply.

Speculating that somehow the electric outlets had some bugging device in them, Krystal asked, "Us – who?" No reply came.

She could only surmise that Goldilocks as well as others were involved in such a devious scheme. Krystal became irritated more so than before. *Such a brazen attitude – to boldly state that 'we bugged your computer' and thought that whole incident was funny – they ought to be taken out and shot!* As Krystal contemplated what purpose their aggravation would have served, she could only think about the married couple who Damian counseled and then shot and killed each other. *That's what they wanted us to do – to get so frustrated and be at each other's throat to the point that we would kill each other,* Krystal concluded. Almost ready to vomit, Krystal decided to once again confront the FBI about surveillance in her house.

With that resolve a long line of letters were written by Krystal, including ones to the Cleveland Office of the FBI and Director Robert Snuggles. This time Krystal produced copies of her hospital unpaid bills, as well as others and then claiming that her mental health had been damaged. She demanded that they provide her with the tape from the 1987 conversation as well as $10 million be placed in her bank account for damages done to her and her household. She then wrote to the FBI office in Washington, D.C. as well.

The following evening she heard a noise downstairs, and sounded like something hitting the window. Her dog, Pepper, had been laying on the couch next to it. In the morning, she found a bullet hole in the storm window. She called the Sheriff's Department and they sent out Cory

Dumas, who Krystal suspected as causing problems in her household. He virtually laughed off her notion that someone would shoot at her window. When he asked who she thought would do such a thing, she gave him several names, including some coworkers of FarmAgriMark. As soon as she said those names, Cory laughed and would not look at her. He said there was no need to file a report because there was no proof that anyone had shot at the window. Then he walked away laughing.

Later on, Krystal received a letter from the Cleveland office of the FBI. Director Robert Snuggles replied that he had no knowledge of any tape and that if she had any problems in her household she should contact the local law enforcement. Krystal was infuriated, but replaced the window. Two weeks later a similar incident occurred whereby another bullet hole appeared. Once again she called the Sheriff's Department. They sent a different deputy, one who seemed genuinely interested in positively serving the public. The deputy searched in vain for a shell casing. Upon finding none, Krystal indicated that she wanted it in the record that she suspected someone had shot at her window. He obliged and a report was filed.

Krystal managed to find a part-time job as clerk for the Scoria city police department. Working her day job at FarmAgriMark, she filled in as clerk in the evening shift. There wasn't much time left for other activities, but Krystal was able to pay for Joshua's schooling at the Christian school.

Although the Waco, Texas Branch Davidian incident had passed by, it was not without effects on Krystal and Joshua. Since the Branch Davidians had broken away from the Adventist Church, the media wanted to keep the association there. The church, however, bluntly stated that they were not the same as the Adventist Church and were not associated in any way with the Branch Davidians. Leonard Blare liked to visit Krystal in the lab at work and taunt her by talking about the incident in front of her. When he saw no response from her, he would leave. Then Krystal would tell her co-workers that there was no association with her church to the Davidians, and that as Adventists, "we get blamed for everything!" Then Krystal would dismiss any accusations and walk away.

At one point she was looking outside the window at work and

noted a man with long black curly hair dressed in a suit, departing from Leonard's side of the building. Immediately the small still voice said inside her, *he's the one you refer to as Goldilocks!* Krystal watched him for a long time and then conjectured that he probably had quite a hand in the harassment she was undergoing not only in her household, but here at work as well.

In Joshua's school he was put on the spot on how to handle the Waco situation. Joshua, not understanding the dynamics of what was transpiring in Texas, gave a simple answer wishing not to be singled out. Other Adventist children were exposed to similar situations.

The Texas FBI camp was split on what approach to take and finally resorted to allowing the more militant sector taking the offensive and ending the siege. Right after the ATF agents were killed in an attempted raid on the compound, the Adventist Church went to work establishing a fund to help out the families of these ATF agents, along with community service work. The church upheld the writings of their well-known prophet, Ellen White, who wrote about being watchmen and light bearers," mending broken hearts as best they could.

One day Krystal returned home from her full-time job earlier than usual. As she opened the door of her house she could hear a female voice screaming at the dogs. Krystal now had two dogs who came to greet her, but appeared cowed. As Krystal closed the door the screaming stopped. No one else was in the house and Krystal could only surmise that the voices were coming from the planted microphones there. Krystal was not sure whose voice it was, but it was definitely female. Perhaps Brittany, perhaps someone else. At this time she was unsure, but she did not like this taking place.

Although busy with both jobs, Krystal rented the movie, Silence of the Lambs. Upon finishing it, she commented, "If this is your rendition of my story, it stinks!" She figured that the psychologist in the movie was a direct display of Damian and how he acted. And at the end of the movie when the psychologist walked away and Hannibal was to go after him, Krystal balked. "You don't seem to want to stop Damian. I've tried to get his license taken away and you people stopped me! – Everything I do to try to rectify my situation, you stop me! – Your movie really stinks! All the way to high heaven, this whole thing stinks!"

Then once again she chose to read out loud from the Bible, as well as other books. She tried to reiterate what was stated in 1 Peter 3:9, "not wishing for any to perish, but for all to come to repentance." Yet she wondered if she was too late to let them know.

When Pastor Andy accepted a position elsewhere. Krystal was saddened by his departure. His replacement, Pastor Kevin, when first approaching Krystal stated, "I know your story."

Krystal was taken back. "How do you know my story? Is it just what others have told you about me and for that matter what have others told you about me?"

His reply was sharp and cutting, as if he did not wish to hear any more from Krystal.

As Krystal drove home she decided to come down the I-71. As she drove past one exit, a make-shift sign had been erected out of sheet metal roofing and placed very close to the roadway. It read, "Brittany: God bless...." Krystal contemplated that sign. She thought perhaps Ernie placed it there, being a state trooper and traveling along the highways, but she was not sure. She thought about the simple message. *Was it blessing Krystal or was it condemning Brittany? Could it have read God damn Brittany. It could go either way! And maybe both ways!* Regardless someone was letting Krystal know that Brittany was involved in her household as well.

Over the next few years, Krystal would come to the conclusion that others were supplying Pastor Kevin with information, but as before this information was tainted. While teaching the children, two infrequent young visitors became very disruptive in the classroom. Krystal finally remarked to them about their behavior.

Their reply was, "You have to cast us demons out!" Krystal had not been blind. She remembered the incident where she had to wake up Joshua because someone had been trying to play head games with him. Now as she viewed these children, she felt somehow they were being manipulated as well.

Figuring that Damian or someone else was probably working on one child and Brittany on another, Krystal refused to cast them out. Instead she turned to the rest of the class and became involved in their activities. At last the children became so disruptive jumping around the room that they left on their own. When they were gone the other children commented that they were glad they had left. Yet Krystal wondered, *is this head game ever going to stop – would anyone ever see this?*

Upon returning to work at the police department, Krystal did a little investigating on her own. She searched the juvenile file and discovered Brittany had been causing disturbances for Melody and John. There were several accounts where the police had been called regarding instances of stolen money.

The following week at her day job, Leonard Blare sat down across from her at break time and began to talk to her about how his wife's Bible was marked to indicate specific phrases. Krystal became suspicious of his intentions and wondered how much misrepresented Scripture was he selling, to whom and for what price.

Then the following Sabbath, the church clerk related that she received a threatening letter from somewhere in Kentucky telling her to come down and argue the Sabbath. Krystal surmised it was probably Leonard, originally from Kentucky, who sent the letter. The clerk was reassured when she was told to ignore it.

While at church, Krystal continued to read more manuscripts in the church library. "Now and onward till the close of time the people of God should be more earnest, more wide awake, not trusting in their own wisdom, but in the wisdom of their Leader..." Yet Krystal wondered how wide awake was this church. She knew from conversations with Sherita that there was a split in the church whereby the blacks had formed their own conference.

When Krystal asked Sherita about this, Sherita responded by "They didn't meet our needs." She then went on to explain about how Purgatory mentioned in the Quran along with the seven levels below and seven levels above related to the first resurrection. Krystal wondered why the church would ignore any passages related to Purgatory until one day she brought her Quran to church hoping to enlighten anyone. This was not to be as one member vehemently said that it was sacrilegious to bring that book in the church.

At that point Krystal began distancing herself more from the church. Although she did not eat pork, she still was not a vegetarian, and this did not set well with some people. Also she still drank coffee, and although she found working two jobs she needed to stay awake, they did not see her reasoning.

Still knowing that Scoria was strongly Republican and knowing that the majority of law enforcement in town voted for Bush and lost, Krystal pretty much kept to herself. She tried not to talk politics while at the police department, but instead focused more of her time on community service. Realizing that some of the detectives were probably checking Krystal out, she figured that some were probably now involved in the surveillance as well. This proved to be true when Greg Fleuzy remarked to her one day about her plans to fix up her house which she had only voiced in her kitchen that morning.

He stated, "That's never going to happen!" as Krystal was viewing plans in a book at the police station. For several days he touted a sweat shirt that claimed he had been in the FBI academy training. Krystal surmised this action was for show and to taunt her. Yet when she approached others in the department about her house being bugged, they brushed her off.

There were others who taunted her at the police department as well. Two cops who Krystal named Abbott and Costello did not like some of her opinions stated in her own household. As Greg Fleuzy shared what he had discovered he twisted what she said to make it appear otherwise. Officers Abbott and Costello decided to play a game with Krystal. Sneaking up behind Krystal Officer Costello goosed her.

Krystal to his surprise immediately looked over her shoulder calmly, "Is that the only thing you want?"

Offended that she had replied in such a manner and the fact that he was embarrassed in front of Officer Abbott and another cop, he promptly walked away.

Krystal was hurt inside because it just seemed no matter what she did, where she went, nobody would just leave her alone for a reprieve. Instead, the attacks constantly were there. Krystal decided not to speak to Officer Costello when he approached her later and she left for the day.

Krystal had been contacted earlier the next day to come in as a call-in dispatcher/clerk. This person had claimed that she wanted to be part of the detective division and work on cases as Greg Fleuzy did. This made Krystal somewhat suspicious if she was not involved in the surveillance of her house as well.

As Krystal was used to clocking in as soon as she got at the police station, out of automation she did the same thing. Those ending second shift and those beginning third shift were standing around in the hallway waiting to clock in or out Krystal went ahead and clocked in, this immediately brought a teasing. They proceeded to tell her that she had to wait to exactly 11 p.m. to clock in. At the same time Officer Abbott was trying to get Krystal's attention, but she was concentrating on the issue at hand.

"So what happens now?" she asked. "Do I get taken out and shot at sunrise?"

"Yes!" came the immediate reply from both Officers Sigorski and Mashinski, who responded jokingly.

"Over a time card?" Krystal posed. When they nodded in agreement smirking, she continued, "This sure is a tough place to work! – No wonder you go through so many clerks." She took their joking one step further. "I want to know something – where do you bury all the bodies?"

They immediately claimed they could not reveal such information in a jovial context. As Krystal placed her card in the bottom of the rack, Officer Abbott continued to try to get Krystal's attention.

"You can stand in line right here," as he motioned making space for her to stand between him and Officer Costello.

"No, that's all right. I'll stand in the back of the bus," next to Sigorski and Mashinski. She did not wish to invoke any of the type of response that she encountered the other day.

The conversation continued with Officer Abbott beginning to brag about the previous encounter in the hallway between Krystal and Officer Costello. Krystal had hoped that such an occurrence had been put aside and forgotten, but to Krystal's dismay, it was brought out in the open, just like a raw wound that someone picks at and opens it up so that it bleeds more. Krystal stared at the reactions of Officer Costello, as well as her friends, Sigorski and Mashinski.

Officer Abbott continued to pour out the details including, "We got her good! – We goosed her!"

However, Krystal noticed that the response from Sigorski and Mashinski was totally unlike that of Abbott's. In fact they verbally protested doing such an action.

All Abbott could reply was with, "Costello did it!"

Krystal thought, *yeah, Costello did it all right – with you promoting him.*

When Sigorski and Mashinski asked Krystal if that was true, all she could feel was a lump in her throat. It was bad enough the incident had occurred the first time, but to have to now brought out in the open for all to hear was just too much for Krystal to take. She knew that now the whole department had heard all about it.

She responded with a stifled, "I was had!"

Sigorski and Mashinski then began to berate those involved in the original incident. As Krystal searched her mailbox for any memos, she decided she had had enough of this conversation. As she made her way to the doorway of the office, Costello advanced towards her with a "hi."

Krystal was not happy with what had taken place now and she was in no mood to be cordial to anyone. So she replied with a strained and disgusted "hi."

As she sat in the office, Abbott came around the corner and then remarked to the others as he returned to the hallway, "She's just sitting there!"

Krystal thought, *so what's it to you? If I chose to sit here and not talk to anyone that's my business.* Relieved when the 11 hour arrived and the hallway cleared, she walked down to the pop machine.

She returned to her desk and waited for the dispatcher to collect the second shift reports so that Krystal could enter them in the daily log. In the meantime she did a little reading. Not long afterwards Officer Costello returned to the police station and approached her asking for change for $20. Krystal proceeded to fulfill his request, but she did it silently and rapidly.

He commented, "I thought maybe I could have a little fun with you."

She quickly replied angrily, "I don't think that's possible with you."

"Yes, it is."

"No, it isn't. Because the next thing I knew I was out in the hallway being screwed over, literally. – Personally, I'd like a little more privacy when I'm getting screwed. If you don't like me, just say so. That way I'll ignore you and you can ignore me and we'll get along just fine!"

"I don't want it that way! – I mean what I say that I like you."

"You have a strange way of showing affection. First, you tell me that you like me. Then you run down the hallway to see what other fun you can make of me with your friends. – That is what you were doing, was it not?" Finally Costello admitted that that part was true, but trying to reiterate that he liked Krystal.

"That doesn't make any sense. Why would you tell someone you like them and then run down the hallway to make fun of that same person? What did I ever do to you to deserve this kind of treatment?"

He really had no answer.

She continued, "Maybe you're part of the group that when someone like me goes over to dispatch, you're sitting on the outside waiting for them to mess up so you can tear them down."

Krystal was not sure who was involved in that group, but she had heard about it previously from two of the dispatchers. She was not happy with this group trying to see if they could get rid of the dispatchers, as if it were some sort of trophy they were earning for the most people they destroyed. Since the other dispatchers were all female, Krystal could only surmise that those harassing them had no use for females unless they were subservient to their male desires.

Costello flatly denied that he had anything to do with such an action.

Krystal continued still searching for a reason why she had been treated to look like a fool. "You know, I could get the rest of the women here together and we could come up with something about you to embarrass you with."

He immediately protested, "I wouldn't like that at all!"

"Then why do it to me? Is your testosterone level too high? Or maybe you have too much jock itch!" She felt that perhaps it was just the fact that she was a woman and someone had a preconceived idea about women. Krystal could only surmise what that preconceived idea might be. He protested her comment and started to walk away angrily.

"I just want to know why!" She shouted to him.

"It's because you're always reading out of that book," he commented noting that she had been reading out of her Bible.

"This?" she inquired and then began to chuckle inside. *That's about par for the course,* she thought. She was not unaccustomed to being ridiculed, but she felt the situation definitely needed clarification. And she was still trying to figure out exactly who was in her house watching her so she pursued her train of thought.

"Look," she said. "I'm not reading this to make an impression on you or anyone else. I'm not even telling you to read this. As selfish as this may sound, I'm reading it just for me. – When I come in here, they really don't give me that much work to do. So when I'm done with my work, I read. Somebody has to baby-sit the window and take care of the fines and bonds. So I have to do something to pass the rest of the time. If you don't care to read it that's your business, and I really don't care if you don't read it. – I'm reading it for me."

Then pointing to a picture in the beginning of her Bible of Jesus in the garden of Gethsemane, she inquired, "You see this guy? I happen to like Him! He saved my life a couple of times!" Then trying to explain herself a little better, she went on. "I put up with a lot of crap on the outside. So when I come in here it's like seeking a little rest and relaxation. Ever since I came down to this planet, I've had to put up with nonsense. So when I come in here and read this book, I'm trying to get re-fortified so that I can better handle all the loony bins that are out there." Costello said nothing.

Krystal went on. "Don't tell me. Let me guess. – I'll bet you think I some kind of sexual prude who reads this book and knows absolutely nothing about sex!" She did not give him any time to answer that. Instead she went on to describe her former lifestyle before she met Christ.

When he balked at some of her story, she finally told him. "You know I can tear you up one side and down the other, and I don't need a knife to do it with!" His face paled as she spoke. "You don't want to make me mad!" she exclaimed. Then he departed.

The next evening when once more the same clerk called off sick, Krystal took her place. Both Sigorski and Mashinski commented, "Hey, you're still alive! – You didn't get shot at sunrise!"

Partaking of the joke Krystal responded, "They told me if I clean up my act and straighten up and fly right, they'll let me live just one more day!" Then she laughed with them.

Once again Abbott tried to distract Krystal by commenting that she could stand in line right in between Abbott and Costello.

However, Krystal remarked, "That's okay. I'll go stand in the back of the bus!" indicating behind Sigorski. When she proceeded to walk in that direction, Abbott yelled out, "Hey, you ain't no nigger!" Costello remarked, "Black person!" and Abbott tried to correct himself.

Krystal decided to seize the opportunity. Walking backwards to where the two were standing she looked at Abbott and in black dialect said, "Say what?" Abbott repeated his corrected statement.

Then Krystal nonchalantly stated, "Oh, no master! My mammy done told me I'z only white on the outside." Then getting a gleam in Krystal's eye and smile across her face, she exclaimed, "But I sho' is black on the inside!" As she said so, Abbott began to retreat away from her.

Krystal further stated, "And black is beautiful! I am somebody! And you don't treat me this way. – Badge or no badge! I am somebody!" Then pointing her finger directly at him, she stated, "Now, you got that?" By now Abbott was plastered up against the wall and could not even look at Krystal.

Putting her arm down, Krystal began to mumble in a manner like she had seen some black people do. "Tell me I got a problem. –You're the one with a problem!" All those standing in the hallway loudly applauded as Krystal moved to the back of the line next to Sigorski.

Abbott shouted out, "You're mean!"

Undaunted Krystal responded, "Yeah, and I eat nails for breakfast, too!"

Then both Sigorski and Mashinski both commented that Abbott definitely deserved that and had it coming to him. For quite some time Abbott left her alone.

Later at the police department, she ran the license plate, LY777, through the LEADS system to determine the owner of such plate. As she did so, she discovered that it belonged to Robert Snuggles, living on Tulip Lane (which was the old Nike Site road), at the house that was built on what was to be Krystal's share of the property. The read-out also stated that he worked for the federal government, and Krystal knew he was head of the Cleveland office of the FBI.

One morning, Krystal went to her home town to take Martha grocery shopping. As they were stopped at the stoplight, Krystal noticed a silver/gray car behind her with the license plate LY 777. As she looked at the driver in her side and rearview mirrors, she noted it was the same bald-headed person who had driven up to the half-finished house on the piece of swampland she had looked at. Figuring it was Director Robert Snuggles, she decided to let him know what she thought of his tactic of "trying to imitate her father" by claiming he sold life insurance and using his license plate. She also was angry at his lack of responsibility in his letters of reply to Krystal and his ignoring of the problems that existed in her household.

As Krystal engaged in idle talk with Martha, she rolled down her window to act like she was adjusting her side mirror, all the time making sure she had the attention of Director Robert Snuggles. When he looked at her, she promptly 'flipped him the bird' in her side mirror. Noting that he saw it, he just shrugged his shoulders, but Krystal glared at him in her rearview mirror. When the light turned green, she revved the engine somewhat to indicate she was not done with him yet. After they finished grocery shopping, Krystal left Marth's house and returned to her own home.

Krystal continued to read aloud from Ellen White's writings. Krystal now viewed herself as a soldier in the making in the Lord's army and began to draw on strength from the only Source she knew who could give her an abundant supply. It was not by chance that she was quite independent. She was raised that way for a purpose. When alone on the battlefield and in her fox hole, she would rely on the strength from her Preserver of Life when all others around her may be failing.

Krystal knew very well that she was not perfect. She was just as human as anyone else. She was living on a planet marred with sin and imperfection along with others who had fallen short of the glory of God. Even the prophets in the Bible were not perfect. Yet God still used them, and in their imperfections they would grow in His knowledge and His grace to fulfill His purpose.

At times the loneliness was quite a burden to bear. Yet many times when she was reading aloud, she felt a presence in the room. There were times also when resting she could feel the hand of someone stroking her head as a sign of reassurance.

She felt her heart was shredded and at one point expressed this sentiment very emphatically outloud. Yet something else seemed to take over as she stated, "Either you start mending my heart, or He is going to take me away from you!" At that moment she felt herself go invisible and then reappear again. She knew that such a feat could only be performed by the Preserver of Life. Later on as she watched TV, an interesting ad came across depicting the same thing and she knew then that what she had felt was true and others had seen it.

One evening at the police station a highway patrol trooper approached the window, but kept his back to Krystal. She managed to partly look at his face, not realizing it was Don Klapper from COINTELPRO at Kent State. He ignored her stare as he asked for background checks for seven people who were supposedly involved in a special protection job. As she glanced at the list she noted her neighbor's name, Randy Hellman, amongst others. Due for shift change, she left the request with the next clerk.

As she turned into her drive, she noted a van at Randy's house with Grey Fleuzy. Randy and Greg spent much time talking and then Greg left.

The following day, Krystal noted a camper parked in Randy's yard directly facing Krystal's house. When this caught the attention of her dogs, one of them barked and looked back at Krystal as if to say, *there's something going on here*. As Krystal approached she noticed Randy in the camper with a high tech mounted camera.

Krystal shouted as she came forward in his direction, "You're not going to do this to me, too!" Her dog barked alongside her as if to confirm this. Even Randy's dog turned in his direction and began barking at him. Randy, however, only hid in the back of the camper.

A few days later Krystal enrolled in the Citizen's Academy offered by the police. She spent several weeks in the course when Greg Fleuzy gave a speech one evening. His topic was night viewing with a high tech camera.

He bluntly stated, "We can see everything you do, even at night!" As he said this he looked directly at Krystal. She had suspected that someone was watching her in the bedroom and was taking pictures of her nude as well in the bathroom, and getting their jollies. Although she could not prove anything, she became angry.

Finally, in February 1995, in desperation and rage, she sent another letter in general to the Cleveland office of the FBI. She reiterated needing $10 million for damages in her household. She quoted that there was no justice in her case and she demanded that they do something.

A few days later two FBI agents showed up on her porch. One was Agent Art Castle from the local office. The other was Agent Alex Flippant from the Cleveland office. Both showed their badges with Agent Flippant claiming he was a psychologist.

Agent Flippant's first question to Krystal was, "Are you taking any medications?" Then started to chuckle.

Krystal was offended by his brazen attitude, and stated, "You don't understand what I've been going through!"

When Agent Castle showed her the letter they received and asked if it was hers, she responded affirmatively and undauntedly. Both agents bore surprised looks on their faces. Then Krystal went on to describe the tactics of Damian, how she knew him from the psychiatric hospital where she had worked, and how he had been harassing her in her own household. She expressed that she wanted to know who else was there. These agents claimed the FBI was not involved in the surveillance.

Krystal thought, *maybe not you, but maybe someone else.* Feeling that she wasn't getting anywhere in the conversation, she told them that she heard someone had shot Damian. She banked on the premise that if Damian was working for the FBI, they would be upset to hear this. As suspected they did become upset.

They demanded that she cease and desist writing letters to the FBI. Before leaving, Agent Castle asked if there were any connections with the CIA.

Krystal responded, "Maybe Damian's working for them as well!" With that she walked back inside and shut the door. Disgusted that she really got nowhere, she contemplated her next step.

The next day she was called into the police department and they asked that she leave her position citing her letters. All Krystal could say was, "This was something they should have been handled a long time ago!" So in early 1995 she walked out of that job.

She heard nothing from the FBI, and decided she had had enough of the community's lack of response in dealing with her issues. Packing up all the computer parts Wilbur had left in the garage, she hauled several car loads to the recycling bins in plain sight in Scoria,

"Make me look like a fool! -You people are the fools!" she cried as she drove off.

CHAPTER
13

From time to time Krystal wondered about the pardoned Iran-Contra affair, CIA agents by President Bush; *were they here or somewhere else causing problems?* When her brother, Matt, returned for a visit, he claimed that he had been hearing how great pork was for the body. Krystal became suspicious. *If the CIA knows that I don't eat pork, what better way to cause division in this household by promoting it in some way for someone else – Perhaps Matt's truck is bugged as well.*

On Matt's next visit, things seemed to be going better for him. As he sat in the living room conversing with her, Krystal silently prayed for his protection and welfare. When she looked in Matt's direction, she saw a faint image of Henry standing right behind Matt. It disappeared almost immediately, but she felt that Matt was in good hands. She did not mention it to him, as he departed with his semi to the West Coast and then up to Alaska.

Krystal became involved with prison ministry, writing letters to recently converted inmates to her faith. Krystal scrutinized how genuine his faith was questioning basic tenants. He responded truthfully and correctly retelling his life story. Realizing that he needed supplies such as an alarm clock, she used what little money she had and sent it to him in the nearby prison. He responded gratefully for her thoughtfulness.

This did not go unnoticed. Some of the watchers ridiculed her with TV ads. Others kept silent. Deciding to visit she entered the prison lobby. A still small voice said, *once you go through that gate, you're not coming back out.* Unsure why she returned to her car.

Later the local newspaper that Danny Boy had uncovered a "plot" in the prison whereby a gun was passed behind bars. *No wonder I was warned,* concluded Krystal. *Somebody meant to shoot me there.*

Krystal never returned to the prison. Upon his release she learned that some of the silent watchers taught him to drive and he was able to obtain a driver's license. She felt reassured that there were some good people in the law enforcement ranks.

In spring of 1994, Richard Nixon passed away. When Krystal heard that police were called out to guard the funeral procession, Krystal laughed. "Let the dead bury the dead!" she cried out loud. "I'll stay here. I don't need to see his funeral."

Then to help ventilate some of her feelings, she baked a devil's food chocolate cake. Decorating the chocolate frosting with marching candy dinosaurs she stated out loud, "You've heard of the marching Weathermen and such at Kent State? Well, now we have the marching dinosaurs." In the middle she formed a large question mark. "We don't know what went wrong with your line of thinking."

For the next several days she enjoyed her cake. This did not go unnoticed in the community as word spread what she did. Leonard once again began to harass her at work. This time he claimed he was going to become a court bailiff. The news made Krystal feel ill at ease. To vent her feelings, she retreated to the basement hazardous waste room. Having securely shut all doors, she began smashing glass jars of samples to be disposed of.

"How could this community be so stupid?" she shouted. After she felt release of her emotions, she returned upstairs. Soon afterwards, she learned Leonard's application for bailiff was denied. Again, Krystal felt at least someone was listening to her.

Relaxing in front of her TV one evening, an ad displayed a black Jeep Cherokee recklessly scaling a stone wall protecting a house. Krystal frequently stated that she built a wall around her heart, she pondered on this scene. Later she discovered that Woolly Bully, an FBI agent from Burning Bridges owned a Jeep Cherokee.

If the FBI are involved with this surveillance, perhaps he was one that tried to take me at church, she speculated. Although Krystal attended church, she was never acquainted with the conference elders. One Sabbath it was announced that Bryan Mallard from the conference would be giving the sermon. Although the sermon was excellent and Krystal really enjoyed it, she was not able to meet directly with Bryan Mallard.

A few weeks later the local church body decided to send Krystal to a workshop held at the conference offices. While there, as she looked at one of the elders nodding to her, a voice came to her stating emphatically, *that's Bryan Mallard!* Immediately Krystal's mouth dropped open. Realizing someone else had replaced the true Bryan Mallard for the church sermon weeks ago, she desired to found out who it was. She discovered that her suspicions were true about the church surveillance and that Woolly Bully had given Bryan Mallard's sermon.

Krystal contemplated, *was the church threatened by Woolly Bully since I did not come with them? Is that why he gave the sermon and not Bryan? Was the FBI trying to get closer to me in some devious way?* Krystal could only concluded that it was another attempt to fool her so she would comply with their wishes.

The following Sabbath before leading out the song service she boldly proclaimed that she knew the church was bugged. "You can come here – You might learn something!" Then she continued with her duties. Yet, some of the congregation disagreed with her statement.

Joshua was building his Christian faith as well through the church and his schooling. He commented that the household was quieter since Wilbur moved out. Yet he enjoyed being with Wilbur in their activities. He often commented to Krystal that the divorce was not the worst thing that could happen to him. As a result a deep bond developed between Krystal and Joshua. Although Krystal did not share all the details of what she knew, she did from time to time relay some things to him. She did not tell him about the visit from Agents Castle and Flippant. Nor did she relate the TV ad several days later depicting Agent Castle before a firing squad. Goldilocks stood in the forefront holding a letter he claimed was all a joke. Krystal wondered if Agent Castle knew that Goldilocks was stabbing him in the back like this. Krystal never revealed her suspicious about the two church members who died. Perhaps Goldilocks was involved, and this thought began to frustrate her. No longer working at the police department, she continued her work at FarmAgriMark.

When she learned that Matt stopped for a visit at Martha's, Krystal visited them. This time Matt relayed semi brakes failed not only once, but several times during the year. As a result his crashed, yet he remained unscathed. A passerby in a white car remarked that he was still alive. Also, Matt relayed he no longer ate pork, and drastically changed his eating habits. Krystal felt Henry was definitely looking after Matt.

She was excited and shared this good news with her church. Once more from the podium she spoke of God's ever protecting care for even those who may be lost, but can be found. Krystal claimed, "God protects his own!" as she encouraged the congregation.

Later that week, Krystal noticed another ad on her TV. This time it featured someone looking exactly like Robert Gates, former director of the CIA. Standing by a white car and smiling, he sarcastically claimed responsibility for Matt's accidents. He might as well has said, *I can do whatever I want now and you can't do anything to stop me.* Irritated Krystal shut the TV off wondering why he would be so brazen to admit such.

Since the FBI told her to contact local law enforcement if she felt her house was bugged, she did so. She met with Sheriff Manuel Porlaborda expressing her concern and disgust. She asked about Cory Dumas, Danny Boy, Damian Madden, and Leonard. Sheriff Porlaborda was well acquainted with all of them. He claimed Damian was living out of the area, but was consulted frequently. Krystal had already surmised that a spoof had been played on her and that he was indeed alive. Krystal became adamant that she did not want any such people in her household. Sheriff Porlaborda assured her that if he found out any of his sheriffs were participating in such acts, disciplinary action would be taken.

Shifting topics he talked about his upcoming reelection. When Krystal asked about Leonard, Sheriff Porlaborda stated that he was a good guy and they had used him several times for various things. Disgusted and almost vomiting, Krystal left feeling very unsatisfied that anything would be done to correct her situation.

Several Sabbaths later, a group of youth came to visit and give their testimony about how they came to change their lives. One black youth dressed in a nice suit and tie related his previous gang activities and murders. Then he relayed about a redeeming message he heard from a woman. He then looked directly at Krystal and was beaming. It was then that Krystal realized her message and story told in the restaurant in 1987 had somehow been circulating. *And what better place,* thought Krystal, *to the black people who helped me out in the past.*

Another time while teaching the adult lesson, a gentleman sat down in the last pew. He appeared like one of the previous elders who had died. As Krystal continued with the lesson, she kept looking in his direction. He continually acknowledged Krystal's comments and finally stated, "You know exactly what you're talking about." She thanked him for his comments and encouragement. Then he just disappeared with Krystal not noticing when he left.

Visiting Martha once more, Krystal noted now several homes had been built on their former property. Director Snuggles had already moved into his house. Krystal brought along a letter she had written to make Martha aware. She wondered if Director Snuggles was involved with distorting her message through movies. She reasoned if so, then he probably forged her signature. She was well acquainted with the copyright law and that no agreement occurred between her and anyone else. She speculated, *if they can forge my name, I can forge theirs!* She then used copies of previous FBI letterhead and explained the misconception over the well. To add insult to injury she forged Director Robert Suggles' signature. Martha read the letter and now understood some things. *This way,* thought Krystal, *with mom's house being bugged as well, and with Director Snuggles just over the hill in his house, he's sure to see what I've done and it will be right in his face!*

Krystal return home somewhat satisfied. Money was still an issue for her and decided to supplement her income with newspaper delivery. The day after she filed her application for such, she received lay-off notification from FarmAgriMark. She along with others filed for unemployment compensation, and she was able to keep bills paid with her secondary job.

When the unemployment ran out, she took several part-time jobs, including a criminal record search for Pinkerton Security. At least she was able to keep Joshua in the Christian school and keep bills paid on time.

Even though she had talked with the sheriff's department, the bugging still continued. On one such occasion, she walked outside to get a breath of fresh air. Putting seed in the bird feeders she heard a voice behind him, though she saw no one.

"Krystal, what's going on in this house? – What is all of this that's happening here?"

"You wouldn't believe what I've had to put up with!" Krystal replied. Reassured that this was a heavenly message, she walked back inside feeling more confident.

When she arrived to pick up her newspapers for delivery a few nights later, the presses broke down and delayed the process. The time delay tired her and made for a long sleepless night. When this breakdown continued, Krystal concluded it was occurring once too often. She suspected someone was either trying to get her to quit or tire her enough so that she would crash on the road. *Just another attempt to wear me down*, surmised Krystal.

Arriving the following evening, everything was working fine to begin with. Then equipment malfunctioned, as if someone had pulled a switch. Krystal looked up and said a quick prayer. When the bundle binding machine acted up again, Krystal looked over at it and a Power came through her. A "laser" light shot out from her eyes to the machine. There was a pop, and it immediately stopped malfunctioning, and began running smoothly. Although no one inside had seen exactly what had happened, those conducting surveillance had.

Officer Costello interrupted Krystal's radio station on her car, when she sat waiting for her papers. He stated who he was and said that he had seen what had happened inside. Then he commeted about 'taking care of Saddam Hussein' questioning the absurdity of having her go and do such.

Krystal retorted, "If the CIA sees this, they'll think I can do anything, but I have no power in of myself. All power comes from up above and it's not at my direction to use. I am a vessel and I get used when He feels it's necessary – not anyone else!"

Later when she returned home, her dog greeted her at the door pawing her, as if to say *watch what I do*. Then he grabbed a plastic bag and shook his head ferociously from side to side. He stopped and looked at her as if to say, *that's what I would do with them!* Krystal patted his head in agreement, reassured that there were invisible angels who were observing and recording such events for the Judgment.

At some point, she heard a news report on the radio that Damian this time had been shot and the person who did this had to really struggle with him. Yet nothing appeared in the paper and Krystal wondered about this. *I suppose though if Damian had been involved in everything I suspect, a thorough investigation would take time. Perhaps they would not want to release the news of his death just yet.*

She listened for more news, but now there were reports about cryogenics that the CIA was developing. Recalling that while president, George H.W. Bush tried creating the illusion of a "New World" with Saddam out of Kuwait. Those believing this engaged in shuffling of stocks on the market with lots of sell-offs. Insurance companies were not spared of these sell-offs. Krystal knew this was the same old world it had been and not new and wondered if he was somehow trying to create a false resurrection.

Later when she drove into Scoria, she saw Damian in his a gray Trans Am. Having been pulled over by the police, his features appeared very bright and shiny. A voice over her car radio exclaimed, "He's back!"

Krystal never saw Damian after that, but felt that he was still around. She did not believe his death had been real, but considered the talk about the cryogenics. Maybe he had been shot, but they were trying to keep him alive. Maybe it was to keep this "game" going, she didn't know.

The game continued with the Jon Benet Ramsey murder in December, 1996. There were several ads on Krystal's TV as well as radio trying to indicate that this was a hoax as a spoof being played by Madonna. Krystal had to get completely away from the Scoria community and began scanning through newspaper articles to discover that it was an actual murder. Once again Krystal realized her house was still being bugged.

Later becoming involved in women's jail ministry nearby. She felt confident in relaying her story of how she was lost and then found. Many inmates felt encouraged by this.

Then Krystal secured a full-time position doing medical transcription at Burning Bridges General Hospital. Working third shift, she could not keep her newspaper delivery job. Working on incentive, Krystal produced a lot of work. She saw the opportunity at last to dwindle down her debts, particularly the $10,000 remaining from her past psychiatric stays.

After her shift one morning, she stopped to pick up some groceries. She noted at the far end of the parking lot there was an isolated car with a chubby, gray-haired man, sitting in it. She looked at him wondering what he was doing. As soon as she got in the store, she noted the overhead radio volume increased, and then an ad claiming how great the FBI was and all the wonderful things they did. Krystal began to get a headache, and quickly exited the store. She noted the car at the end of the parking lot was gone.

Still irritated not only with this incident, she wrote another letter to the FBI. This time she asked for $250,000, the penalty for copyright infringement. She sent the letter to Agent Art Castle.

As anticipated, two agents showed up at her doorstep. One was chubby with gray hair, who she recognized from the car in the parking lot. The other was rather scraggly-looking. Neither showed her a proper FBI badge. Krystal noted that the gray-haired man was driving a black Jeep Cherokee, just like the one she had seen in the TV ad, recklessly scaling a rock wall surrounding a house. He claimed he had been at her house before. When Krystal stated it was not him before, but Agent Castle and Agent Flippant, he changed the subject and told her not to send any more letters.

"I'll put the cuffs right on you now if you don't stop!" he asserted and kept reiterating that he was there before. Krystal thought, *I suppose because I've been in the hospital, he thinks he can jerk me around – like I'm some kind of retard or something, but I'm not going to let him do this to me!*

Krystal never did catch the name of this agent, but referred to him as Woolly Bully, because of his brazen attitude towards her. He went on to talk about several things including the fact that Agent Art Castle was now retired and no longer in charge of the case. Then he smiled a sickening grin at Krystal. Undaunted Krystal calmly let him know that she knew Agent Castle was retired.

His grin faded and becoming angry he claimed, "That doesn't matter now. I'm heading the investigation!" Krystal made no comment only thinking, *what investigation? – The FBI has been denying this all along!*

When he once again threatened her with handcuffs, she glared at him thinking, *You go right ahead – I have enough hospital records now that I'll claim by reason of insanity and you won't do anything with me.* Yet she said nothing and just stared at him, recalling that Solomon in the Bible in all his wisdom recognized there was a time to be quiet and not argue with fools!

She asked about the FBI possibly bugging her house, and he denied such. She decided it was futile to ask any more. He already lied to her about being on her porch previously. *Why would he tell me anything different now?* She looked at the black Jeep Cherokee and thought about the ad she had seen. *He's lying about this as well*! she concluded. Then he reiterated that she was not to write any more letters or he would arrest her for doing such. Krystal went back inside feeling left with nothing but lies and hopelessness of a morbid situation.

Later Krystal wrote to the CIA as well as FBI in Washington DC to try to get any records they might have on her. When she finally received letters to the negative, she relayed out loud her dismay in her kitchen. Someone listening in, indicated their presence, and so responded to them.

"Oh, so you're here!" not knowing exactly who it was. "I'm surprised the walls are still standing, since there are so many bugs in this house!"

Krystal then explained that there was no such thing as the well and that she knew Director Snuggles was driving the car with the license plate, LY777.

She explained, "I don't know what you're trying to prove – my dad is dead, and you're not him." Aware that Director Snuggles possibly was trying to portray Krystal's dad, she wondered just how far this 'fake resurrection' game was going to go.

At one point she looked up at a picture of Christ hanging in her kitchen and said, "Oh, Irving, I had a piece of swampland for sale and they bought that too!" She referred to Director Snuggles new house with a basement full of water.

"Well," she claimed, "I may be a dumb Polack, but at least I don't have a swimming pool for a basement!" She exclaimed that it was fair that Director Snuggles bought into that falsehood and claimed, "all's fair in love and war, and this is war, so it's fair!" She still wasn't sure who was listening in, but had to be several law enforcement people as well as FBI.

Pondering over the events, she concluded that there probably were some decent FBI agents somewhere in the bureau, but Woolly Bully certainly was not one of them. She concluded that Woolly Bully was nothing more than a "fat ass," reminding her of some old fat southern sheriff who felt he could push his weight around just because he has a badge on his chest. *And what about Goldilocks? He certainly was no knight in shining armor either.* She concluded that they probably should have formed a special sect of the FBI, known as the PLO – Pathological Liars Organization.

For therapy, Krystal made up a file in which an FBI agent was investigating her case and reporting to her now and again. This file never left her house, but Krystal utilized it for blowing off steam and injecting humor into a situation that underneath only aggravated her. However, this therapy file helped alleviate the tension she would feel.

Krystal continued working in medical transcription. Her boss, Barbie Sue Dull, was not someone Krystal could warm up to, and she wondered about her motives. Yet Krystal did her work without any issues and dwindled down her debts. She wondered how the rest of the country was fairing under the economic situation.

She noted a lot of materialism in the housing industry building not houses, but rather mansions with cathedral ceilings and ranging anywhere $200,000 to $400,000 just in her area. Even her former property boasted many of these mansions. She recalled that before ancient Israel was taken into captivity, they too had built extravagant mansions complete with ornate wood paneling and other trappings. Krystal lamented, *I pity this country, because when the time of tribulation comes upon you, your mansion will be worthless and useless – and you too will be taken into captivity.*

Again TV ads appeared noting Italian wines with Goldilocks claiming he had "turned over a new leaf." Krystal was very skeptical of his attitude and bluntly stated so.

A few nights later when she arrived at work, a person in the medical records section told Krystal, "They're having a horse race in there!"

Unsure when she meant, Krystal she noted everyone else was dressed up complete with new hairdos. She was told by one co-worker that Barbie Sue Dull had arranged for everyone to participate in this "horse race" to see how fast the work could get done. The boss decided to have everyone work on the same work type and utilize Krystal's abbreviations and shorthand from her word processing program. This was an older processing system. Krystal considered the possibility that if everyone concentrates on one work type using her abbreviations, the system may crash.

As suspected, malfunctions began to arise. The keyboards were clacking louder than usual, almost sounding like horse hooves. Often the abbreviations would copy something else. Krystal warned the others of possible impending disaster, but they ignored her. She contemplated, *if they want a horse race, they're going to burn up their computers with such stupidity!*

Finally, the system crashed and nobody could type. Two people then came in the room; one from data processing and the other from medical records. Not only had this affected their system in medical records, but now none of the doctors anywhere in the hospital could view patient records on the computer system. Both the data processing person and medical records person asked if anyone would volunteer to take the time and help get the system back.

Krystal immediately said she would. She wanted to "jump this horse racetrack" and do something productive. It was a lengthy process and basically Krystal had to send some reports with lots of errors in it to dislodge a bunch of crammed reports that had shut down the system. It took over an hour when finally they told Krystal that it was starting to work. As the rest of the system started to come back up and the doctors were able to view records, Krystal thought, *no one is ever going to know that this crashed and what has happened here tonight. – Maybe I need to send up a few flares.*

So Krystal purposely included a few mistakes in the next set of reports which she knew would go to certain doctors. *Hopefully, they'll wonder how the reports came through the system that way and start questioning some things.* By the time Krystal left at 7:00 a.m. the system was working fine. Krystal left a note for her boss explaining what happened.

Later in the morning Barbie Sue Dull called Krystal at home and began screaming that it would have been impossible to restart the system if it crashed. Then she claimed there were others complaining about Krystal's attitude. Krystal asked her from whom, but Barbie only continued to scream at her. At last Barbie claimed that she had "seen her doing things at work!"

How interesting, thought Krystal. *If you saw me when you were not there, then that could only mean the watchers allowed you to see me via their cameras.* Krystal now suspected the surveillance extended to her work place.

Finally, Barbie stated that she was going to show her boss the note Krystal left on her desk. Krystal just barked back, "Go ahead! And while you're at it why don't you really find out what's going on in data processing and the rest of the hospital. I did help to bring the crashed system back up!"

When she hung up, Krystal tried to relieve her headache by lying down. As soon as she did, the phone kept ringing. When she answered, no one was on the other end of the line. Then she heard a lot of drilling and dull pounding noises throughout the house. Although Krystal was not sure, in time she discovered Goldilocks had set up the "horse race" event at the hospital. Yet once more nothing seemed to be done about it.

The noisy harassment continued and included Randy Hellmen setting off firecrackers from a boat parked in his yard. The firecrackers were once more aimed in the direction of Krystal's house. Randy had been placing "dog treats" on Krystal's property so that her dogs would go outside and gobble them up. Laced with laxatives, when Krystal returned home in the morning, she had a mess to clean up. She always let her dogs out before she left for work, and normally this would not have happened.

When she finally noticed that fecal secretions were becoming filled with mucus, she knew that these treats were tearing the dogs' insides up as well. She suspected that Leonard was behind the formulations as he was now working in the animal pharmaceutical portion of the company. He would have access to supplies. Judging from his previous harassment of her, she figured this would not stop just because she had been laid off from the company.

Exasperated by all the events as well as lack of sleep, Krystal once more appeared out of sorts to Wilbur when he came to visit. He took her to the hospital. Although Krystal admits she was out of sorts, she did not appreciate another psychiatrist just glancing at her previous record and claiming that she was schizophrenic. She only stayed a couple of days gaining sleep to make up for the past few days. She not only returned home, but returned to work. No one said anything to her for a long time.

Krystal took work home as in-house work was getting behind at the hospital. As she worked, she became aware there were others watching her, and began a "countdown". She surmised they would try to burn down the house. She wasn't sure exactly how that could be done, but wondered if a surge through the outlets would spark a fire. When the countdown was almost completed, she heard a click and then nothing.

She stated, "What's the matter? Didn't your trick go off like you thought?" Her house then remained quiet for quick a long time.

Later Greg Fleuzy lost his polic detective credentials with the police department and was charged with soliciting sexual favors for grades. He stated he was moving to Delaware and co-drive semis with his brother.

There were others in the sheriff's department who also were demoted and lost their standing. Yet no compensation for damages done in her household came in Krystal's direction. When she wrote to the police department, requesting that something be done, no reply came. When Trooper Otto Hartsel tried to come forward with lots of evidence. He was turned away and eventually forced to leave not only the area, but the state as well. Once more, justice was denied to Krystal as she knew legally she could not prosecute anyone without concrete evidence. She also knew that policemen didn't like to turn on other policemen as it created ill feelings in the department and lack of adequate backup would result.

Krystal began to relax knowing that some of the irritating sheriffs were gone. Having paid off her bills, she bought herself a few things. Slowly she began working on her book again, saving her files to disk in case anything would happen to her system. As soon as she got to the chapter where she tried to recall the events of the 1987 conversation, once more as anticipated her computer started to act up again.

Krystal took a break from the hospital work in spring of 2000, taking on some outside work at home. She dropped her hospitalization, reasoning that if she had no insurance, the hospital could not keep her for a psych admission and stay. She purchased outside insurance that only covered her if her and Joshua had an accident. As the work load built up at the hospital, Barbie Sue Dull was forced to ask Krystal if she would return. Krystal contemplated it for a while, and then realizing that she made better money there than at home, she decided to return. This time Barbie claimed that Krystal could work whatever schedule she wanted on second shift. This pleased Krystal as third shift had really been a strain on her. So Krystal accepted.

When Barbie approached her one day talking about the health insurance benefits at the hospital and that Krystal should once more enroll in the program, Krystal replied that she had insurance elsewhere.

"So it's not the insurance you want?" grinned Barbie. "Then why are you working so hard?" Krystal did not respond, but noted Barbie's reactions and wanted to know why Barbie was so concerned about Krystal having hospital insurance.

I just wonder, she pondered, *who else was behind getting me admitted this last time?*

Later a meeting took place in the conference room where a satellite feature was playing on the TV that had no connection to the discussion at hand. Krystal noted that this TV segment featured, "PsychLink" and was a panel of three doctors discussing a woman's mental illness and how "sick" she was. In this feature, one doctor appeared very similar to Damian Madden and another appeared like a wimpy older Dr. Klone. Krystal only watched for a while and when Barbie came in to conduct the meeting, she made sure she left the TV program playing until it finished.

When Barbie shut the TV off, she began discussing other unrelated items. Then Krystal questioned Barbie about procedures for handling certain reports, noting that Barbie would not look in her direction.

Hmm, thought Krystal, *perhaps you're guilty of playing this game and your guilt keeps you from looking me straight in the eye.* Krystal returned home to work on her book.

Eventually she replaced her home computer and continued with her story, bypassing the 1987 conversation chapter for now, but surging ahead with other information and insight that she had gained. This time when she was telling the story, she put in everyone's real name. 'That way,' she thought, 'hopefully the good guys doing surveillance will start checking things out, and finding out this is all true.'

When the close-call election results were finally disclosed at the end of 2000 George W. Bush had been declared the winner. Knowing that the Bush camp had returned to the area to see what she would do, Krystal declared, "I suppose you want to know what I'm going to do about Saddam. Well, for one thing God had been very silent in those matters. – The fact is some of you are no better than he is. Just suppose he makes it into the kingdom of God before you do. – What will you do then? – You've tried doing things your way and they didn't work. Now we'll do things Our way!"

When she was finished she composed a letter to Saddam. She commented she had no e-mail address for him, and no one came forth to provide one. Then she mailed her letter along with an explanation to several forms of Adventist public media, in the hopes that somehow it would arrive in Saddam's hands. As soon as she had done so, a light from out of nowhere showed brightly in her room. It was not a light as from a lamp or other electric equipment, but a light in of itself. Instead, this was a Light sent from the Source to indicate that Krystal was pursuing the course the Preserver of Life wanted. This Light was witnessed by those conducting the surveillance so that they might understand and come to know the truth in Krystal's household. Not sure if her letter would reach it's destination, she prayed that this Light would guide the way.

At work there still were problems. One female ER doctor continually had the dictation system cut her off. Krystal wondered, *she's an intelligent female doctor and I think she's Jewish. Now who in this community does not like intelligent females?* Once more her attention was directed to both Damian and Goldilocks. On a hunch, Krystal began to investigate where Damian was hiding now. To her surprise Krystal discovered that the State Psychology Review Board denied his license to practice psychology. She also discovered the public record including 400 pages that was accessible.

Searching through these records, she found much of what she surmised about him. One female patient had kept a journal and in it Krystal discovered that Damian had been abusing women for a long, long time. While Krystal was going through these documents, several double murder/ suicides took place in the community. At last, Krystal suspected much like before in Scoria, that someone was prompting these to occur. After all Damian had bragged to Krystal long ago that he thought it was funny a husband and wife would get so exasperated with each other they would commit murder. When Krystal revealed her concerns to those conducting surveillance, some of the good ones had already checked out the murder/suicide in Scoria. At that house, they discovered planted bugging devices.

Now that Burning Bridges was encountering several double murder/ suicides within a span of just a few weeks, Krystal could no longer contain herself. She wrote once more to the Cleveland Office of the FBI, asking for her file. She completed the necessary paperwork, and when at last she received what they sent, she found it was grossly incomplete with several blatant errors. It only included some of the letters to the Cleveland office, but none that she had sent to Director Snuggles. There was nothing from the Kent State interview. Reading through it she called out the errors. One agent had written that there was a man coming to the household and "may be an ex-husband."

Krystal declared, "Well, then why don't you go down to the damn courthouse and find out if it's an ex-husband or not!" She remarked about several other notes.

When at last she uncovered Agent Art Castle's notes from the interview on her porch whereby she discussed Damian, she noted Agent Castle had included a lot of what she had said. Knowing that they blocked out names and that they only discussed Damian, Krystal found that there was a line drawn to the marked-out name, stating 'she knew him from the psychiatric hospital." In front of Damian's name was S.A. which was not blocked out and stood for 'Special Agent.'

She cried out, "You knew he was working with you guys all this time. And you let him continue even though he was destroying my household as well as others!" With that she proceeded to began to appeal her case to the U.S. Department of Justice. In the meantime September 11, 2001 occurred and so many things were put on hold, including Krystal's search for records.

Later Krystal discovered that no one was willing to bone up to the fact that politics had taken preference over justice as well as common sense. Krystal eventually learned that the director of the Cleveland office of the FBI who replaced retired Director Snuggles had been promoted to assistant director in Washington, D.C.

What made things worse was the promotion of the movie Erin Brockovich which stared Julia Roberts and was about somehow who fought the justice system and won. "Was this a slap in the face?" declared Krystal. "I am trying to find justice there and all I see is some stupid movie about how someone can win, and I can't?" ventilating to those listening in.

Krystal thought, *This whole justice system is awry. – They refused to listen to what I had to say in 1987 and now they're trying to cover their tracks and they can't. This will be an interesting Judgment!*

Krystal spent more time combing through the Quran and wondered why those in the government were so blind to the fact that all the Muslims were not evil. Yes, there were radicals such as Al-Qaeda that attacked American planes and the Pentagon on September 11, 2001. Those who followed the basic tenants of the Quran followed a similar line with Christianity. When other similar tragedies occurred, many Muslims were first to give aid to others. Unfortunately, not everyone would look at events as Krystal did. *I guess it's easier to hate someone than try to learn more about them and get along with them,* Krystal surmised.

CHAPTER
14

fter the 9/11 tragedies occurred, Krystal kept her beliefs to herself and attended church, but was quite dismayed with other peoples' attitudes toward non-Adventist faiths. She distanced herself from the congregation even more so. Yet she found articles in their magazines whereby the authors correctly talked about casting out demons. She wrote acknowledging letters to them. However, there were also articles displaying ignorance on accomplishing this feat, and this Krystal found very distressing.

She learned in the Arab nations, Adventists had set up centers for Adventist-Muslim relations to pray together. It was obvious to Krystal that there was a bridging taking place in the religious world, more so than any political realm. Krystal also realized that the black church seemed more in tune with Krystal's religious beliefs than the white church.

She had enjoyed working at the police department, even though there were those who worked against her. She decided to enroll in an online detective course. She still worked at the hospital, but wanted to do something different.

With Joshua now attending college and not wishing to return to the area, Krystal thought about moving to a different community. With interest rates down, she approached Randy Hellman who expressed interest in buying it. She found a nice home in the Burning Bridges area, closer to the hospital, and moved in 2003. Although she was closer to Woolly Bully, she felt maybe she would get more answers to her questions, one way or another.

Krystal felt with the upcoming 2004 election someone might try once more demanding she do something about Saddam Hussein. Krystal concluded that although Saddam was ruthless, some of our own CIA and FBI agents were just as bad, especially with their previous threats. In anticipation of trouble, Krystal purchased a 0.45 caliber semi-automatic pistol for defense.

When it became apparent that Martha could no longer live alone having fallen several times, Darlene and Krystal agreed upon nursing home placement. Subsequently, both sisters worked at settling Martha's affairs when she would die.

While at her new home, Krystal continued with her detective course. She hoped for gainful employment when she finished. However, state policy changed regarding requirements, and once again Krystal could not pursue this line of work.

She continued reading the Quran noting in Sura 2:30 "When your Lord said to the angels, 'I am placing on the earth one that shall rule as My Deputy,' they replied: "Will You put there one that will do evil and shed blood, when we have for so long sung Your praises and sanctified Your name?' He said, 'I know what you know not.'

Was it possible that the Lord foresaw what I would turn out to be and be able to come to terms with my life and where it lead? Was this the plan all along? And if so, was the FBI and CIA afraid of people coming together? Rather than fighting wars, would it be such a bad thing to work for peaceful solutions? Krystal contemplated on the significance of such an idea. She also contemplated the statue of St. Michael in front of her home church that she learned about when she was so young. It was unlike any other statues representing him. He had a sword and shield at his side, but his arm was across his chest as if signifying protection. She recalled that the first words of St. Michael's prayer was "defend us in battle." This gesture in the statue seemed to represent this.

In the meantime, President George W. Bush vowed to invade Iraq in search of weapons of mass destruction. Krystal openly opposed this war and wrote several public letters noting such. Then she got a mailing form a historical group with former President George H.W. Bush on their planning committee seeking donations for a museum. When Krystal saw the former President Bush's signature on the enclosures, she fired off a letter not only to the organization, but to former President Bush as well. She expressed her concern supporting soldiers in the field, but wondered about the ones who never came home, either physically or mentally from the wars. She cited all the veteran's organizations she already donated to and did not include museums.

As was expected her letter was ignored, and in fact they sent another appeal for money. This time she just threw all the requests away. "You didn't listen to me before, and you still don't want to listen to me," she declared. "There's no sense beating a dead horse!"

As the war in Iraq continued, eventually Saddam Hussein was captured at the end of December 2003. Taken to a secure location he was held prisoner. With that news Krystal began to surge ahead with her book spending as much of the winter months on it as possible. She also noted that during Saddam's trial, he continually read from the Quran, and she wondered if he had received her letter.

Then she thought, *what if my book gets written from a slightly different prospective?* With those thoughts in mind she set about outlining how the book would come together. Krystal was able to continue her new approach to her book, even recalling more from the 1987 conversation in Friendly's. This time, she made it through the chapter without her computer crashing.

Eventually, she finished the book and sent it off for publication in 2004. In the original version, she did not have all the answers that she wished. She wanted to end the story with character assassination of Damian. So she portrayed him as being shot. Yet those on the outside who like to spin things, tried to indicate that is what happened to him.

As soon as her book was published, she heard remarks about 'what is she going to write in the sequel?' It was then Krystal knew that the people let go from the Scoria sheriff's department and police department, had not traveled very far, but instead were still following her. Several from the sheriff's department managed to transfer to the Burning Bridges Sheriff's Department, including Keith Munson, who frequently posted pornographic pictures on her Facebook feed or e-mail.

Eventually he was caught and arrested for other charges unrelated to Krystal. Others from Scoria such as Randy Hellman and Tyler Grove continued their harassment, but to a lesser degree. Then there was the element of Woolly Bully and because Krystal was closer to the FBI office where he was located, he continued to be behind the scenes of taking ideas from her computer as well, and utilizing them in any way to help political agendas.

Leonard Blare, on the other hand, took a different approach and with disguise became a different person in the community.

In January 2004, Krystal's older brother passed away. She made sure that Martha was aware of this event and that Krystal would attend the funeral. Of course, Martha was sad to know that her oldest son had died, and she wondered why it couldn't have been her.

Krystal had to fly out of state. When the funeral was over, she stayed another day and then returned home. As she had boarded her plane and was seated ready for departure, the pilot came on the loud speaker and announced that the instruments were showing something odd, and that they would be boarding another plane to take off. As they boarded the second plane, Krystal discovered that the first plane had just come from Miami. Krystal was aware that old crony CIA agents resided in Florida, and *wondered how far would these people go to get rid of me? Would they disrupt a plane so that something drastic would happen in flight?* Knowing what she knew about how devious some CIA agents could be, it would not surprise her. She vowed that she would probably never fly again because it posed an issue she did not want to have to deal with.

In early March 2004 Krystal received information regarding her class reunion and follow up. When she viewed the "In Memoriam" section were several classmates' names, she noted Chrysha's name. Saddened she decided not to attend the reunion. Krystal wondered if there had been more to Chrysha's death than what was revealed through old high school classmates. After several months, she found out that someone had approached Chrysha and wanted her to denounce all that Krystal was. Chrysha would not do it for her long-time friend, and

Krystal only surmised that perhaps Chrysha's death was orchestrated because of that.

What if, Krystal surmised, *since Matt was plagued by Robert Gates trying to destroy him by cutting brake lines on his truck – what if Robert Gates ventured down the West Coast and found Chrysha? Would he have tried to force her to go as a sacrifice in Krystal's place or try to discredit Krystal?'* Krystal started delving into this matter considering the likelihood that Chrysha had been murdered in one form or another either by him or someone like him. With the CIA being so ruthless, nothing would stop someone from injecting another with a cancer producing agent, and having it take its effect on them.

When President Bush marked the one-year anniversary of the war in Iraq on March 19, 2004, Krystal once again became upset with the whole matter as he claimed "Mission Accomplished." A trial had begun regarding the fate of Saddam Hussein, and it dragged on for a long time.

In the meantime, Krystal continued to visit Martha at the nursing home. Her eyesight was beginning to deteriorate and so she began refusing to read the newspaper. Her hearing had always been strained as she was deaf in one ear. Yet Krystal strove to help her understand by writing out items that would be important to her.

As the house and property were still in Martha's name, payment for the nursing home care was made through the assets she still owned. Darlene had these assets put into a trust fund, however, with hindsight it would have been better to have put the house and property in the sisters' names as if sold. At any rate, the assets dwindled down. Darlene began preparing to sell the house, and somewhere along the line she was told that she could only ask $250,000 tops for the sale, according to some source from Medicare.

Krystal thought, *now isn't that interesting! $250,000 was what I asked for from the FBI with regards to copyright infringement on my materials taken from my computer.* She could only surmise that Agent Snuggles was behind this and how much he could interfere with this sale along with Bush and Cheney and others.

At one point while visiting the nursing home, writing notes for Martha to read. Krystal overheard the nurses in the hallway directly outside the room. One explained, "We're saving her for George." Both made sure that Krystal saw and heard them. Krystal could only think of Bush senior and wondered how much of Martha's care was being directed by outside interference.

Days later, Darlene stated she could not attend an intake session for Martha's care. Krystal went in Darlene's place. Upon arrival at the nursing home, Krystal was confronted first by one of the office secretaries, who claimed that all the nursing notes were not back yet from transcription. This secretary had the attitude and gestures remarkably similar to Krystal's boss, Barbie Sue Dull. Krystal remarked that she knew how transcription worked with outsourcing materials. So it was not surprising to her. Then an activities person came into the room, as well a head nurse. When they began going over Martha's care, Krystal realized that they had Martha on a roller coaster of care. They would take her blood sugar, feeding her breakfast, not wait the two-hour time after eating to check blood sugar once more. Then they gave her insulin as the sugar level was too high, and feed her again because the sugar level dropped. Also, Martha was developing a blackness to her toes on her left side, which Krystal began to wonder about diabetic gangrene developing. Krystal became very adamant questioning this nurse and it became apparent to Krystal that either this nurse knew very little about diabetic care or that she was being prompted by someone else. In short, Krystal made sure that by the time she left, Martha's care was under a stricter regimen.

When talking this meeting over with Darlene, and it was agreed to put Martha under hospice care while in the nursing home, take her off all medications, and allow her to pass on her own.

Krystal approached Martha on the next visit. Martha exclaimed, "I just want to die."

Krystal stroked her hair and leaning close to her ear she whispered, "We're working on it."

At that point Mary totally relaxed as if to say, *thank God, someone's finally heard me!* Mary lasted over two weeks without medications before she finally passed on in January 2005.

At some point during this time frame, there was an attempt on George H.W. Bush's life. Krystal heard about it and wondered what had occurred because she felt one night as she slept that she was accompanying someone "down to hell". Yet something happened along the way and that person did not continue. As she reached the bottom, she noted there was a "well" of sorts. This well she later read about was the "well of souls" referenced in Islam, and that some of the souls were released.

Krystal discovered to her dismay several days later that indeed an attempt on Bush's life had occurred, but there were individuals who "brought him back to life." However, Bush was not the same person as before, as if the cryogenics had distorted his brain function. By this time Krystal had completed the detective course and procured her identification card and papers, only to find out that the State of Ohio changed some rules on proceeding with private investigation work. Krystal thought, *another wrench thrown in my plans.*

Unknown to Krystal, while Damian was reading her book he began to discretely send anonymous notes about what was happening. Although Krystal was unsure who was feeding this information, she wondered if her Higher Power was working on him to change as well.

In 2006 Krystal made some more changes in her life. She chose to retire from the hospital and work part-time at home for other companies. This seemed to help relieve any other stressful situations that might arise. The only other thing she had to contend with is that Wilbur ended up requiring home-care for some time. Realizing that this would have been a strain on her if she had to go to his house all the time, she moved him into her house requiring a rent payment from. They were still divorced and she reiterated to him that fact. So no close relationships occurred, but the household for the most part was now stable in terms of any interference on a large scale.

Although there were still the troublesome sheriffs in the area who came from Scoria, they only caused issues now and then, and Krystal was more aware of their 'games.' Also, there was this other person helping her on the outside, which became a blessing in itself.

When Saddam Hussein's trial finally concluded, on December 2006 he was executed. Krystal still wondered about whether her message reached him or not prior to his execution.

By this time Krystal had grown quite weary of trying to explain to the Adventist church that Scriptures and the Quran complemented each other in so many ways. Yet, in the local church they refused to listen to her, even if she tried to describe some of the issues she had to deal with concerning her household in the past. Since they treated her like a second class citizen, she mentally began making plans to eventually leave the Adventist church.

Before she left though, she thought she should correct her relationship with Lydia, who had bullied Kyrstal in the very beginning. So Krystal confessed to Lydia about the letter while doing foot washing. Yet, Lydia did not seem to understand the significance and bragged to others on how she was right regarding how Krystal treated her, rather than accepting the confession for what it was. It was soon after this event that Krystal left the church.

She worshipped at home utilizing music she had recorded years earlier, and felt comfortable reading both Scripture and the Quran. She considered herself a Christian Jewish Muslim, because she could see overlaps in all three religions. She also wondered, as she looked back over her life, *what did the FBI and CIA suspect about me so long ago, when they approached her family about me being a sacrifice? Could it have been something to do with bridging other nations, cultures, religions in a more cohesive manner? Were they afraid of her being female, Catholic, of Polish descent, or a combination of all these factors? Just what were they afraid could happen?*

Late in 2007 the older Dr. Klone passed away. Krystal attended the funeral service and overheard his wife proclaim that he had been doing so well until now. Krystal wondered if someone underhandedly did something so that he would be one less friend of Krystal's. When young Dr. Klone passed away of a heart attack in 2012, again Krystal wondered what was behind it. Supposedly there was some drug abuse involved, yet Krystal contemplated that he could have been set up as well.

Then in 2015, contact was made with a long last cousin, who had grown up under Grandma Kruczysinki's care. Both Darlene and Krystal met with this cousin who had discovered a family history series at the local library. It apparently had been up in Cleveland and was then brought down to this local library. Krystal copied some pages from it and then later looked them over. She questioned some things such as claiming that some of the family came over from Switzerland in the mid to later 1800's as 'Seven day Adventists.' Yet Krystal knew that they were known as Millerites at the time and not Adventists as such. So Krystal questioned if someone could have altered this history knowing that she had been an Adventist. *I guess they didn't plan on me leaving the Adventist church at some point,* Krystal surmised. *What would they write about me bridging the Quran with Scripture? How could they explain that I feel I'm a Christian Jewish Muslin?*

Once again, harassment started in her household, but she now knew that Woolly Bully was still playing his game. Krystal had developed a personal e-mail account that she used to ventilate her feelings, much like she had done previously. So she considered it her diary and would write herself notes and answer them as if she were writing to an actual person. Woolly Bully viewed this as well. After a time Krystal realized that he was reading her e-mails, and so became disgusted with his stealing of her ideas and suggestions for dealing with some issues locally as well as further away. These in turn were then channeled into political notes for Republican candidates, of course, still under the guidance of George H.W. Bush.

When it became apparent that the Republicans were going to back Donald Trump for president, Krystal thought back to her conversation in Friendly's in 1987. She had talked about voting for Donald Duck regarding his character, and she also commented that she played Pinochle and talked about using trump cards to win.

Could it be that because Bush and Cheney were solely interested in oil, making money and such business deals, that they had started to formulate a plan pushing forth Donald Trump at some point? Krystal wondered strongly about this.

Then in late 2016 George H.W. Bush claimed he was going to vote for Hillary, and Dick Cheney voiced he would vote for Trump. Krystal wondered if George had stated that for her benefit. Krystal's ideas, however, taken from her computer, were then used politically to favor Trump.

One afternoon in late 2016 as Krystal was strolling through her wooded area, she came upon a small orange scroll, that when she opened it up it appeared to be the colors of vomit. There were no other pieces of orange material anywhere else around. She brought it back to the house and described it all who were listening in. She claimed it revealed the Almighty's view and judgment of Trump. Later on a few days later, she would find a silver scroll, about the same size, and that was her Judgment.

When the votes were counted and Trump became President, Krystal knew we were definitely headed into the time of tribulation as revealed in Matthew Chapter 24 spoken by Christ Himself.

At last Krystal decided something had to be done drastically, as she became frustrated with this plagiarism and theft of her ideas. She had already purchased a semi-automatic pistol, but she knew that if she shot an FBI agent, she would go to federal prison. Finally, after seeking guidance from her Higher Power, she wrote a very nasty note to him via her personal e-mail account, and once it had been read by him and read, he was struck by an unknown Presence who took the life out of him. Later that morning, fellow agents would discover Woolly Bully sitting at his desk with pen in hand and his computer open to Krystal's message, but he was dead. This occurred in January 2017.

In other areas of concern, there were attacks on Jewish synagogues that took place, and Krystal noted that many times the Muslim groups were the first to come to their aid and help out as much as possible.

When George H.W. Bush finally died on November 30, 2018, Krystal knew this time he was going to stay down. As she read Revelation Chapter 9, she became acutely aware that there was now a connection to the well of souls encountered several years earlier when an attempt was made on Bush's life and he was brought back via cryogenics. Though Krystal felt that the CIA's attempt proved futile, she wondered where Dick Cheney was and what he was up to, now that his buddy was gone for sure.

One recent incident in March 2020 that had Krystal really question "bugging devices" and if they were used on others, occurred at a manufacturing plant that Randy Hellman worked at. Apparently a fire started at one of the machines and the fire spread. Krystal wondered who was at the machine and if that person was of a different color than white, or was it a woman or both or religious or political beliefs. In any case, it seemed possible that a person could have been targeted.

Nothing more was ever publically reported and Krystal wondered if the investigation was still ongoing.

Then of course, came the COVID-19 pandemic, and Krystal wondered if this was something that would bring people together even though the pains of deaths that occurred would bring such dread and sorrow. Yet there were so many lies and perverted rumors surrounding this mostly coming from Trump's White House, that it became tiresome to deal with. *And when would all those lies end?* Krystal knew that the final Judgment would be the only answer. She only wished others could see that and be prepared.

Yet, this type of thing had been going on all her life, and she wondered when it would end. Then hate erupted again in the form of blacks being attacked by police and other whites, and riots once again ensued. Not only that, but people began attacking each other, no matter what color, what religion, what political beliefs. It was as though people had to vent, but could only take it out on others, rather than looking inward to see if change needed to be made. Then take the 'log out of your own eye first, before you take the speck out of someone else's' admonition from Christ Himself didn't seem to be factoring in, and even churches in general were drifting away from Christ's message.

Yet Krystal wondered how she could get her message across – there is a Judgment coming and it will not go well for many people. She was reminded of Christ's own words in Matthew 24:37, it will be like in the time of Noah when so few listened, and then were destroyed. Krystal could only see angels above weeping for those who wouldn't listen.

Even though Krystal was very aware that the unrest all over the globe had been going on since time began, the amount of hatred and violence expressed towards other people appears to be at an all-time high.

In Malachi Chapter 4 verses 5 and 6 talk about Elijah the prophet returning before the day of the Lord. The purpose is to restore the hearts of children to fathers and fathers to children. Some have interpreted this as just addressing the family unit. Yet Krystal can see it as a need for reconciliation among all peoples, not just family. As it is written, if that does not happen the Lord will smite the land with a curse. Krystal wondered if that would happen.

Krystal's only hope is that there were many, as noted by John in the book of Revelation, who would be counted in the kingdom. Many times these peoples' voices are silent, yet they appear to acknowledge a message of understanding and working with one another. Perhaps with enough of these people listening, there would not be a curse on the land. Krystal leaves that choice up to the individual to decide.

I was sitting at my desk looking out the window of the Maxine O'Day Detective Agency, when a woman carrying a large package walked in.

"Hi, I'm Krystal Kruczyinski. I'd like to apply for a position in your detective agency. Here's my resume," she stated.

I looked it over and made some comments. "I see you've had training through the detective training course. That's quite a higher standard!" Then I asked her, "Have you ever had any experience doing detective work?"

"Well," she began as she brought out a large black notebook from the package she was carrying. "I've been involved in this investigation for some time, but I've hit some snags. I was hoping you could help me with this matter."

"Hmm, that's quite a file you've got there. Let me look it over and I'll get back with you."

"I must say, there are some things in there that are quite disturbing," she stated.

As I quickly scanned through the material she had, I noted it involved the FBI and CIA. "This may take some time, but I'll see what I can do."

Then she thanked me and left my office.

So, I Maxine O'Day began to look into the matter and began to help her write her book.

When the original book was published, this last scene was written to depict where the book would eventually end up. In Revelation chapter

10, it talks about a little book that ends up in Heaven's hands and becomes one of the books that end up in Judgment. Krystal recalled that in Friendly's in 1987, her Source declared that her 'book would do the trick,' including bringing others to know the Source personally.

This revised edition illuminates more of what was transpiring behind the scenes as more information was uncovered.

References

Israel, Fred – The FBI, 1986, Chelsea House Publishing, New York, NY.

Ellis, Rafaela – The Central Intelligence Agency, 1987, Chelsea House Publishing, New York, NY.

Norton, W.W. – Hoover, The Man And His Secrets, 1991

Library of Congress – Secret Police – KGB – Soviet Exhibit on "Attacks on Intelligentsia: Suppressing Dissidents." – Telegrams and Letters from March 5, 16 and 25, 1971.

Kessler, Ronald – Inside the CIA, 1992, Pocket Books, New York, NY.

Trento, Joseph J. – The Secret History of the CIA, 2001, Prima Publishing, Roseville, California.

Kent State/May 4 – Echos Through A Decade, 1982, Edited by Scott L. Bills. Kent State University Press, Kent, Ohio.

Testimonies for the Church by Ellen G. White, Volumes 1-9, 1948, reprinted 1995, Pacific Press Publishing Association, Boise, Idaho. (Volume 8, p. 399 [p. 188])

Selected Messages by Ellen G. White, Volumes 1-3, reprinted 1995, Pacific Press Publishing Association, Boise, Idaho. (Volume 3, p. 411 [p.188])

Jesus Christ, Superstar, A Rock Opera by Andrew Lloyd Webber and Tim Rice, Musical Excerpts, 1970 by Leeds Music Corporation, New York, New York.

The New American Standard Bible, Collins Word Publishing, 1973.

The Koran (Quran), Penguin Classics, 1999.